THEOSIS IN THE THEOLOGY OF THOMAS TORRANCE

Torrance's vision of *Theosis* (deification/divinisation) is explored through his doctrine of creation and anthropology, his characterisation of the incarnation, his accounts of reconciliation and union with Christ, and his theology of church and sacraments. Myk Habets' study distinguishes Torrance's Reformed vision of *theosis* from other possible accounts of salvation as divinisation as they are found, for instance, within patristic thought and Eastern Orthodoxy.

This book presents the first critique of the theology of T.F. Torrance to focus on *theosis*, and examines a model of *theosis* within the realm of reformed theology built upon Western theology.

ASHGATE NEW CRITICAL THINKING IN RELIGION, THEOLOGY AND BIBLICAL STUDIES

The *Ashgate New Critical Thinking in Religion, Theology and Biblical Studies* series brings high quality research monograph publishing back into focus for authors, international libraries, and student, academic and research readers. Headed by an international editorial advisory board of acclaimed scholars spanning the breadth of religious studies, theology and biblical studies, this open-ended monograph series presents cutting-edge research from both established and new authors in the field. With specialist focus yet clear contextual presentation of contemporary research, books in the series take research into important new directions and open the field to new critical debate within the discipline, in areas of related study, and in key areas for contemporary society.

Other Recently Published Titles in the Series:

The Challenges of the Pentecostal, Charismatic and Messianic Jewish Movements
The Tensions of the Spirit
Peter Hocken

Reading Anselm's Proslogion
The History of Anselm's Argument and its Significance Today
Ian Logan

Jürgen Moltmann's Ethics of Hope
Eschatological Possibilities For Moral Action
Timothy Harvie

Phenomenology and Eschatology
Not Yet in the Now
Edited by Neal DeRoo and John Panteleimon Manoussakis

The Identity of Christian Morality
Ann Marie Mealey

Evagrius Ponticus
The Making of a Gnostic
Julia Konstantinovsky

Exodus Church and Civil Society
Public Theology and Social Theory in the Work of Jürgen Moltmann
Scott R. Paeth

Theosis in the Theology of Thomas Torrance

MYK HABETS
Carey Baptist College, New Zealand

2009

ASHGATE

Published by
Ashgate Publishing Limited
Wey Court East
Union Road
Farnham
Surrey, GU9 7PT
England

Ashgate Publishing Company
Suite 420
101 Cherry Street
Burlington
VT 05401-4405
USA

www.ashgate.com

British Library Cataloguing in Publication Data
Habets, Myk.
Theosis in the theology of Thomas Torrance. – (Ashgate new critical thinking in religion, theology and biblical studies)
1. Torrance, Thomas F. (Thomas Forsyth), 1913–2007.
2. Deification (Christianity) 3. Deification (Christianity) – History of doctrines.
I. Title II. Series
234–dc22

Library of Congress Cataloging-in-Publication Data
Habets, Myk.
Theosis in the theology of Thomas Torrance / Myk Habets.
p. cm. — (New critical thinking in religion, theology, and biblical studies)
Includes bibliographical references and index.
ISBN 978-0-7546-6799-5 (hardcover : alk. paper) 1. Torrance, Thomas F. (Thomas Forsyth), 1913–2007. 2. Deification (Christianity) I. Title.
BT767.8.H33 2009
230'.044092—dc22

2009004418

ISBN 978-0-7546-6799-5
EISBN 978-0-7546-9407-6

Mixed Sources
Product group from well-managed forests and other controlled sources
www.fsc.org Cert no. SA-COC-1565
© 1996 Forest Stewardship Council
FSC

Printed and bound in Great Britain by
MPG Books Group, UK

In memory of Tom Torrance (1913–2007), for inspiring so many of us to think through more clearly the contours of a scientific theology that glorifies the triune God of grace.

Contents

Preface

The Christian tradition, both East and West, has developed various models and theories of the atonement as explanations of what it means to speak of the reconciling activity of God in Christ. Central to these has been the claim that God has reconciled the world to himself in Christ. One way of testifying to the reconciling love of God has been the adoption of the metaphor *theosis* ('divinisation', 'deification') as an explanation of salvation. While central to Eastern Orthodoxy, a doctrine of *theosis* also has a rich tradition within Western, especially Reformed theology.

The Reformed theologian, Thomas Forsyth Torrance, represents an attempt to construct a soteriology that incorporates both Eastern and Western models of the atonement around the controlling metaphor of *theosis*. A close reading of his theology presents a robust and clearly articulated doctrine of *theosis* as a key way of expressing God's reconciling activity in Christ. As the true Man and the last Adam, Christ represents the *archē* and *telos* of human existence, the one in whose image all humanity has been created and into whose likeness all humanity is destined to be transformed from glory to glory. Through the Incarnation the Son becomes human without ceasing to be divine, to unite humanity and divinity together and effect a 'deification' of human nature, mediated to men and women who are said to be 'in Christ' by the work of the Holy Spirit. By means of a 'wonderful exchange' Christ takes what is ours and gives us what is his. For Torrance, this is the heart of atonement.

The goal of humanity is worship, something Torrance defines as the gift of participating through the Spirit in the incarnate Son's communion with the Father. The *locus* of worship, and thus of *theosis*, is the church, the communion of saints created by the fellowship of the Holy Spirit. Throughout Torrance's doctrines of creation, anthropology, incarnation, reconciliation, and pneumato-ecclesiology, the concept of *theosis* plays a central and constitutive role in explaining a Christian theology of salvation. *Theosis* is thus foundational to Torrance's theology and is one way in which he holds together in systematic fashion his diverse theological *oeuvre*.

I owe a debt of gratitude to many people for their support and encouragement over the duration of this project. I especially wish to thank Professor Ivor Davidson whose theological insight made the project *much* better than it would otherwise have been. To my colleagues, students, and friends at Carey Baptist College, Laidlaw College, and Otago University, I wish to express my deep gratitude for providing ongoing centres of theological discussion and encouragement.

The process of academic research is a journey, but one that is not made entirely alone. Many people have generously helped me with their time and knowledge. I especially wish to acknowledge the enthusiasm shown to my project by Professor Elmer Colyer and Professor Paul Molnar; along with Fr. Thomas Weinandy, O.F.M.

Cap., Professor Alister McGrath, and Professor Alan Torrance. A special word of thanks goes to Professor Thomas Torrance himself for encouraging comments on the nature of the project.

I am grateful to those family and friends who listened and helped by reading and commenting on various stages of the work, especially Peter Lineham and Peter McGhee. Last but certainly not least, to my wife Odele – my favourite theological interlocutor – I owe the greatest thanks and love. *Perichoresis*, my dear!

Myk Habets
Doctor Serviens Ecclesiae
Auckland, New Zealand

Introduction
Approaching T.F. Torrance and the Theme of *Theosis*

Introduction

Throughout his career The Very Reverend Professor Thomas Forsyth (T.F.) Torrance (1913–2007), presented a doctrine of *theosis*, an understanding of which illuminates his incarnational view of the atonement. In his espousal of *theosis* Torrance has advocated a distinctively Eastern model of salvation and yet has managed to do so without jettisoning his own Reformed theological models, usually associated with an emphasis upon humanity's being in union with Christ. Certainly, for Torrance, the two concepts or models of reconciliation – *theosis* and union with Christ – are not incompatible but are, rather, complementary. While union with God and *theosis* are not identical they are closely related. In her study of the patristic use of *theosis*, Anna Williams concludes:

> [W]e can safely say that where we find references to human participation in divine life, there we assuredly have a claim specifically of theosis. This kind of claim regarding participation in divine life is carefully to be distinguished, however, from the idea of divine indwelling in the human person...A second infallible marker of the doctrine, then, is the union of God and humanity, when this union is conceived as humanity's incorporation into God, rather than God's into humanity.[1]

While utilising the concept of *theosis* Torrance recognises that for much of the Western tradition this language may appear strange. This leads him to state: 'let us not quarrel about the word *theosis*, offensive though it may be to us, but follow its intention'.[2] He explains that intention thus:

> *Theosis* is an attempt to express the staggering significance of Pentecost as the coming from on high, from outside of us and beyond us, of divine power, or rather as the coming of Almighty God, the Maker of heaven and earth, to dwell with sinful mortal man, and therefore as the emancipation of man from imprisonment

---

[1] Anna N. Williams, *The Ground of Union: Deification in Aquinas and Palamas* (New York: Oxford University Press, 1999), p. 32.

[2] Thomas F. Torrance, *Theology in Reconstruction* (Grand Rapids: Eerdmans, 1965), p. 243.

> in himself and the lifting of him up to partake of the living presence and saving acts of God the Creator and Redeemer.[3]

Due to the reluctance of much Western theology to accept notions of *theosis* Torrance rarely uses the technical vocabulary of *theosis* and nowhere does he explicitly deal with the issues at any length. His theology is, however, profoundly compatible with, and shaped by, the central themes associated with doctrines of *theosis*. While the formal exposition of *theosis* may be absent, a strong case can be made that Torrance's entire theology is significantly influenced by the conceptuality of creaturely salvation as a process of *theosis*. The questions this study seeks to address are these: What is *theosis* as used by Torrance? How does he utilise this idea in his theology? At what points is his theology of *theosis* open to critique? In answering these questions we shall have recourse to consider Eastern traditions of *theosis*, Western and Reformed models of atonement, Torrance's immediate antecedents and mentors, and those who have sought to interact critically with his proposals.

Echoing the thoughts of Elmer Colyer we may ask the question: How can we gain an integrated view of Torrance's theology from the discussions of various aspects of his position found in his diverse publications? Colyer's suggested answer is instructive, by indwelling the corpus of Torrance's writings until we gain an insight into it.[4] The following represents an attempt to 'indwell' Torrance's work, and to deploy creative imagination in a manner that is tested and controlled by Torrance's own concerns.

Alister McGrath opens his biography with the statement, 'Thomas Forsyth Torrance is widely regarded, particularly outside Great Britain, as the most significant British academic theologian of the twentieth century';[5] and Elmer Colyer states, 'there is a growing consensus that Thomas F. Torrance is one of the premier theologians in the second half of the twentieth century'.[6] Torrance is a theologian's theologian and for that reason alone he rewards his commentators with stimulating and fruitful study.

Given the immense volume of Torrance's writings (over six hundred published works) it is somewhat surprising to find that apart from a number of unpublished doctoral theses there has to date been no comprehensive critique of his theology as a whole.[7] Furthermore, it does not appear that any sustained critique of Torrance's soteriology in particular has ever been attempted. In the words of Colin Gunton,

---

[3] Ibid., p. 244.

[4] Elmer M. Colyer, *How To Read T.F. Torrance: Understanding his Trinitarian and Scientific Theology* (Downers Grove: IVP, 2001), p. 337.

[5] Alister E. McGrath, *T.F. Torrance; An Intellectual Biography* (Edinburgh: T & T Clark, 1999), p. xi.

[6] Colyer, *How To Read T.F. Torrance*, p. 11.

[7] In order to address this gap in 2003 the 'Thomas F. Torrance Theological Fellowship' was formed, meeting as a sub-group of the AAR. See http://www.tftorrance.org/.

'it appears remarkable, scandalous even, that there is so little detailed secondary discussion of [Torrance's] work'.[8] Presently there are only two book-length treatments of Torrance's theology: an intellectual biography by Alister McGrath,[9] and a theological guide by Elmer Colyer.[10] Book-length critiques of specific aspects of his work are also conspicuous by their absence; those that do exist are confined to a few monographs and a number of unpublished theses, mostly associated with Torrance's 'scientific theology' and epistemology as it relates to the knowledge of God.[11] While Torrance is clearly a major force on the contemporary theological landscape his work is relatively unexamined in terms of its potential for both development and critique. With this in mind, a study of *theosis* in Torrance's work could have important implications for Western models of soteriology in contemporary discussion.[12]

Torrance writes theology from within the Protestant Reformed tradition, mediated, as it were, by Patristic theology, especially that of Athanasius, on the one hand, and the influence of Karl Barth on the other hand. Throughout his writings he shows an admiration for and reliance upon the theology of John Calvin. However, while accepting much of Calvin's theological thought Torrance is scathing of the way in which he believes Calvin was systematised in later Calvinism, particularly by the seventeenth-century Protestant scholastics.[13] Out of such scholasticism

---

[8] Colin Gunton, 'Foreword', in Jason H-K. Yeung, *Being and Knowing: An Examination of T.F. Torrance's Christological Science* (Hong Kong: China Alliance Press, 1996), p. xvii.

[9] McGrath, *T.F. Torrance.*

[10] Colyer, *How To Read T.F. Torrance*. Also see Elmer M. Colyer, *The Promise of Trinitarian Theology: Theologians in Dialogue with T.F. Torrance,* ed. Elmer M. Colyer (Lanham, Md.: Rowman & Littlefield, 2001).

[11] Recent exceptions to this include the volume on the Torrance brothers' theology, especially christology, ed. Gerrit S. Dawson, *An Introduction to Torrance Theology: Discovering the Incarnate Saviour* (London: T & T Clark, 2007).

[12] See Myk Habets, 'Reforming Theōsis', in *Theōsis: Deification in Christian Theology*, eds Stephen Finlan and Vladimir Kharlamov (Eugene, OR.: Pickwick Publications, 2006), pp. 146–67.

[13] This concern is shared by his brother James B. Torrance; see especially: 'The Concept of Federal Theology – Was Calvin a Federal Theologian?' in *Calvinus Sacrae Scripturae professor*, ed. Wilhelm H. Neuser (Grand Rapids: Eerdmans, 1994), pp. 15–40; 'Strengths and Weaknesses of the Westminster Theology', in *The Westminster Confession in the Church Today: Papers Presented for the Church of Scotland Panel on Doctrine*, ed. Alasdair I.C. Heron (Edinburgh: St Andrew Press, 1982), pp. 40–53. The views held by Thomas F. and James B. Torrance have been seriously challenged by a number of recent studies, among which see *Protestant Scholasticism: Essays in Reassessment*, eds Carl R. Trueman and R. Scott Clark (Carlisle: Paternoster, 1999); Richard A. Muller, *Post-Reformation Reformed Dogmatics*, 2nd edn 4 vols (Grand Rapids: Baker, 2002); and Carl R. Trueman, 'Calvin and Calvinism' in *Cambridge Companion to Calvin*, ed. Donald K. McKim (Cambridge: Cambridge University Press, 2004), pp. 225–44.

(and Enlightenment science) have arisen a number of dualisms that, according to Torrance, threaten to derail or at least sidetrack much contemporary theological (and scientific) endeavour. In Torrance's own work he has set himself the task of removing all *a priori* dualisms that have crept into contemporary theology.[14]

His former lecturer at Edinburgh University, Hugh Ross Mackintosh, introduced Torrance to the work of Karl Barth, an acquaintance his mother had enhanced when she gave her son a copy of Barth's *Credo* when he entered the Faculty of Divinity at New College. It was this interest and admiration for Barth that prompted Torrance to study under Barth at Basel in 1937–38. Torrance's love for and respect of Barth's theology never waned. Torrance would go on to oversee the translation of the *Church Dogmatics* into English (1956–75), in addition to devoting several monographs to Barth's life and work. In one sense his entire writing career has been an attempt to critically explicate the central concerns of Barth's theological method.

Torrance has consistently sought to work out a 'scientific theology', a methodology he professes to have learned from several key influences, most notably John Philoponos, Albert Einstein, and Michael Polanyi. He also claims that this methodology is modelled in the theology of Anselm of Canterbury and Karl Barth. Theological thinking, as with all scientific thinking, must be properly realist. It is out of this 'theological realism' that Torrance sees the *homoousion* as a faithful expression and model of the oneness in being in the relation of the incarnate Son with the Father. Ultimately, Torrance's theological realism is grounded in God and calls the church back to a truly 'rational worship of God' (*logike latreia*).[15] From the basis of such a scientific theology Torrance constructs a doctrine of *theosis.*

Theosis as a Theological Motif

What exactly is *theosis*? This section briefly examines a definition of the term in its biblical and historical perspectives. In this way a context will be established for discussing Torrance's use and development of *theosis* in his own theological construction. In order to assess *theosis* we need to pursue two complementary lines of enquiry: the first etymological, the second historical. Only the broad

---

[14] See the little work of Alan G. Marley, *T.F. Torrance: The Rejection of Dualism* (Edinburgh: Handsel Press, 1992).

[15] This point is made clear in Thomas F. Torrance, 'Theological Realism', in *The Philosophical Frontiers of Christian Theology: Essays Presented to D.M. MacKinnon,* eds Brian Hebblethwaite and Stewart Sutherland (Cambridge: Cambridge University Press, 1982), p. 193.

brushstrokes of both themes will be presented here as the history and use of the concept of *theosis* have been rehearsed many times in scholarly literature.[16]

The Semantics of Theosis

Theosis is largely synonymous with another term *theopoiesis*.[17] Literally, *theosis* means 'becoming god', and *theopoiesis* 'making divine' or 'making into a god'.[18] In English *theosis* is typically translated as 'divinisation' or 'deification', although many scholars, both Western and Eastern, see both of these English renderings as inadequate and even misleading.[19] Pelikan argues for the retention of the transliterated form *theosis* on account of the 'grave handicaps' both English terms pose to Western readers.[20] The argument against the use of 'divinisation' and 'deification' is that the Greek term *theosis* means something far deeper than these English words can express. I follow the advice of Pelikan and others and simply transliterate the Greek term in most instances.

Theosis *in Historical Perspective*

The use of the concept of *theosis* has a rich pedigree extending back through the early church to Scripture itself. While mostly associated with the Greek patristic theologians and Eastern Orthodoxy, the doctrine also has a developed use in the West, something often overlooked by its contemporary detractors and Eastern advocates alike. After some cursory comments on the use of *theosis* in Scripture

---

16 Two works are considered to be more or less authoritative on the subject: Jules Gross, *La divinisation du chrétien d'après les pères grecs: Contribution historique à la doctrine de la grâce* (Paris: J. Gabalda, 1938) [ET: *The Divinization of the Christian According to the Greek Fathers*, trans. Paul A. Onica (Anaheim, CA.: A & C Press, 2002)]; and Myrrha Lot-Borodine, *La Deification de l'homme selon la doctrine des Peres grecs* (Paris: Cerf, 1970). Other significant works include: Norman Russell, *The Doctrine of Deification in the Greek Patristic Tradition* (Oxford: Oxford University Press, 2004); *Theōsis: Deification in Christian Theology*; and *Partakers of the Divine Nature: The History and Development of Deification in the Christian Traditions*, eds Michael J. Christensen., and Jeffery A. Wittung (Madison: Fairleigh Dickinson University Press, 2007).

17 For a comprehensive review of the semantics of *theosis* consult Russell, *The Doctrine of Deification in the Greek Patristic Tradition*, Appendix 2: 'The Greek Vocabularly of Deification', pp. 333–44.

18 Geoffrey W.H. Lampe, *A Patristic Greek Lexicon* (Oxford: Clarendon, 1961), p. 649.

19 For instance Nikos Nissiotis in *Die Theologie der Ostkirche im ökumenischen Dialog: Kirche und Welt in orthodoxer Sicht* (Stuttgart: Evangelisches Verlagswerk, 1968), pp. 50–51.

20 Jaroslav Pelikan, 'Orthodox Theology in the West: The Reformation', in *The Legacy of St. Vladimir,* eds John Breck, John Meyendorff, and Eleana Silk (Crestwood, NY.: St Vladimir's Seminary Press, 1990), p. 164.

and the east, a brief review of its western use will provide a context from which to examine Torrance's own proposals.

In the Old Testament, the teaching of the creation of human beings in the image and likeness of God and the call of the chosen people through the covenant to a closer communion with God prepared for the development of the theme in the New Testament. The New Testament teaching that God's Son becomes man so that man (humanity) may participate in God through the adoption of the Spirit is elaborated on especially. While the specific antecedents are limited to a few texts, chiefly Jn 10.34 (Ps 82.6); Jn 17.20–23; Acts 17.28; and 2 Pet 1.4, 'In fact', Studer comments,

> [T]he biblical foundation is much more solid than it seems, as long as we know how to use the Scriptural evidence without forcing it. Texts concerning man as God's image (Gen 1.26f), divine sonship (Gal 4.5ff.; Rom 8.15), imitation of God (Mt 5.4–48) and of Christ (Phil 2.5–11), as well as texts presenting the new life of Christians as a pledge and anticipation of future glory (1 Cor 13.12; 2 Cor 3.18; 1 Jn 3.1–3), must all be considered in this light.[21]

A doctrine of *theosis* was one of the fundamental themes of the Fathers who took the idea from Scripture and began to reinterpret *theosis* in their own cultural and philosophical environments, not least that of Platonism.[22] Not only are the actual words *theosis* and *theopoiesis* relevant but also the reality of those terms as expressed by many other words, both Greek and Latin, such as *aptharsia*, *methexis*, *koinonia*, *henosis*, *glorificatio*, *profectus ad Deum* and others.[23] With each development of the idea certain philosophical premises found their way into the particular expression of the doctrine of *theosis*, the extent of which forms a large part of historical interest and comment on the doctrine.[24]

---

[21] Basil Studer, 'Divinization', in *Encyclopedia of the Early Church*, 2 vols, ed. Angelo Di Beradina (New York: Oxford University Press), vol. 1. p. 242.

[22] Russell, *The Doctrine of Deification in the Greek Patristic Tradition*, pp. 1–2, identifies three usages of the term 'deification'; the nominal, analogical and metaphorical.

[23] For a summary see Stephen Finlan and Vladimir Kharlamov, 'Introduction', in *Theōsis: Deification in Christian Theology*, pp. 1–8. Anna N. Williams, 'Deification in the *Summa Theologiae:* A Structural Interpretation of the *Prima Pars*', *Thomist* 61 (1997): p. 222, reminds us of the Fathers' 'quasi-technical vocabulary' for *theosis* in terms of three 'virtual synonyms': participation, union and adoption, in addition to a number of related but secondary phrases such as: grace, virtue, knowledge, light, contemplation, glory and vision.

[24] See in this regard Mark D. Nispel, 'Christian Deification and the Early *Testimonia*', *Vigiliae Christianae* 53 (1999): pp. 289–304, who seeks the origins of 'deification' concepts in the early church arguing that they are derived from the church's christological use of Psalm 82 in the East and West, not, as J. Gross and others have argued, simply from the Hellenistic milieu in which the early fathers dwelt. See Carl Mosser, 'The Earliest Patristic Interpretations of Psalm 82, Jewish Antecedents, and the Origin of Christian Deification', *Journal of Theological Studies* 56 (2005): pp. 30–74.

It was only in the fourth century that *theosis* came in for expansive treatment. Athanasius stands out as one of its main architects.[25] He reasons that when God assumed humanity and became incarnate, he opened the way for people to ascend to him, assume divinity, and become 'in-godded'. In one of his letters to Adelphus, Athanasius makes his famous statement that the Son of God became man 'that he might deify us in himself'.[26] Elsewhere he writes that Christ 'was made man that we might be made God'.[27] When understood within the broader theological logic of Athanasius it is clear that by this language he intends to say that *theosis* is the means of salvation whereby the human person is incorporated, not into the divine essence, but into the person of Christ who, by virtue of the hypostatic union, is the mediator of divinity.[28]

In a summary statement of the Athanasian conception of *theosis* we read simply that 'He deified that which He put on, and more than that, "gave" it graciously to the race of man'.[29] By this time *theosis* was a firmly established christological doctrine and was most often used to demonstrate, against the Arians, the full humanity and full deity of the Incarnate Christ (and the deity of the Holy Spirit). With Athanasius the doctrine of *theosis* has become, to use the words of Dalmais, an 'uncontested truth'.[30]

Eastern Orthodoxy has consistently asserted the doctrine of 'deification'. With Pseudo-Dionysius, Maximus the Confessor, John of Damascus, Symeon the New Theologian, Nicholas Cabasilas, and finally Gregory Palamas, the Eastern Orthodox understanding of *theosis* came to mature expression.[31] According to Palamas, the image in humans is an indistinct image of God and not, like the Son, an exact image. For Palamas, as in Irenaeus before him, the image applies to the whole person, body and soul. As God contains and infuses life into the world

---

[25] For an exhaustive list of his cognates for *theosis* see Guido Müller, *Lexicon Athanasianum* (Berlin: Walter De Gruyter & Co, 1952), cols. 8–9; 24–5; 182; 498; 628–9; 765; 1516.

[26] Athanasius, *Letter 60, to Adelphus*, 4 (*NPNF*, 2nd series, vol. 4. pp. 1334–40).

[27] Athanasius, *On the Incarnation,* 54 (*NPNF*, 2nd series, vol. 4. pp. 340–41).

[28] Athanasius, *Defence of the Nicene Definition*, 14 (*NPNF*, 2nd series, vol. 4. p. 516). See Alan L. Kolp, 'Partakers of the Divine Nature. The Use of 2 Peter 1.4 by Athanasius', *Studia Patristica* 17 (1982): pp. 1018–23; and Hamilton Hess, 'The Place of Divinization in Athanasian Soteriology', *Studia Patristica* 26 (1993): pp. 369–74.

[29] Athanasius, *Contra Arianos,* 42 (*NPNF*, 2nd series, vol. 4. p. 855).

[30] Irénée-H, Dalmais, 'Divinisation. II: Patristrique grèque', in *Dictionnaire de spiritualité, ascétique et mystique, doctrine et histoire*, vol. 3 (Paris: Beauchesne, 1937–), col. 1380.

[31] For a comprehensive study of Palamas see Georgios I. Mantzaridis, *The Deification of Man: St Gregory Palamas and the Orthodox Tradition*, trans. Liadain Sherrard (1963. Crestwood, NY.: St Vladimir's Seminary Press, 1984); and of Cabasilas see Panayiotis Nellas, *Deification in Christ*, trans. Norman Russell (1979. Crestwood, NY.: St Vladimir's Seminary Press, 1987).

through his Spirit, so human intellect, through its spirit, contains and vitalises the body attached to it. The human soul, according to both Palamas and the Orthodox tradition, is not held captive within the body so that it strives for release, as the Platonists taught. Mantzaridis explains that, 'From the moment of his creation, man strives to approach his archetype, God, and so to be deified. This movement of man from "image" to archetype is generally expressed in the fathers by the phrase from Scripture "after His likeness"'.[32]

'For St Paul the "image of the invisible God" is Christ. And man, as we shall see, is the image of the Image.' The goal of humanity is to realise true and full human personhood, or to express the image of God fully. If that image is Christ then the goal of human existence is to achieve the image of Christ, or what in Orthodox language is termed 'Christification'.[33] In this way men and women are the 'image of the Image'. Nellas remarks, '...man, having been created "in the image" of the infinite God, is called by his own nature – and this is precisely the sense of "in the image" from this point of view – to transcend the limited boundaries of creation and to become infinite'.[34]

Torrance draws upon many of these familiar Orthodox themes and adapts them in significant ways before applying the key insights to his own doctrine of *theosis*. What we find in Torrance's work is a creative continuity with certain features of Orthodox thought alongside a rejection of other themes in that same tradition. While libertarian free will, determinacy, and sacramental striving towards perfection are rejected, the notion that humans are the image of the Image, who is ultimately Jesus Christ, is accepted, along with a nuanced version of *theosis*.

Doctrines of *theosis* are clearly deeply established within Eastern Christianity and to this day they remain a central thread in Greek and Russian theology. But what of the Latin West? While the theme of *theosis* is not a dominant one in the West it is certainly not without its supporters. In company with the Greek theologians Augustine speaks of the essential link between the incarnation of the Son and the divinisation of the human. Lampe maintains that,

> Augustine repeats more often, perhaps, than any of the Greek theologians, the theme of the 'interchange of places'. 'The Word', he says, became what we are that we might attain what we are not. For we are not God; but we can see God with the mind and interior eye of the heart. 'God hates you as you are, in order to make you what you are not yet. You will be what he is', but Augustine hastens to add that this means that we shall be God's image in the sense in which a man's reflection in a mirror is his image inasmuch as it is *like* him, not in the sense in

32 Mantzaridis, *The Deification of Man*, p. 21.

33 Nellas, *Deification in Christ*, p. 24.

34 Ibid., p. 28.

which a man's son is his image inasmuch as he *is* actually what his father is 'according to substance.[35]

In Augustine's discussions on *theosis* it is clear that we are made partakers of the divine nature by grace, not by nature.[36] For Augustine this means by adoption – sonship by grace; this is a direct consequence of human nature being assumed by God in the incarnation.

Thomas Aquinas makes significant use of the doctrine of *theosis* in his voluminous theological works.[37] One commentator concludes her study of the *Summa Theologiae* with these words: 'In view of this particular structure of Thomas's doctrine of God, theological anthropology, Christology, and the connection between them, it is no exaggeration to say the *Summa* lacks a question on deification because the subject of its every part is deification.'[38] To cite just one example, where Aquinas seeks to establish that God alone is the cause of grace he writes: 'It is…necessary that God alone should deify, bestowing a partaking of the divine nature.'[39] Aquinas's use of *theosis* provides a metaphysical bridge between the Uncreated and created by appealing to the idea that nature can be ascribed to a subject in two ways: essentially, and by participation. Arguably *theosis* functions in the second use of the term 'nature'.

---

35 Geoffrey W.H. Lampe, 'Theology in the Patristic Period', in *A History of Christian Doctrine*, ed. Hubert Cuncliffe-Jones (Philadelphia: Fortress, 1978), pp. 153–4. See the studies of Gerald Bonner, 'Deification, Divinization', in *Augustine Through the Ages: An Encyclopedia*, ed. Allan D. Fitzgerald (Grand Rapids: Eerdmans, 1999), pp. 265–6; 'Deificare', in *Augustinus-Lexikon*, ed. Cornelius Mayer (Basel: Schwabe & Co., 1996), vol. 2. pp. 265–7; *God's Decree and Man's Destiny: Studies in the Thought of Augustine of Hippo* (London: Variorum Reprints, 1987); and 'Augustine's Conception of Deification', *Journal of Theological Studies* ns 37 (1986): pp. 369–86.

36 This is clearly brought out in the newly discovered sermons of Augustine, especially the so-called *Dolbeau* 6 or *Mainz* 13, where Augustine supplies an extended meditation on deification amongst an exposition of Ps 81. See Francois Dolbeau, 'Nouveau sermons de saint Augustin pour la conversion des paiens et des donatistes (V)', *Revue des Etudes Augustiniennes* 39 (1993): pp. 57–108; and *The Works of Saint Augustine: Newly Discovered Sermons*, trans. Edmund Hill (Hyde Park, N.Y.: New City, 1990).

37 For comprehensive treatment see Williams, *The Ground of Union*, and the literature that looks at Thomas' idea of participation as a philosophical concept such as Francis J. Klauder, *A Philosophy Rooted in Love: The Dominant Themes in the Perennial Philosophy of St. Thomas Aquinas* (Lanham, MD.: University Press of America, 1994).

38 Williams, 'Deification in the *Summa Theologiae:* A Structural Interpretation of the *Prima Pars*', p. 255.

39 Thomas Aquinas, *Summa Theologiae* I–II, q.112, a.1 (Westminster, MD.: Christian Classics, 1980). Other examples include I–II, q.3, a.1 ad 2; I–II, q.50, a.6; II–II, q.2, obj.1; III, q.1, a.2; III, q.2, a,1, ad 3; III, q.16, a.7, ad 3; and in one of his *opscula* on the Feast of Corpus Christi: 'The only-begotten Son of God, wishing to make us sharers in his divine nature, assumed our nature…that made man he might make men gods' (*opscula* 57).

Not only did the early church, the Fathers, and the scholastics adopt a doctrine of *theosis*, so too did the Protestant Reformers. Since the mid-1970s a new interpretation of Luther known as the 'Finnish School' or 'Helsinki Circle' has arisen under the influence of Tuomo Mannermaa.[40] The central thesis of this school is that for the so-called 'later' Luther, salvation is conceived as union with Christ, based around Luther's phrase '*in ipsa fide Christus adest*' ('in faith itself Christ is really present'). The Finnish School argues that for Luther faith is a real participation in Christ; that in faith a believer receives the righteousness of God in Christ, not only in a nominal and external way, but genuinely and inwardly. This insight radically challenges traditional Luther scholarship. If the forensic model of justification argues that through faith we are *declared* righteous, while in actuality we are not *made* righteous, this new reading of Luther argues that through faith we participate in the *whole* Christ, who in his divine person actually communicates the righteousness of God. If such an interpretation is correct (and there is considerable debate),[41] then herein lies, arguably, a sufficient bridge from Reformation thought to the Orthodox idea of salvation, understood as *theosis*.

A concept of *theosis* is also present in the theology of Calvin, albeit in quite what way scholars dispute.[42] Given Torrance's interest in Calvin's theology, his use of *theosis* is an important backdrop for Torrance's. For Calvin, the concept of *theosis*

---

40 See *Union With Christ: The New Finnish Interpretation of Luther,* eds Carl E. Braaten, and Robert W. Jenson (Grand Rapids: Eerdmans, 1998); along with Rainer Hauke, *Gott-Haben – um Gottes Willen. Andreas Osianders Theosisgedanke und die Diskussion um die Grundlagen der evangelisch verstandenen Rechtfertigung. Versuch einer Neubewertung eines umstrittenen Gedankens,* (Frankfurt-am-Main: Peter Lang, 1999); *Luther und Theosis: Vergöttlichung als Thema der abendländischen Theologie,* eds Simo Peura, and Antti Raunio (Helsinki: Luther-Agricola-Gesellschaft, 1990); Joachim Heubach, *Luther und Theosis* (Erlangen: Martin-Luther-Verlag, 1990); and Reinhard Flogaus, *Theosis bei Palamas und Luther: ein Beitrag zum ökumenishcen Gespräch* (Göttingen: Vendenhoek and Ruprecht, 1997).

41 The Finnish interpretation is not without its ardent critics, see for instance, Timothy J. Wengert, '*Union With Christ: The New Finnish Interpretation of Luther:* Review Article', *Theology Today* 56 (1999): pp. 432–4; and Carl R. Trueman, 'Is the Finnish Line a New Beginning? A Critical Assessment of the Reading of Luther Offered by the Helsinki Circle', in *The Wages of Spin: Critical Writings on Historical and Contemporary Evangelicalism* (Fearn: Mentor, 2004), pp. 129–48. Also important are the collection of essays in *Luther und Theosis.*

42 Frederick W. Norris, 'Deification: Consensual and Cogent', *Scottish Journal of Theology* 49 (1996): p. 420, believes it is not present at all. Others argue it is clearly there, for example J. Todd Billings, *Calvin, Participation, and the Gift: The Activity of Believes in Union with Christ (*Oxford: Oxford University press, 2007); and Carl Mosser, 'The Greatest Possible Blessing: Calvin and Deification', *Scottish Journal of Theology* 55 (2002): pp. 36–57. Cf. Jonathan Slater, 'Salvation as Participation in the Humanity of the Mediator in Calvin's *Institutes of the Christian Religion*: A Reply to Carl Mosser', *Scottish Journal of Theology* 58 (2005): pp. 39–58.

comes closest to what is more commonly in the West termed 'union with Christ'. It has been argued that the *unio mystica* is central to Calvin's theology.[43] If this is true, and there is good evidence to believe that it is, then logically the doctrine of *theosis* is also of importance to Calvin's theology.[44] In one of his rare uses of the word 'deification', Calvin writes, in reference to 2 Pt 1.4: 'We should notice that it is the purpose of the Gospel to make us sooner or later like God; indeed it is, so to speak, a kind of deification.'[45] Echoing the same thought as Eastern Orthodox writers, Calvin, when writing about the thought of humans partaking of the divine nature, makes it plain that this does not mean we partake of the divine *essence* but the divine *likeness*. 'The apostles', writes Calvin, 'were simply concerned to say that when we have put off all the vices of the flesh we shall be partakers of divine immortality and the glory of blessedness, and thus we shall be in a way with God so far as our capacity allows.'[46]

For Calvin, the process of partaking of the divine nature is initiated in our election for salvation, effected in our union with Christ, and made possible in two interrelated ways. The first is by the incarnation of the Son, which represents a divinising of humanity through the humanising of divinity. In his *Institutes* Calvin speaks of partaking of the divine nature in terms of the *mirifica commutatio* whereby,

> Having become with us the Son of Man, he [Christ] has made us with himself sons of God. By his own descent to the earth he has prepared our ascent to heaven. Having received our mortality, he has bestowed on us his immortality. Having undertaken our weakness, he has made us strong in his strength. Having submitted to our poverty, he has transferred to us his riches. Having taken upon himself the burden of unrighteousness with which we were oppressed, he has clothed us with his righteousness.[47]

---

[43] See for instance Wilhelm Kolfhaus, *Christusgemeinschaft bei Calvin* (Neukirchener Verlag: BGLRK3, 1939); Charles Partee, 'Calvin's Central Dogma Again', *Sixteenth Century Journal* 18 (1987): pp. 191–9; and Dennis E. Tamburello, *Union With Christ: John Calvin and the Mysticism of St. Bernard* (Louisville: Westminster John Knox, 1994).

[44] John Calvin, *Calvin's New Testament Commentaries*. vol. 12. *Hebrews and 1 and 2 Peter*, trans. William B. Johnston, eds David W. Torrance, and Thomas F. Torrance (Grand Rapids: Eerdmans, 1963), p. 330; John Calvin, *Institutes of the Christian Religion*, Library of Christian Classics, vols 20–21, ed. John T. McNeill, trans. Ford L. Battles (Philadelphia: Westminster Press, 1960), 1.13.14; 2.7.1; 3.2.24; 3.11.10; 3.25.10; 4.17.2, 4, 11. (All references to Calvin's *Institutes* are to the 1559 edition in the Battles translation, unless otherwise stated.)

[45] Calvin, *Calvin's New Testament Commentaries*. vol. 12. *Hebrews and 1 and 2 Peter*, p. 330.

[46] Ibid.

[47] Calvin, *Institutes*, 4.17.2.

The second way in which union with Christ is effected is through the work of the Holy Spirit. This partaking of the divine nature, or more specifically of Christ, is then experienced and further developed through the sacraments and the life of piety lived out in the Spirit's power.

In Calvin's treatment of *theosis* the doctrine of the Trinity provides the foundation and the context within which the 'deification' of humans is set. Calvin's doctrine of *theosis*, like its classical antecedents, is built around the hypostatic union. *Theosis* is only possible because human nature has been deified in the theandric person of the Mediator. As men and women are united to Christ, his divinity deifies them.[48] Mosser concludes: 'The believer's union with Christ and the Father, the indwelling presence of the Spirit in our hearts, restoration of the divine image, being made like Jesus and our eventual glorification are each important themes in Calvin's soteriology and eschatology. They are all pervaded by the language of theosis.'[49]

Later Protestant thought also adopted *theosis* as a theme. This is evident in Anglican theology, for example. Arthur Allchin looks at the doctrine of *theosis* as it is to be found in representative Anglican theologians during the last four centuries and in the process uncovers a surprisingly rich heritage in theologians as diverse as Richard Hooker, John Henry Newman, Edward B. Pusey, and Clive S. Lewis.[50] Most notable in this regard is the so-called Oxford Movement (1833–45), which reasserted many patristic themes including *theosis*.[51] Louth has shown the extent to which the appeal to the Fathers was present in these Anglican writers precisely in their appropriation of a doctrine of 'deification'.[52] The leaders of the Oxford Movement recovered a patristic doctrine of *theosis* that speaks of a real participation between God and humanity in the work of redemption and sanctification. What Keble, Newman, Pusey and DuBose all asserted was the radical nature of this union and the disciplined life of holiness that it called forth from the faithful. As

---

48 See David Willis-Watkins, 'The Unio Mystica and the Assurance of Faith According to Calvin', in *Calvin: Erbe und Auftrag*, ed. Willem van't Spijker (Kampen: Kok Pharos, 1991), p. 78.

49 Mosser, 'The Greatest Possible Blessing: Calvin and Deification', p. 55.

50 Arthur M. Allchin, *Participation in God: A Forgotten Strand in Anglican Tradition* (Wilton, Conn.: Morehouse-Barlow, 1988). Also Edmund Newey, 'The Form of Reason: Participation in the Work of Richard Hooker, Benjamin Wichcote, Ralph Cudworth and Jeremy Taylor', *Modern Theology* 18 (2002): pp. 1-26; Dan Edwards, 'Deification and the Anglican Doctrine of Human Nature: A Reassessment of the Historical Significance of Henry Porcher DuBose', *Anglican and Episcopal History* 58 (1989): pp. 196–212; and Myk Habets, 'Walking *In Mirabilibus Supra Me*: How C.S. Lewis Transposes *Theosis*' (unpublished paper).

51 For a brief overview see E. Charles Miller, Jr., *Toward a Fuller Vision* (Wilton: Morehouse-Barlow, 1984).

52 Andrew Louth, 'Manhood into God: The Oxford Movement, the Fathers and the Deification of Man', in *Essays Catholic and Radical*, eds Kenneth Leech and Rowan Williams (London: Bowerdean Press, 1983), pp. 70–80.

with the patristic authors, the architects of the Oxford Movement emphasised an immediacy of contact with God that, in their opinion, was most clearly formulated by articulating a notion of *theosis.*

Methodism, under the teaching of the Wesley brothers, also evinces the effects of a doctrine of *theosis.*[53] Various studies have identified in both John and Charles Wesley a significant influence of Eastern mysticism alongside their Western distinctives.[54] According to McCormick:

> The eastern tradition maintains that *theosis*, the 'way' into this deifying union or restoration of the *imago dei*, comes by way of the mysterious coinciding of a gift of divine energy and human freedom… It is just such an understanding of *theosis* which Wesley seems to employ as the organizing principle of his *ordo salutis*. And, as Wesley wrote his *ordo salutis* to the tune of *theosis*, it is probably better to understand it as a *via salutis*: that is to say, we are *becoming* 'like' God by the energy of love (coinciding with our freedom) as He was *becoming* what we are in condescending love.[55]

Finally, the link between Wesley's theology and the subsequent Holiness tradition and Pentecostalism is crucial to note in that Pentecostalism is open to a doctrine of *theosis* and is currently exploring the theme, most notably in relation to Roman Catholic-Pentecostal dialogue.[56] As the fastest growing religion on the planet, Pentecostalism is having a pervasive effect on world and Protestant theology, and doctrines of *theosis* are proving popular and powerful within this tradition.[57]

---

53 Jürgen Moltmann, *The Spirit of Life: A Universal Affirmation,* trans. M. Kohl (Minneapolis: Fortress, 1992), p. 165, has pointed out Wesley's adoption of *theosis* and provides original and secondary sources. See also Randy L. Maddox, 'John Wesley and Eastern Orthodoxy: Influences, Convergences and Divergences', *Asbury Theological Journal* 45 (1990): pp. 29–53.

54 See in this regard Nicholas Lossky, *Lancelot Andrewes the Preacher [1555–1626]: The Origins of the Mystical Theology of the Church of England* (Oxford: Clarendon, 1986), who highlights how the Anglican writers Lancelot Andrewes (1555–1626) and Thomas Ken (1637–1710) influenced the theological perspectives of both John and Charles Wesley.

55 Steve K. McCormick, 'Theosis in Chrysostom and Wesley: An Eastern Paradigm on Faith and Love', http://www.wesley.nu.edu/theojrnl/26-30/26-3.htm (accessed 3.7.02). A recent Wesleyan articulation of *theosis* is found in Thomas C. Oden, *Systematic Theology*, vol. 3. *Life in the Spirit* (Peabody, MA.: Prince Press, 1992), pp. 207–12.

56 See in Veli-Matti, Kärkkäinen, *Spiritus ubi vult spirat: Pneumatology in Roman Catholic-Pentecostal Dialogue (1972–1989),* Schriften der Luther-Agricola-Gesellschaft 42 (Helsinki: Luther-Agricola Society, 1998); and *Ad ultimum terrae: Evengelization, Proselytism and Common Witness in the Roman Catholic-Pentecostal Dialogue 1990–1997* (Frankfurt: Peter Lang, 1999).

57 As one example see Veli-Matti, Kärkkäinen, *One With God: Salvation as Deification and Justification* (Collegeville, Mn.: Liturgical Press, 2004).

It may well be argued that historically a doctrine of *theosis* has not been neglected in the Western tradition at all; it has been there all along, albeit often in an underdeveloped form. With the republication of many Eastern Orthodox texts on *theosis* into English, and the recent calls from a number of contemporary Western theologians to reintroduce *theosis* onto the Western soteriological agenda,[58] *theosis* is one of a number of patristic themes to which appeal is currently made both to recall the church to its theological sources and to aid it in confronting the challenges of a postmodern era. It is also being used by a number of theologians as a possible way of ecumenical advancement.[59] It is into this context that Torrance's use of *theosis* may be considered, given his expertise in the patristic literature, his commitment to Reformed theology, his critical development of key Barthian insights, and his own constructive insights into the development of a scientific theology.

Conclusion

Direct references to *theosis* within Torrance's work are relatively few and yet his work is significantly influenced by the conceptuality of it,[60] a feature often misunderstood or ignored in critical studies on his theology. In an address delivered to the World Alliance of Reformed Churches, in Frankfurt, 5 August 1964, Torrance pleaded for:

> [A] reconsideration by the Reformed Churches of what the Greek fathers called *theosis*. This is usually unfortunately translated *deification*, but it has nothing to

---

58 A brief list includes: Oden, *Systematic Theology.* vol. 3. pp. 207–12; Daniel B. Clendenin, *Eastern Orthodox Christianity: A Western Perspective* (Grand Rapids: Baker, 1994); Thomas Oden, 'Partakers of Divinity: The Orthodox Doctrine of Theosis', *Journal of the Evangelical Theological Society* 37 (1994): pp. 365–79; Clark H. Pinnock, *Flame of Love: A Theology of the Holy Spirit* (Downers Grove: IVP, 1996), pp. 149–83; Gary D. Badcock, *Light of Truth and Fire of Love: A Theology of the Holy Spirit* (Grand Rapids: Eerdmans, 1997), pp. 35–61; Robert V. Rakestraw, 'Becoming Like God: An Evangelical Doctrine of Theosis', *Journal of the Evangelical Theological Society* 40 (1997): pp. 257–69; David Cunningham, *These Three Are One: The Practice of Trinitarian Theology* (Oxford: Blackwell, 1998), pp. 165–95; Robert W. Jenson, *Systematic Theology.* vol. 2 (New York: Oxford University Press, 1999), pp. 296–98; 311–12; 322–3; 340–46; Bruce Marshall, 'Justification as Declaration and Deification', *International Journal of Systematic Theology* 4 (2002): pp. 3–28; and Kärkkäinen, *One With God.*

59 See for example Veli-Matti, Kärkkäinen, 'The Ecumenical Potential of Pneumatology', *Gregorium* 80 (1999): pp. 121–45; 'The Doctrine of Theosis and its Ecumenical Potential', *Sobornost* 23 (2001): pp. 45–77; and *One With God.*

60 Only one publication is explicitly dedicated to the theme, Thomas F. Torrance, 'Incarnation and Atonement: Theosis and Henosis in the Light of Modern Scientific Rejection of Dualism', *Society of Ordained Scientists*, Bulletin No. 7 (Edgeware, Middlesex, Spring 1992): pp. 8–20.

> do with the *divinization* of man any more than the Incarnation has to do with the humanization of God. *Theosis* was the term the Fathers used to emphasize the fact that through the Spirit we have to do with God in his utter sublimity, his sheer Godness or holiness; creatures though we are, men on earth, in the Spirit we are made to participate in saving acts that are abruptly and absolutely divine, election, adoption, regeneration or sanctification and we participate in them by grace alone. *Theosis* describes man's involvement in such a mighty act of God upon him that he is raised up to find the true centre of his existence not in himself but in Holy God, where he lives and moves and has his being in the uncreated but creative energy of the Holy Spirit. By *theosis* the Greek fathers wished to express the fact that in the new coming of the Holy Spirit we are up against *God* in the most absolute sense, God in his ultimate holiness or Godness.[61]

Within this quotation we have Torrance's doctrine of *theosis* in summation.

When we examine the direct references to *theosis* in Torrance's work, and then consider the context in which Torrance speaks of *theosis*, it is evident that while Torrance uses the technical vocabulary of *theosis* sparingly, when he does employ it he does so in contexts which are central to his entire theological programme, thus making this doctrine one of considerable importance within his overall theological corpus.[62] In place of the technical vocabulary of *theosis* Torrance deals with this theme under a series of other conceptual equivalents including: union, communion, participation, transcendental determination, reordering, humanising, personalising and atoning exchange.[63] This study examines these themes in their theological contexts and what emerges is a complex but coherent Torrancean doctrine of

---

61 Thomas F. Torrance, 'Come, Creator Spirit, For the Renewal of Worship and Witness', in *Theology in Reconstruction*, p. 243. His first use of the term 'deification' appears in a lecture on the Incarnation in *The Doctrine of Jesus Christ: Auburn Lectures 1938–39* (Eugene, Or.: Wipf & Stock, 2002), p. 73, where Torrance is arguing against any Ebionism that advocates the deification of the Man Jesus to God.

62 Torrance is ready to use the phrase 'partakers of the divine nature' [cf. Thomas F. Torrance, *Space, Time and Resurrection* (1976. Edinburgh: T & T Clark, 1998), pp. 135–6], and yet he also notes that 1 Pt 2.4 is perhaps best translated 'partners of the Deity', Thomas F. Torrance, *The Christian Doctrine of God: One Being Three Persons* (Edinburgh: T & T Clark, 1996), p. 95, fn. 52. He also decries any 'debased' understanding of this verse in Thomas F. Torrance, *The Trinitarian Faith: The Evangelical Theology of the Ancient Catholic Church* (Edinburgh: T & T Clark, 1995), p. 140. He does maintain, however, that a doctrine of *theosis* is not simply derived from 2 Pt 1.4 but from a variety of texts, and also that he is following, in large measure, Athanasius who, although Torrance dislikes some of his phrases, essentially got it right. Other key texts Torrance draws upon for his doctrine of *theosis* include but are not limited to Jn 10.35, and Phil 2.9–10.

63 Eastern Orthodoxy also uses a number of synonyms, analogies, and cognates for *theosis* which Clendenin, 'Partakers of Divinity: The Orthodox Doctrine of Theosis', p. 374, lists as: transformation, union, participation, partaking, intermingling, elevation, interpenetration, transmutation, commingling, assimilation, reintegration, adoption, recreation.

theosis. However, it is not one that is without critical questions, deficiencies, and indications for further study.

Through a descriptive and critical exposition of *theosis* in Torrance's theology it will be evident that *theosis* is of fundamental importance to his soteriology. Under patristic, Reformation, and modern influences, *theosis* becomes an integral consequence of his scientific dogmatics, especially as it relates to the *homoousion* and to the doctrine of the Trinity. As an essential part of his Christian dogmatics, the concept of *theosis* in Torrance's approach is one way to unify the various *loci* of theology. While not *the* central point of his dogmatics, it is a necessarily crucial integrating theme within his overall theological *oeuvre*.

Chapter 1 investigates Torrance's doctrines of creation and theological anthropology, emphasising his christological-teleological reading of the *imago Dei* and of his account of the way in which creation is proleptically conditioned by redemption. Because Jesus Christ is the true human being, theological anthropology is actually a correlate to christology. As a result, the essential aspects of the reordering of creation to conform to the nature of the Incarnate Son are compatible with a doctrine of *theosis*. But more than mere compatibility is in view. Torrance's doctrines of creation and anthropology provide the necessary backdrop against which his doctrine of *theosis* is developed. On account of the contingent and proleptic nature of creation Torrance's use of *theosis* takes on a universal range, with consequences extending to the cosmos, which will one day be redeemed and perfected.

The second chapter assesses Torrance's christology and highlights a central theme of his entire theology: that is, that the Incarnation is redemptive and thus Christ's entire life is an act of 'divinisation'. Through the Word incarnate, revelation of God is given and received by means of Christ's vicarious humanity, and union with God in Christ is made a reality. In the life of Christ we have the divinisation of humanity, but not, according to Torrance, in the way many have perceived.

Building upon the doctrine of Christ's vicarious humanity, Chapter 3 forms the heart of the study. It examines Torrance's soteriology directly, exploring the actual dynamics of how the believer is brought into relationship with the True Man, Jesus Christ, and through him into a relationship with the Triune God. Drawing upon a reading of Calvin that makes union with Christ central, Torrance highlights how this union brings the believer into the gift of all the benefits of Christ, and seeks to show that justification as a forensic declaration and 'deification' as an actual participation in the divine life are ultimately compatible within his Reformed theology.

In Chapter 4 the crucial roles of the Holy Spirit and ecclesiology are analysed, since it is by the Spirit that union and communion with Christ become a reality in the life of the believer in the context of the church. The role of pneumatology, often said to be a somewhat underdeveloped area in Western theology, is developed by Torrance as the Holy Spirit brings revelation, reconciliation, and transformation to the believer in Christ and in the Spirit. The work of God within the individual is never separate from the church, and thus Torrance develops his ecclesiology as the locus of *theosis*. The sacraments, priesthood, prayer, ministry and worship are seen as central ecclesial acts through which believers are progressively 'deified'. While Torrance incorporates the Holy Spirit and the church into his theology there are critical issues and deficiencies in his account of *theosis* that I shall note.

The conclusion draws together the various threads of the present study. While Torrance's vision of *theosis* is robust and pervasive, it is often implicit, undeveloped, and very rarely interacts with critical scholarship. Through a presentation of how Torrance's theology is more than compatible with doctrines of *theosis* and through a critical engagement with contemporary scholarship, the rudiments of a doctrine of *theosis* compatible with Reformed theology are presented, but it is argued that this doctrine requires further development and refinement beyond that which Torrance provides.

Chapter 1
Creation and Theological Anthropology

Creation: God and the World

According to Torrance, *theosis* is initially accomplished in the work of the Incarnate Son Jesus Christ, then, by extension, in the experience of particular human persons. However, as in the patristic tradition and the theologies of Eastern Orthodoxy, the entire creation is somehow involved or caught up in the 'deification' of humanity. It is not that creation experiences *theosis* as such, but rather that there is a cosmic scope to *theosis* that Torrance, no less than his Eastern colleagues, emphasises.

Fundamental to Torrance's doctrines of creation and anthropology is an assumption that finds expression thus: 'it is distinctive of Christian theology that it treats of God in his relation to the world and of God in his relation to himself, not of one without the other.'[1] Torrance makes it clear that Creator and creation must be thought of in vital relation to each other. More specifically, 'a theology that is restricted to the relation between man and God is deficient and primitive, for it has not advanced from *mythos* to *logos*, from thinking out of a centre in the human subject to thinking out of a centre in objective reality...'.[2] The nature of the specific form of this relationship between creation and redemption is the all-important issue at hand.

Torrance envisages a realist theology as operating within a triadic structure. The specific form this 'complex of relations' takes for Torrance is that of God-humanity-world, not simply God-humanity as has so often been the case in formal, especially evangelical theology, nor God-world as is so often apparent in some contemporary ecological approaches. We cannot speak of God except within the world in which he has placed us, and the world of which humanity is, by divine creation, a primary constituent element. Hence anthropology and creation are not two independent *loci* of theology; rather, a doctrine of creation is the *locus* of anthropological reflection, or put another way, anthropology is a *focus* of the doctrine of creation. As a concise summary we read: 'Theologically speaking, man and the universe belong together and together constitute what we mean by "world", the world in its relation to God.'[3] This approach becomes all the more evident when humanity is considered in light of the eternal Word of God

---

[1] Thomas F. Torrance, *Reality and Evangelical Theology* (Downers Grove: IVP, 1999), p. 21.

[2] Ibid., p. 27.

[3] Ibid. Wolfhart Pannenberg follows similar lines of enquiry in his second volume of the *Systematic Theology* (Grand Rapids: Eerdmans, 1994), p. 1.

who became incarnate and is identified as the one through whom creation exists. In this way Jesus Christ becomes central to Torrance's doctrines of creation and anthropology, and hence central for an understanding of *theosis*. Given this triadic relation we must interpret *theosis* through the specific sort of relations that exist between God, the world, and humanity. While we shall examine christology in Chapter 2, we must anticipate the general direction it will take in this chapter.

Two interrelated tasks are accomplished within Torrance's doctrine of creation: one is to clarify that creation is not necessary to God but is contingent on the divine will; the other is to stress that participation in the divine nature is grounded in the creature's existence. In presenting *theosis* as integral to the creation of humanity Torrance is drawing upon specific notions of *theosis* held by some of the Fathers, although much of their usage limited the doctrine to the sanctifying work of the hypostatic union in the Son or the graced renewal of the human by the Spirit. Torrance presents both ideas but insists upon the creational aspect as integral to the whole doctrine, something only a few Eastern Orthodox theologians do explicitly.[4]

In order to understand Torrance's doctrine of *theosis* we must start with his doctrine of creation and specifically ask how it is that Creator and creation are related to one another. From this relation we investigate his account of theological anthropology, especially the important doctrine of the *imago Dei* in its trinitarian and teleological dimensions.

Cosmic Consequences of Theosis

Torrance consistently maintains that creation is a work of the Triune God in which all three Persons have a distinctive part to play. Torrance accepts and seeks to expound the formula derived from Basil that states that creation is *from* the Father, *through* the Son, *in* the Holy Spirit.[5] According to Torrance, 'the fact that God is

---

[4] For example: Panagiotes K. Chrestou, *Partakers of God* (Brookline, Mass.: Holy Cross Orthodox Press, 1984), p. 41: 'The world and man had a definite destiny in God's creations, namely, to partake of the goodness and glory of God, which is possible only through communion with him'; and Dumitru Staniloae, *The Experience of God: Orthodox Dogmatic Theology*, vol. 2. *The World: Creation and Deification*, trans. and eds Ioan Ionita and Robert Barringer (1978. Brookline, Mass.: Holy Cross Orthodox Press, 2000), pp. 191–200, commits an entire chapter to developing this idea. Reflecting concerns reminiscent of Torrance, Staniloae is insistent that, 'the human being cannot exist apart from his relationship with nature. The three together make an inseparable whole: *I-Thou-Nature*', p. 198. This moves both Staniloae and Torrance beyond Barth's *I-thou* notion (via Buber) of constitutive relationality towards the 'exocentrism' of Pannenberg. See F. LeRon Shults, 'Constitutive Relationality in Anthropology and Trinity: The Shaping of the *Imago Dei* Doctrine in Barth and Pannenberg', in *Neue Zeitschrift für systematische Theologie und Religionsphilosophie* 39 (1997): pp. 304–22.

[5] See Basil, *De Spiritu Sancto* 16.37–40; Thomas F. Torrance, *The Christian Doctrine of God: One Being Three Persons* (Edinburgh: T & T Clark, 1996), pp. 203–4; and Thomas F. Torrance, *Theology in Reconstruction* (Grand Rapids: Eerdmans, 1965), p. 221. This has

always Father, not always Creator, but *became* Creator, means that it is precisely *as Father* that he is Creator...'.[6] From this axiom Torrance derives certain corollaries of a trinitarian kind. As Father he is Father of the Son and sender of the Spirit, and a trinitarian stamp is found within creation.[7]

Along with recent trends in theology Torrance is able, in this trinitarian construct, to give space to the Spirit as the one who brings creation to its destined end or *telos*.[8] This implies that the Spirit is the *Spiritus Vivificans* who works not only in the church but throughout the entire world, bringing order out of chaos as in the first creation account, and bringing all things to their providential end – communion (*theosis*) with God.

As a way of summarising the distinctive ways in which the Triune God creates, Torrance alludes to a doctrine of *theosis* thus:

> The supreme end for which God has designed his creation and which he activates and rules throughout all his relations with it is the purpose of his Holy Love not to live for himself alone but to bring into being a creaturely realm of heaven and earth which will reflect his glory and within which he may share with others the Communion of Love which constitutes his inner Life as Father, Son and Holy Spirit. It is in the incarnation of God's beloved Son in Jesus Christ, and in our sharing in that relation of the Son to the Father through the Holy Spirit, that the secret of the creation, hidden from the ages, has become disclosed to us.[9]

Here *theosis* is a sharing in the Divine Life in a creaturely way as a direct result of the creation from the Love of the Father through the omnipotent grace of the Son and realised by the life-giving work of the Holy Spirit.[10]

Moving beyond the trinitarian *how* to an investigation of the *purpose* of creation, the cosmic consequences of *theosis* need to be further articulated. Torrance does

---

become a standard theological way of describing the creating-work of the triune God in recent theology. For a similar exploration see Stanley J. Grenz, *Theology for the Community of God* (Carlisle: Paternoster, 1994), pp. 133–9; and Colin E. Gunton, *The Triune Creator: A Historical and Systematic Study* (Grand Rapids: Eerdmans, 1998).

[6] Torrance, *The Christian Doctrine of God*, p. 209.

[7] For an explanation of this 'trinitarian stamp' on creation see Myk Habets, 'How "Creation is Proleptically Conditioned by Redemption"', *Colloquium* (forthcoming).

[8] On recent trends see the seminal essay of D. Lyle Dabney, 'Starting with the Spirit: Why the Last Should Now be First,' in *Starting with the Spirit,* Task of Theology Today II, eds Stephen Pickard and Gordon Preece (Adelaide: ATF, 2001), pp. 3–27.

[9] Torrance, *The Christian Doctrine of God*, p. 218. Torrance goes on to quote in full Eph 1.3–14.

[10] For comparable visions of Triune creation see Emil Bartos, *Deification in Eastern Orthodoxy: An Evaluation and Critique of the Theology of Dumitru Staniloae* (Carlisle: Paternoster, 1999), p. 104, who sums up the position of Staniloae and Eastern Orthodoxy more generally on this point; and the Pannenberg-inspired description by Grenz, *Theology for the Community of God*, p. 138.

this through the concepts of order and re-order and an exploration of the axiom that 'creation is conditioned by redemption'. Out of this discussion Torrance asserts the cosmic consequences of *theosis* and builds a foundation from which to articulate his dynamic and relational doctrine of the *imago Dei* and explain how the incarnate Christ is central, even if in a proleptic way, to both creation and the *imago*, thus making Christ central to his doctrine of *theosis*.

The 'reordering' of creation Within Torrance's work there is a direct and explicit link between God the Father as Creator and the person and work of the Son in the economy. Here creation and redemption are brought together in an insightful synthesis. 'Quite clearly, Christology and Soteriology have and must have critical significance for our understanding of God as almighty and of his distinctive activity in creation and redemption',[11] writes Torrance. Here christology actually conditions the creation in the first place, proleptically influencing its reality. Torrance's vision of creation is here, as elsewhere in his theology, a christocentric one. Creation is not only through Christ, but also for Christ. McGrath identifies a notable point within the history of Christian thought which applies equally to the works of Torrance:

> The Christian understanding of creation leads directly to the conclusion that there is a correspondence – the degree of which requires clarification – between the works of God and the being of God. Creation and redemption are not merely interconnected within the economy of salvation; they can each be argued to embody the character of God.[12]

In the Incarnation redemption intersects and overlaps with creation in such a way that Christ and his Kingdom encompass all of history. Purpose is deliberately built into creation from the beginning and, as with the *theosis* of human beings so with creation itself, perfection is anticipated from the very creation, yet this perfection will not come about mechanistically or 'naturally', but rather through divine grace.

This same theme echoes within the theology of Athanasius, a key influence upon Torrance, who repeatedly emphasised the connection between creation and redemption. According to Athanasius the purpose of the incarnation was not only the restoration of humanity but of the whole created order. He writes:

> It is, then, proper for us to begin the treatment of this subject by speaking of the creation of the universe, and of God its Artificer, so that it may be duly perceived that the renewal of creation has been the work of the self-same Word that made

[11] Thomas F. Torrance, *The Trinitarian Faith: The Evangelical Theology of the Ancient Catholic Church* (Edinburgh: T & T Clark, 1995), pp. 82–3.

[12] Alister E. McGrath, *A Scientific Theology*, vol. 1, *Nature* (Grand Rapids: Eerdmans, 2001), p. 193.

> it at the beginning. For it will appear not inconsonant for the Father to have wrought its salvation in Him by Whose means He made it.[13]

In harmony with Torrance's 'scientific' approach to theology he considers redemption in terms of the relationship between theology and the natural sciences and the mutuality of their commitment to 'order'.[14] Torrance argues that atonement can be seen in terms of a 'reordering' of creation.[15] This applies not only to the human person but also to the entire creation.[16] It is a cosmic consequence of *theosis*, similar to but not identical with certain Greek patristic emphases.[17] Torrance notes how the universe requires 'redemption from disorder':

> In other words, in the whole human life of Jesus the order of creation has been restored; in the midst of our disordered, sin-disrupted existence, there has been lived a human life in perfect order and proportion to the Will of God...This is the order of redemption which reaches back to the original order of creation and far transcends it in the amazing purpose of the divine love, as the order of the new creation.[18]

By means of the life of Christ, and especially his resurrection, reorder was achieved out of disorder. In a similar way to Irenaeus, Torrance considers redemption to entail the restoration and perfection of the God-given order in which the cosmos

---

13 Athanasius, *On the Incarnation* 1.4 (*NPNF*, 2nd series, vol. 4. p. 273).

14 For definitions of 'order' and 'disorder' see Torrance, *The Christian Frame of Mind*, 2nd edn (Colorado Springs: Helmers and Howard, 1989), pp. 102–5; *Divine and Contingent Order* (1981. Edinburgh: T & T Clark, 1998), pp. 113–28; and 'The Concept of Order in Theology and Science,' *The Princeton Seminary Bulletin* 5 (1984): pp. 130–39.

15 On 'order' and 'reorder', see Thomas F. Torrance, 'The Doctrine of Order', *Church Quarterly Review* 160 (1959): pp. 21–36, and Jason H-K. Yeung, *Being and Knowing: An Examination of T.F. Torrance's Christological Science* (Hong Kong: China Alliance Press, 1996), pp. 66–7.

16 Roland Spjuth, *Creation, Contingency and Divine Presence: In the Theologies of Thomas F. Torrance and Eberhard Jüngel* (Lund: Lund University Press, 1995), pp. 173–4, speaks critically of Torrance's 'divinisation' of the world as implying an exchange from contingency to one all-embracing rationality. However, this misses the point and the force of Torrance's argument. Nowhere in Torrance's writings does he advocate the total independence of creation from Creator or suggest that the creation will ever be anything but contingent. In fact, according to Torrance, it is in this very contingency that the freedom of creation is to be found.

17 See H.E.W. Turner, *The Patristic Doctrine of Redemption* (London: Mowbray, 1952), pp. 70–95.

18 Thomas F. Torrance, 'The Doctrine of Order', *Church Quarterly Review* 160 (1959): pp. 22–3. Cf. Torrance, *The Christian Frame of Mind*, p. 103; and 'The Atonement the Singularity of Christ and the Finality of the Cross: The Atonement and the Moral Order', in *Universalism and the Doctrine of Hell*, ed. Nigel M. de S. Cameron (Carlisle: Paternoster, Grand Rapids: Baker, 1992), pp. 250–55.

came into being. Against this backdrop salvation by means of *theosis* can be seen as the humanising of the person not their 'divinisation' *per se*. It is a making perfect in Christ, not a making into another. In McGrath's reading of Torrance, 'Redemption is thus the restoration of humanity, in order that humanity may play its defined role…in the restoration of the universe as a whole'.[19] This universal restoration of which Torrance speaks refers to the cosmic consequences of *theosis* that we see him begin to develop throughout his doctrine of creation.

Because creation is purposive it, no less than human beings, has a *telos*. 'Somehow it is not just man who has fallen but the whole created order along with him, so that we may not isolate our understanding of human evil from natural evil, or moral evil from material evil, the pain and suffering of human being from the suffering and misery, the pain and travail of the whole creation.'[20] From this truth Torrance draws the conclusion 'that real redemption from the power of human sin and guilt involves a radical change in the material world and calls for the complete redemption of the created order'.[21] Torrance's principle is that 'God does not abandon his creation when he has saved man, for all creation, together with man, will be renewed when Christ comes again'.[22]

What will this redemption applied to nature look like, beyond merely saying 'new heaven' and 'new earth'? One can only speculate at this point based upon the scant biblical references. The outcome, if we accept Torrance's grandiose vision of the cosmic consequences of *theosis*, is that harmony, freedom, and contingency will reach its ultimate fulfilment. Alongside these familiar themes we could go beyond what Torrance has stated to a picture he might also agree with – the perfection of the beauty, artistry, and fecundity of the creation itself. John of Patmos could speak of golden streets, foundations of precious stones, and walls of costly jewels (Rev 21.19). The natural scientist could perhaps speak of balanced eco-systems, the extinction of extinction itself, and the ordered-yet-free, harmonious-yet-new, ordering of the natural order. In Torrance's words:

> God made the creation for such a communion that it might sing His praises and reflect in gladness and joy His loving kindness and glory. Hence the restoration of creation involves the restoration of creation to communion and fellowship with Him in which the peace of God reigns over all, the joy and gladness in God the Father fills the whole of creation. Thus in reconciliation of atonement it is not

---

[19] Alister E. McGrath, *T.F. Torrance; An Intellectual Biography* (Edinburgh: T & T Clark, 1999), p. 227.

[20] Torrance, *The Christian Doctrine of God*, p. 226.

[21] Ibid. See Thomas F. Torrance, *Space, Time and Resurrection* (1976. Edinburgh: T & T Clark, 1998), p. 155, where we are pointed to Karl Barth's *Church Dogmatics*, 4 vols (Edinburgh: T & T Clark, 1956–75), III/3, §49, in which the doctrine of creation and its continuous preservation under the Lordship of Christ is discussed. (Hereafter *Church Dogamtics* will be referred to as *CD*.)

[22] Torrance, *The Christian Doctrine of God*, p. 226.

only with obedience and justice that we have to do, but with the worship and adoration of creation, in which it faithfully reflects the Father's glory and love.[23]

From this principle of reordering Torrance affirms a cosmic extension of redemption, with special emphasis on the redemption of the natural order. The order of redemption 'reaches back to the original order of creation and far transcends it in the amazing purpose of the divine love, as the order, of the new creation'.[24] Redemption is not interference or interruption with the created order but is a healing or restoration of a damaged creation.[25]

Creation is thus, in Calvin's famous words, the theatre for God's glory,[26] a theatre, to extend the metaphor, upon which the drama of redemption is being played out, one day to reach its final act under divine grace. This *theatrum Dei* serves the twofold purpose of glorifying God the Creator and leading God's creatures to glorify God. 'The whole of creation is a mirror, a theatre, a world of signs, which God uses in fulfilment of His Covenant relations with men, as the tools and instruments of His Word.'[27] Creation and redemption share a mutual history and Torrance's doctrine of *theosis* brings both together in a creative synthesis. This presupposes a central axiom that deserves direct consideration, that 'creation is conditioned by redemption'.

Creation conditioned by redemption What Torrance constructs is a view of creation 'proleptically' conditioned by redemption.[28] 'With the incarnation, the death and resurrection of Christ in space and time a portentous change has taken place in the universe affecting the way in which we are to understand divine creation

[23] Thomas F. Torrance, 'The Atoning Obedience of Christ', *Moravian Theological Seminary Bulletin* (1959), p. 66. See also *The Mediation of Christ,* 2nd edn (Edinburgh: T & T Clark, 1992), pp. 71–2.

[24] Thomas F. Torrance, *Conflict and Agreement in the Church*, vol. 2. *The Ministry and the Sacraments of the Gospel* (London: Lutterworth, 1960), p. 15. Torrance provides more background to this 'new creation' in 'The Doctrine of Order', pp. 21–36.

[25] Torrance, *Space, Time and Resurrection*, p. 77. See *The Christian Frame of Mind*, p. 42.

[26] Calvin, *Institutes,* 1.5.8, cf. 1.6.2, 1.14.20, 2.6.1, 3.9.2. Thomas F. Torrance, *Reality and Scientific Theology* (Edinburgh: Scottish Academic Press, 1985), p. 67.

[27] Thomas F. Torrance, *The School of Faith: The Catechisms of the Reformed Church,* trans. and ed. with Introduction by Thomas F. Torrance (London: James Clarke and Co., 1959), p. liii. See also 'The Atoning Obedience of Christ', pp. 65–6.

[28] Torrance no doubt inherited this idea from many of the Fathers, most especially Athanasius in whose work the essential connection between creation and redemption is repeatedly emphasised. See Athanasius *On the Incarnation* 1, 2 (*NPNF*, 2nd series, vol. 4. p. 272). Torrance also learned of the idea from H.R. Mackintosh, see Torrance, 'Introduction', *The School of Faith*, p. ciii.

as proleptically conditioned by redemption.'[29] Colyer helpfully summarises the proleptic nature of creation in the following way:

> What Torrance intends, I believe, is that God's ultimate *telos* for creation from the beginning is revealed and actualised in the incarnation, death and resurrection of Christ, a *telos* in which all creation comes to share in the eternal communion of love that God is. This is the ultimate goal of both redemption and creation. It is actually realised in redemption after the Fall, and it is a *telos* that proleptically conditions the creation.[30]

This reading of Torrance is well acknowledged, when, for instance, Spjuth notes Torrance's application of the hypostatic analogy to creation, such that 'the whole universe of creaturely existence' is brought into relationship to the redemption of Christ (the Covenant) and thus is appointed to reflect God's glory. Citing Torrance, Spjuth comments, 'Here there is a covenanted correspondence between the creation and the Creator'.[31] According to Torrance, the whole of creation lives by this hypostatic relation to the Covenant in a form of created correspondence (analogy).[32]

Redemption and creation thus imply one another with redemption conditioning creation. After the Fall the world is in such a precarious state that God the Son unites its creatureliness to himself in order to save it. Without the incarnation neither humanity nor creation more generally could reach its intended created *telos*.[33] In Torrance's work on the resurrection under the subtitle 'the cosmic range of eschatology' we read:

> the range of Christ's mighty acts in incarnation, reconciliation and resurrection apply to the whole universe of things, visible and invisible. The whole creation falls within the range of his Lordship, as he works out his purpose by bringing

---

29 Torrance, *The Christian Doctrine of God*, p. 204. Torrance then cites H.R. Mackintosh to the same effect. Torrance presents the same theme in *The Trinitarian Faith*, p. 102.

30 Elmer M. Colyer, *How To Read T.F. Torrance: Understanding his Trinitarian and Scientific Theology* (Downers Grove: IVP, 2001), p. 164, fn. 34.

31 Spjuth, *Creation, Contingency and Divine Presence*, p. 40; citing Torrance, *The School of Faith*, p. li.

32 Pannenberg echoes remarkably similar themes to Torrance: 'the incarnation cannot be an external appendix to creation nor a mere reaction of the Creator to Adam's sin. From the very first it is the crown of God's world order, the supreme concretion of the active presence of the Logos in creation', *Systematic Theology*, vol. 2, trans. G.W. Bromiley (Grand Rapids: Eerdmans, 1994), p. 64. While Pannenberg comes at this from eschatological premises drastically different from those of Torrance, they do share, at this point at least, a remarkable correspondence. See Wolfhart Pannenberg, *Theology and the Kingdom of God*, ed. Richard J. Neuhaus (Philadelphia: Westminster Press, 1969), p. 67.

33 This has certain implications for a doctrine of election, implications of which Torrance is aware. See Chapter 3, pp. 97–109 and pp. 126–35.

> redemption together with creation, and actualizing the holy will of the Father in everything.[34]

Christ is central to creation as a whole, not simply to humanity.

This, Torrance argues, is the end for which its Creator has designed creation. Here we see a familiar tenet of Torrance's theology, the vicarious work of the incarnate Christ doing for us (creation) what we could not do for ourselves, taking what is ours and making it his own in order to give what is his to make our own. We shall see that Torrance uses other words for this in other contexts, such as 'atoning reconciliation', and 'atoning exchange', but each time the basic idea is the same. Through the incarnation of the Son of God, in his taking to himself of human nature, God himself transfers our creaturely contingent existence into his own experience, so that Jesus Christ secures the origin and end of creation in his own eternal being.[35] For Torrance, such logic is central to *theosis* – the union of divinity and humanity in the person of the incarnate Word and the participation of men and women in him, along with the summing up of all things in Christ: 'For by Him all things were created, both in the heavens and on earth, visible and invisible, whether thrones or dominions or rulers or authorities – all things have been created by Him and for Him. And He is before all things, and in Him all things hold together' (Col 1.16–17). With 'all things' Torrance includes animate and inanimate creation.[36]

Throughout Torrance's doctrine of creation we can see the influence of classical Greek, in contrast to Latin, theology at work. According to classical Greek theology the incarnation and resurrection of Jesus Christ revealed the final cosmic range of God's redeeming purpose. This is evident within Athanasius's *De Incarnatione* and the *Capita Gnostica* of Maximus, for instance.[37] This theology, according to Torrance's reading, is essentially world affirming in character whereas the Latin theology of Tertullian and Augustine, for example, is essentially world denying. Torrance finds much the same contrast between Luther's eschatological outlook, which he believes is basically Augustinian, and Calvin's, which is said to be basically Athanasian. He characterises Luther's as an eschatology of faith and Calvin's as an eschatology of hope.[38] Torrance's reading of the tradition here is unconvincing to many, however, within the logic of his own theological vision Torrance's doctrine of creation is one filled with christological hope.[39]

---

34 Torrance, *Space, Time and Resurrection*, p. 155.

35 Torrance, *The Trinitarian Faith*, p. 102.

36 See the discussion throughout Torrance, *Reality and Scientific Theology*.

37 See Torrance's citations in *Space, Time and Resurrection*, p. 155, fn. 19.

38 This is developed in Thomas F. Torrance, *Kingdom and Church: A Study in the Theology of the Reformation* (Edinburgh: Oliver & Boyd, 1956), pp. 139–40.

39 Paul Helm, *John Calvin's Ideas* (Oxford: Oxford University Press, 2004), pp. 50–52, draws upon the work of Anthony N.S. Lane, *John Calvin: Student of the Church Fathers* (Edinburgh: T & T Clark, 1999), ch. 3, to refute such notions, arguing that the influence of

Torrance's doctrine of creation is an essential ingredient of the account of *theosis* he goes on to build in his anthropology and beyond. The 'deification' of men and women occurs in space and time, in this contingent world, one that is utterly dependent upon God, and a world that, like men and women, awaits final redemption. This worldly redemption is inextricably bound to the 'deification' of believers. While Torrance makes this general point he offers little by way of development or discussion of it, electing to deal more fully with the human dimensions of *theosis* and more specifically its christological properties.

Anthropology: God and Humanity

Having examined Torrance's account of the relation existing between God and the world, we must now assess the God-human relation and explore the way in which Torrance develops his theological anthropology in harmony with his cosmology. If the incarnation proleptically conditions creation, Jesus Christ becomes the central figure, and a theological anthropology has to account for that. In order to do this Torrance develops a dynamic and relational account of the *imago Dei* that develops central emphases of Eastern Orthodox anthropology, along with some explicitly Calvinistic themes. The result of his theological anthropology is an affirmation of the supremacy of the incarnate Christ, the creation of men and women in his image, and a concept of human development that is consonant with certain themes innate to a doctrine of *theosis*.[40]

In a 1940s *Festschrift* for Karl Barth, Torrance argued that the doctrine of humanity was one of the most relevant discussions of the day.[41] The republication of that article nearly twenty years later reflected its abiding relevance for Torrance. As with other aspects of his theology, anthropology is not a subject developed separately but one that stands within the nexus of his scientific trinitarian theology.[42] Anthropology comes within the broad contours of creation and so it too

---

Athanasius and the Cappadocians on Calvin must remain speculative since there is no hard evidence that Calvin had access to their writings. It does appear this is an overstatement given Calvin's citation of Greek theologians, however Helm's work is a strong caution against Torrance's reading of Calvin.

40 The doctrine of the Primacy of Christ is important and a topic which Torrance deals with to some degree in *The Christian Doctrine of God*, p. 210; *The Doctrine of Jesus Christ: Auburn Lectures 1938–39* (Eugene, Or.: Wipf & Stock, 2002), p. 137; and *The Mediation of Christ*, pp. 110, 116. For a detailed discussion of Torrance as a modified Scotist see Myk Habets, 'On Getting First Things First: Assessing Claims for the Primacy of Christ', *New Blackfriars* 90 (2009): pp. 343–64.

41 Torrance, *Theology in Reconstruction*, p. 99, reprinted from 'The Word of God and the Nature of Man', in *Reformation Old and New: Festschrift for Karl Barth,* ed. F.W. Camfield (London: Lutterworth Press, 1947), pp. 121–41.

42 For Torrance's theological anthropology see especially: *Calvin's Doctrine of Man* (London: Lutterworth, 1949); 'Man, Priest of Creation', in *The Ground and Grammar of*

is contingent, and thus subject to what has already been said about creation more generally. As with his overall christocentric treatment of the doctrine of creation, Torrance's anthropology is formed in light of the humanity of Christ and his redemptive mission.[43] With the incarnation, the coming of God as man, profound implications for the understanding of humanity and their relation to God occurred. There arose a distinctively Christian anthropology in which 'man is given a unique place in the creative and providential purpose of God for the universe, as the creature who exists as a spiritual and physical being on the boundary between heaven and earth, eternity and time, grace and nature'.[44] Because humanity exists on the boundary of two worlds humanity alone is 'the one constituent of the universe through whom the creation discloses its astonishing order and harmony and comes to expression in such a way as to prize and glorify God the Father Almighty, Creator of all things visible and invisible'.[45]

Torrance develops his doctrine of humanity through the interconnection between the knowledge of God and the knowledge of self (Calvin),[46] which constitutes the very life of humanity. Human persons are created to know God – that is their chief end (*telos*) and so one is not truly a *person* unless one knows God.[47] What this knowing consists of is our present theme.

The Imago Dei *and The Proleptic Self*

While the concept of the *imago Dei* is clearly central to a theological anthropology, what this *imago* consists of offers no easy definition within the history of Christian thought. Two views have dominated the discussion: the structural/substantial position, and the relational one.[48] The first view argues that there is a constitutive

---

Theology (Charlottesville: University of Virginia Press, 1980), pp. 1–14; 'The Goodness and Dignity of Man in the Christian Tradition', *Modern Theology* 4 (1988): pp. 309–22; 'Man, Mediator of Order', in *The Christian Frame of Mind,* pp. 29–48; and 'The Soul and Person in Theological Perspective', in *Religion, Reason, and the Self: Essays in Honour of Hywel D. Lewis*, eds Stewart R. Sutherland and T.A. Roberts (Cardiff: University of Wales Press, 1989), pp. 103–18.

43 Torrance, 'The Goodness and Dignity of Man in the Christian Tradition', p. 309.

44 Torrance, 'The Soul and Person in Theological Perspective', p. 104.

45 Ibid. See further in 'The Goodness and Dignity of Man in the Christian Tradition', p. 311; and *The Christian Frame of Mind*, pp. 32–3.

46 Calvin, *Institutes*, 1.1.1.

47 'Therefore, we may say, man has been made in such a way that he is not truly a man except in the realisation of his creaturely dependence on the grace of God, and that he cannot retain his life except in a motion of thankful acknowledgment of the sheer grace of God as Creator and Father in whose Word man's life is deposited, and in the continuous communication of which alone may life be possessed', Torrance, *Theology in Reconstruction*, p. 102.

48 See a history of these two positions in Stanley J. Grenz, *The Social God and the Relational Self: A Trinitarian Theology of the Imago Dei* (Louisville: Westminster John

and thus substantial aspect of the human creature that qualifies the *imago Dei*, most notably the possession of a rational nature. The second view argues that human persons are created with the capacity to enter into full loving relationships with God and with others and it is this that qualifies the *imago Dei*. As Grenz reminds us, 'the standard description looks to the Reformation as marking the transition from the predominance of the first to heightened interest in the second'.[49] More recently a third view has come to prominence, also drawing on patristic support: the teleological view of the *imago*. This view retains key aspects of the first two but develops these in considerably different ways. It is this third view that Torrance presents in his theology and one which is in harmony with his theology of *theosis* – the participation of the human being in the life of God as the intended goal or *telos* of human persons, based upon the centrality of Jesus Christ.

Torrance's articulation of the image of God, one that is in fact embedded within Irenaeus's doctrine of recapitulation, the Eastern Orthodox quest for 'divinisation', the Reformers' relational view, and Barth's christological *imago* – is that of human destiny, goal, or *telos*. This third alternative offers a way beyond the static category of substance and the rather 'slippery' category of relation, in favour of a more robust definition that is at once biblical, traditional, and contemporary.[50] Torrance's theological anthropology fits naturally into this category as he takes seriously the teleological orientation of creation,[51] humanity included, and finds this model most conducive to a doctrine of *theosis*.

A central axiom of Torrance's anthropology is that even more is gained in Christ than was lost in Adam. We see this same view in a variety of thinkers.[52] According to Luther, although humankind lost the image of God through sin,

---

Knox Press, 2001), pp. 141–77. Millard J. Erickson, *Christian Theology*, 2nd edn (Grand Rapids: Baker, 1998), pp. 517–36, offers a three-tier taxonomy consisting of the substantive, relational, and functional views. However, the functional view is merely a *result* of the *imago Dei*.

49 Grenz, *The Social God and the Relational Self*, p. 142.

50 This 'third view' is being explored by: Philip E. Hughes, *The True Image; The Origin and Destiny of Man in Christ* (Grand Rapids: Eerdmans, 1989); Wolfhart Pannenberg, *Systematic Theology*, 3 vols, trans. G.W. Bromiley (Grand Rapids: Eerdmans, 1991, 1994, 1998); Eberhard Jüngel, 'Humanity in Correspondence to God: Remarks on the Image of God as a Basic Concept in Theological Anthropology', in *Theological Essays* (Edinburgh: T & T Clark, 1989), pp. 124–53; Grenz, *The Social God and the Relational Self*; and T.A. Smail, 'In the Image of the Triune God', *International Journal of Systematic Theology* 5 (2003): pp. 22–32.

51 Eric G. Flett, 'Priests of Creation, Mediators of Order: The Human Person as a Cultural Being in Thomas F. Torrance's Theological Anthropology', *Scottish Journal of Theology* 58 (2005): pp. 161–83, correctly describes the human person in Torrance's anthropology as 'an eschatological being determined by Christ and oriented towards the future', p. 163.

52 Savvas Agourides, 'Salvation According to the Orthodox Tradition', *Ecumenical Review* 21 (1969): p. 192.

the Holy Spirit and the Word of God can restore it. This restoration is ultimately eschatological, initiated in time and space, but, importantly for our study, is of an even higher order than the condition that was lost in the Fall. The perfection of the divine image is the eternal life for which Adam was 'fitted'.[53] According to Calvin what is restored to humanity in redemption far exceeds a return to the supposed perfection of Adam and Eve before the fall.[54] Consequently, the *imago Dei* is thus inherently teleological, or, as Gunton reminds us, it is properly *eschatological*.[55] Here we reach a main feature of Torrance's soteriology.

Like many in the early church Torrance believes the *imago* is an inherent rationality within men and women – a rationality that enables them to perceive the order of the creation and to praise and worship the one from whom this order came – the Creator. In this regard Torrance affirms aspects of a substantive definition of the *imago*.[56] However, this is only a partial description of the *imago Dei* according to Torrance. With Karl Barth in the foreground (and Calvin in the background), Torrance also vigorously defends a relational interpretation of the *imago*. Humans are created to 'correspond' with (Barth), or be a 'mirror' to (Calvin) God. However, Torrance develops this relational view beyond that of Barth along lines similar to Pannenberg, that of human destiny.[57] Men and women are persons-in-becoming. Jesus Christ, the incarnate Word of God, is the complete person, *the Imago Dei* in perfection and the one into whom men and women are being transformed, from glory to glory (2 Cor 3.18; Rom 8.29; 1 Jn 3.2 etc).[58]

Torrance rejects the static categories of nature and grace in his discussion of the human person in the *imago Dei*. He argues that Reformed theology in general, rejects any notion of the *imago Dei* that sees it as purely a natural possession of the human person.[59] For Torrance, a fundamental aspect of *theosis* is knowledge of

---

53 Martin Luther, *Lectures on Genesis*, in *Luther's Works*, American Edition, ed. Jaroslav Pelikan, trans. G.V. Schlick. (St. Louis: Concordia, 1958), 1, pp. 64–5.

54 John Calvin, *Commentary on Genesis*, vol. 1 of *Calvin's Commentaries*, trans. J. King (Grand Rapids: Baker, 1981), p. 296.

55 Gunton, *The Triune Creator*.

56 This is evidenced by his endorsement of Colin Gunton's essay 'The Lord Who is the Spirit', in *The One, The Three and the Many* (Cambridge: Cambridge University Press, 1993), pp. 180–209. Torrance clarifies that this substantial aspect of the *imago*, as I am calling it, is not independent of God but is created precisely by the Holy Spirit: 'While the creature does not have any continuity in relation to God that belongs to the creature in itself, it does have a relation to God which is continuously given and unceasingly sustained by the presence of the Holy Spirit', Torrance, *The Christian Doctrine of God*, p. 152, fn. 51.

57 See the best study to date; Kam M. Wong, *Wolfhart Pannenberg on Human Destiny* (Aldershot: Ashgate, 2008).

58 Tom Smail, 'In the Image of the Triune God', p. 23 offers a good summary of the biblical material read in this fashion.

59 Torrance, *Theology in Reconstruction*, pp. 105–6.

God.[60] Here Torrance departs from certain features of Latin theology on the beatific vision as the supreme goal of *theosis*.[61] From Calvin, Barth, and the East, Torrance argues that knowledge of God, while not isolated from beatific vision (light) is the supreme *telos*. 'We do not know God unless we know that our knowing is due to God alone', writes Torrance, 'otherwise the light shines in the darkness, and the darkness comprehends it not'.[62] Within this Reformed context of the grace of God and the note of unbounded thanksgiving as the true life-answer of created humanity to the Father, Torrance constructs his theological anthropology and in turn contributes towards constructing a doctrine of *theosis*.

If humanity is created to know God and to revel in the joy this knowledge brings (worship), then *theosis* is the attainment of that knowledge and the joyous communion it creates. The problem with this is, of course, the fact that humanity has fallen. Any discussion of humanity created in the *imago Dei* must deal with the fact of the Fall and its consequences. For Torrance, the Fall of humanity resulted in total depravity, in Calvinistic fashion.[63] Total depravity does not entail, according to Torrance's reading of Reformed theology, a thorough ontological break in humanity's relation with God, but it does mean the essential relation in which true human nature is grounded has been perverted and turned into its opposite, something which only makes sense in a relational-teleological understanding of the *imago Dei*.[64] Sin is properly of the mind and drags humanity into an active rebellion against God. It is only by the grace of God that human beings still exist at all. The *imago Dei* is not destroyed by the Fall but 'continues to hang over man as a destiny which he can realise no longer, and as a judgment upon his actual state of perversity'.[65] As a consequence, Torrance follows Barth and Calvin in maintaining that the *imago Dei* can now only be found in Jesus Christ, not in the creature properly speaking. He writes, '...justification by grace alone declares in no uncertain terms that fallen man is utterly destitute of *justitia originalis* or *imago dei*. It must be imputed by free grace'.[66]

There are tensions within Torrance's anthropology (as in Calvin's). On the one hand he argues the *imago* is an inherent rationality within all humans. On the other hand he argues the *imago* no longer remains in the creature after the Fall as creatures are utterly depraved. The sole existence of the *imago Dei* is found in Christ and in

---

[60] A favourite text Torrance draws on repeatedly to express this is Mat 11.27. See for instance 'The Christ Who Loves Me', in *A Passion for Christ: Vision that Ignites Ministry*, eds Gerrit Dawson and Jock Stein (Edinburgh: The Handsel Press, 1999), p. 9.

[61] See further in Chapter 3, pp. 131–5.

[62] Torrance, *Theology in Reconstruction*, p. 101.

[63] For Torrance, *Calvin's Doctrine of Man*, p. 83, within the logic of Calvin's theology total depravity is necessitated by the fact of the corollary of total grace. Because the Gospel speaks of salvation in total terms we must speak of depravity in total terms as well.

[64] Torrance, *Theology in Reconstruction*, p. 107.

[65] Ibid.

[66] Ibid., p. 109.

those in communion with him. For sure this communion is only possible through the incarnate Son and by the Holy Spirit, but the inherent capacity for communion with God is there nonetheless. How do we account for this tension? Our options are, as I see it, twofold: first, Torrance is inconsistent, or second, there is a deeper explanation. It is my conviction that Torrance is so influenced by Calvin's anthropology that he adopts his 'perspectival approach', to use Engel's words.[67] From the perspective of traditionally conceived explanations of the *imago Dei* in substantial terms, the *imago Dei* has been obliterated in fallen creatures. And yet, from a christological perspective the *imago* is present, incipiently, as all humans have a capacity for God because the incarnation proleptically conditions creation. Outside of a saving relationship with Christ this avails them the condemnation of God. Savingly reconciled to Christ his *Imago* becomes theirs through the Holy Spirit. In this way Christ alone naturally possess the *imago Dei*, he shares this realised *imago* with creatures by grace, and those not in Christ 'make more out of the *imago dei* than they ought' as they 'continue to sin against the Word and Law of God'.[68]

Within creation, the theatre of God's glory, all creation is purposely brought into existence in order to glorify God, and it is in this context that Torrance speaks of men and women as the 'priests of creation'.[69] Their task is to represent creation to the Creator in a worshipful and joyous response. But nature fails in its realisation of such a human vocation. Humanity has failed in its duty as the priests of creation; it refuses to sing the praises of all creation to God. It is precisely at this point that Torrance introduces the astounding claim that God in Christ Jesus does for us what we could not do for ourselves. Torrance's anthropology is christological, soteriological, and eschatological. These three features inform his theological anthropology at every point.

Within Torrance's theology *theosis* consists in being recreated in Christ Jesus who alone is *the* Image of God. Until men and women are renewed and brought face to face with God in Christ, we cannot know what it means either to know God or to know ourselves as *persons*.

> …the coming of God in Christ, and his self-communication to man, have taken such a form in the Incarnation, that it is there only that we may see human nature set forth in its truth as creature made to be the child of the heavenly Father. Thus there can be no question of trying to understand man out of himself, or from his relation to the world, he must be understood primarily from the Word made flesh.[70]

---

67 Mary P. Engel, *John Calvin's Perspectival Anthropology* (Atlanta: Scholars Press, 1988).

68 Torrance, *Theology in Reconstruction*, p. 109.

69 This theme is explored further in this chapter at pp. 45–7.

70 Torrance, *Theology in Reconstruction*, p. 102. Torrance continues to distance himself from the form of 'Calvinism' that transferred to nature what belongs to grace. Torrance argues that after Calvin there came into being a strange amalgamation of Thomistic logic and the Reformation view of humanity.

In the incarnation the eternal Son of God assumes fallen human nature and redeems it thus restoring and fulfilling the divine *telos* for humanity of union and communion with God (*theosis*).[71] With Athanasius, Torrance speaks of Jesus as 'the Dominical Man' and 'the principle of ways' which God has provided for us. By this he means that the incarnate Christ has an archetypal significance for human beings.[72] He even suggests that: 'every human being is ontologically bound to him. It is in Jesus Christ the incarnate Creator, then, that the being of all men, whether they believe or not, is creatively grounded and is unceasingly sustained'.[73]

The chief end and true felicity of humanity involves, according to Torrance, knowledge of oneself as a creature utterly dependent on the grace of God.

> [M]an has been created an intelligent being in order to know God in such a way that in the act of knowing man is brought to re-live consciously, and in a qualitatively different fashion, the very movement of grace in which he is created and maintained in being, so as to be carried beyond himself in responsible union with God in whom he finds his true life and felicity.[74]

Herein lies one of the main components of *theosis* within Torrance's anthropology. The *imago Dei* lies ahead of each human person and can only be realised in the person of the incarnate Son, Jesus Christ. The *imago Dei* is our destiny and true *telos*, not something inherent within each human person, waiting to be realised through some self-effort, self-examination, process of spiritual awakening, or mysticism.[75] The realising of the *imago Dei* is *theosis* within Torrance's anthropology and as with the rest of his thought, is actioned entirely by grace, that is, in the incarnate Son of God. 'In other words, the fall of man means that the

---

[71] This is a reversal of the fall which resulted in sin which Torrance defines as shattered communion in Torrance, 'The Atoning Obedience of Christ', pp. 65–6.

[72] Torrance, 'The Soul and Person in Theological Perspective', pp. 115–16.

[73] Torrance, 'The Atonement the Singularity of Christ', p. 244. Torrance is not implying that all people, by right of this ontological bond, are saved. Quite the opposite! The article in question is one in which Torrance is arguing for the singularity of Christ in an otherwise pluralistic world. His point is that because Jesus Christ is the Creator Incarnate, then all creation, men and women especially, are ontologically related to him. His logic goes as follows: if Christ in his incarnation represents all humanity, then in his atonement he must represent to the same extent all humanity. Any other view is to separate atonement from incarnation and revert back to an old dualist notion: a 'schizoid notion of the incarnation', ibid., p. 246.

[74] Torrance, *Theology in Reconstruction*, p. 101.

[75] In place of 'mysticism' Torrance prefers to speak of 'intuitive', non-logical knowing that arises under the constraint of reality upon the mind. See his 'Intuitive and Abstractive Knowledge: From Duns Scotus to Calvin', in *De Doctrina Ioannis Duns Scoti. Congressus Scotisticus Internationalis*, ed. Carl Balic (Rome: Societas Internationalis Scotistica, 1968), pp. 291–305. See Myk Habets, 'Thomas Forsyth Torrance: Mystical Theologian *Sui Generis*', *Princeton Theological Review* 14 (2008): pp. 91–104.

imago dei can be interpreted only in eschatological terms.'[76] These eschatological terms are entwined with christological action.

> [T]he original intention of God becomes event in man's existence only by the Word, and the *imago* is possessed only in faith and hope until we see Christ as he is and become like him. In Christ, therefore, we see the *Imago Dei* to be the ground of our existence beyond our existence, but which becomes sacramental event here and now in the hearing of faith, as we are sealed with the Holy Spirit until the redemption of the purchased possession.[77]

For Torrance, a christocentric understanding of creation is formed around the ontological claim that Christ is the meaning and purpose of creation.[78] In this way Torrance appropriates key Barthian insights.[79] The soteriological objectivism within Barth sees everything that takes place in creation as being subordinated to and proleptically conditioned by the incarnation of the Son of God and the redemption he brings.[80] Torrance develops this theme in his own distinctive but no less christocentric way.[81] Jesus Christ himself is the true Image of God to which all creation will one day be conformed. In *The Christian Doctrine of God* Torrance wrote concerning Christ:

> We can also say in the light of the incarnation that as the Word made flesh, the Word by whom all things that are made were made, Jesus Christ is the fulfilment of God's eternal purpose for his creation, that it is in Jesus Christ himself that all things in heaven and earth are reconciled, and that the whole created universe consists in him as its Head.[82]

---

[76] Torrance, *Theology in Reconstruction*, p. 108. Torrance refers the reader to Calvin's *Commentaries* on *Romans* (5.12), and *1 Corinthians* (15.45); and his *Sermons on Job* (14.1–2; 33.1–2; and 39.8–9).

[77] Ibid., p. 109.

[78] See Barth, *CD*, III/1, pp. 42–329.

[79] Torrance is not a 'Barthian' who simply restates and defends Barth's own views, contra the view of Richard A. Muller, 'The Barth Legacy: New Athanasius or Origen Redivivus? A Response to T.F. Torrance', *Thomist* 54 (1990): pp. 673–704.

[80] George Hunsinger, *How to Read Karl Barth: The Shape of His Theology* (Oxford: Oxford University Press, 1991), 105–14. Barth's position has occasioned disagreement from many quarters, see Ian G. Barbour, *Religion in an Age of Science: The Gifford Lectures 1989–1991* (London: SCM, 1990), pp. 10–16; and Gustav Wingren, *The Flight From Creation* (Minneapolis: Augsburg, 1971), p. 19.

[81] For a definition of 'christocentric' within his theology see Torrance, 'The Place of Christology in Biblical and Dogmatic Theology', in *Theology in Reconstruction*, pp. 128–49, originally a 1956 article written in honour of Karl Barth which acknowledged his indebtedness to the second half-volume of his prolegomena to the *Kirchliche Dogmatik*.

[82] Torrance, *The Christian Doctrine of God*, p. 199.

From this fulfilment of all things in Christ, Torrance contends that we can read this back into the beginning of creation. 'As the First and the Last, the Alpha and Omega, the Lord Jesus Christ gathers up all things from the beginning in himself as the Head of the created universe in the consummation of God's eternal purpose of Love. ...'[83] In an explicit reference to what a doctrine of *theosis* within Torrance's anthropology represents we read that the omnipotence of God evidenced in the incarnation represents his:

> Becoming what we are in our lost and damned condition in order to save us and reconcile us to himself in the undoing of all disorder and in the triumph of divine Love and Light over all darkness and evil. In the resurrection of Jesus God has manifested the measureless extent of his power to share with us to the uttermost our perdition and condemnation in order to lift us up to share with him his divine Life and Light, delivering us from the power of darkness and translating us into his Kingdom.[84]

Torrance goes on to provide a concise summary of *theosis* in these terms: 'In other words, the sovereignty of God is the grace of the Lord Jesus Christ, who, though he was rich, for our sakes became poor that we through his poverty might become rich.'[85] Here we find a direct echo of the patristic framing of the doctrine of *theosis*. Given Torrance's expertise as a patristic scholar, this allusion is hardly accidental.

Torrance is clear that in the self-humiliation of God in Jesus Christ, his *kenosis*, there is no abandonment of divine power or attributes, no ceasing to be God, but rather an exercise of his 'omnipotent grace' within the limitations of our contingent existence in space and time.[86] Thus the Son became human without ceasing to be divine in order to make creatures participate in the divine communion without ceasing to be creatures. For Torrance the incarnation of the Son of God is:

> The fact that he who freely created the universe has once and for all become incarnate within it, means that as the Creator God wills freely to coexist with his creaturely children, and therefore that the continuing existence of the universe is ontologically bound to the crucified and risen Jesus and destined to partake in the consummation of God's eternal purpose in him.[87]

What does this mean for the man or woman who is not in Christ? Torrance argues that we do not fully know. What we do know is that for the believer in Christ their 'human nature as body of [their] mind and mind of [their] body is affirmed with a

---

83 Ibid.

84 Ibid., pp. 215–16.

85 Ibid., p. 216.

86 Torrance's views against the so-called 'kenotic-christology' were developed as early as his Auburn lectures, see Torrance, *The Doctrine of Jesus Christ*, pp. 108–30.

87 Torrance, *The Christian Doctrine of God*, p. 217.

spiritual wholeness and a new ontological interrelation with others that transcends [their] original creation, for now [they] exist not just alongside of the Creator, but in such a way that [their] human being is anchored in the very Being of God'.[88]

Body, Soul and Spirit

In utilising the language that a human person is a 'body of his soul and soul of his body',[89] Torrance rejects a trichotomous view of the human person (as body, soul, and spirit) in favour of a dichotomy of body and soul, related to God 'through the power and presence of God's Spirit, and thereby endowed with the capacity to think and act in accordance with the nature (*kataphysin*) of what is other than himself'.[90] The human spirit is actually an essential and dynamic correlate of the divine 'Spirit' – not a third object distinct from body and soul. The presence of the Holy Spirit in the human results in a 'transcendental determination' implanted within each of us. This phrase, 'transcendental determination', effectively functions within Torrance's anthropology as another cognate for *theosis*. The human person is created with a goal (*telos*) in view, to participate in the triune relationship of the Father for the Son in or by the Holy Spirit. This transcendental determination of the Spirit impels the human movement toward God, this movement may be characterised as *theosis*.[91]

What drives the human being to personality and relatedness is the Holy Spirit who is the bond of union between the Father and the Son in the Triunity and between Creator and creature in space-time. The S/spirit of men and women is not

[88] Torrance, 'The Goodness and Dignity of Man in the Christian Tradition', p. 321.

[89] Torrance, *The Christian Frame of Mind*, p. 29. Cf. *The Trinitarian Faith*, 150; and *The Soul and Person of the Unborn Child*, p. 7. Torrance's use of this phrase derives from Athanasius in *De Incarnationis* 15; *Contra Arianos* 2.53–4; 3.20, 30–35; etc. It is also evident that Torrance has developed this idea from Karl Barth. Barth's anthropology spoke of the person as 'the soul of his body', in Barth, *CD*, III/2, p. 325. Barth appeared to give priority to the soul whereas Torrance wishes to see the soul and body as coterminous. While Barth makes the 'soul of the body' the point of human contact with God, Torrance posits the S/spirit as the real point of contact. This is a subtle distinction in their respective works and not one that should be pressed. See *CD*, III/2, pp. 378–97.

[90] Torrance, 'The Soul and Person in Theological Perspective', p. 110.

[91] Wolfhart Pannenberg, *Toward a Theology of Nature: Essays on Science and Faith*, ed. Ted Peters (Louisville: Westminster John Knox Press, 1993), p. 133, speaks of an 'ecological self-transcendence' inherent to living organisms which corresponds to the biblical idea of a spiritual origin of life. This is wedded to a field of energy which in turn is wedded to a concept of spirit. While Pannenberg's idea of 'self-transcendence' sounds similar to Torrance's 'transcendental determination', the fundamental difference lies in the identity of the S/spirit. For Torrance 'spirit' in this context is always the Holy Spirit while for Pannenberg 'spirit', as with much philosophy, identifies an anthropological predicate as much as it does a divine Person.

some 'spark of the divine' (Origen)[92] but the 'ontological qualification of his soul' brought about and maintained by the Holy Spirit.[93] In this way the human person is capable of thinking objectively of what is other than them – it is the very essence of their human rationality and relationality. As Torrance clarifies:

> It is not through any alleged participation in the essence of God, as Hellenic religion and philosophy maintained, but through the objective orientation of man in soul and body to God, the Source and Ground of all creaturely rationality and freedom, that man is constituted a rational subject and agent, i.e. a *person.*[94]

What makes men and women so distinctive is that as unitary beings – body of their soul and soul of their body – they span two 'worlds' – the physical and spiritual – and are thereby able to reach knowledge of the created contingent order and divulge the secrets of its vast intelligibility.[95] As a result a correspondence between God and humanity is spanned by human persons created in the *imago Dei.*

Impetus for Torrance's anthropology comes from Patristic sources which recast terms from Middle Platonism into a distinctively Christian anthropology, the two most important being *soul* and *person.*[96] Like the rest of creation, the soul and body are created *ex nihilo* and are contingent rather than immortal.[97] The soul and body of human beings are 'continuously sustained by the creative presence of God and are given immortality through the grace of a relation with God who only has immortality'.[98] Despite the absence of the technical vocabulary of *theosis* here we find an implicit reference to the doctrine when Torrance speaks (in Orthodox terms) of the mortal gaining immortality. This graced relation to God is initiated in space-time but extends to the eschaton in which the resurrection of the whole being of the person as body and soul is realised. Resurrection is to a creaturely

---

92 David Cairns, *The Image of God in Man*, 2nd edn (London: Collins, 1973), pp. 66–78.

93 Torrance, 'The Soul and Person in Theological Perspective', p. 110.

94 Ibid., p. 113.

95 Torrance, *The Christian Frame of Mind*, p. 33. For this reason Torrance terms humanity the 'mediator of order'. For more on Torrance's conception of the body-soul relation see Flett, 'Priests of Creation, Mediators of Order', pp. 164–8, and sympathetic to Torrance's anthropology see Ray S. Anderson, 'On Being Human: The Spiritual Saga of a Creaturely Soul', in *Whatever Happened to the Soul? Scientific and Theological Portraits of Human Nature*, eds Warren S. Brown, Nancey Murphey and H. Newton Malony (Minneapolis: Fortress, 1998), pp. 175–94.

96 As G.L.C. Frank, 'The Spirituality of the Orthodox Tradition', *Studia Historiae Ecclesiasticae* 18 (1992): p. 5, commented, 'A careful reading of the Fathers reveals that they did not uncritically accept the platonic premise of the soul's kinship with the divine. Too much in the tradition spoke against it'.

97 See Torrance, *Transformation and Convergence*, pp. 333–49.

98 Torrance, 'The Soul and Person in Theological Perspective', p. 105.

participation in the uncreated eternal Life of God, a kind of *theosis*.[99] Torrance sees the resurrection not only as deliverance from corruption but also as an ontological act in which true creaturehood is restored through the intimate relation with the creative Source of all being.[100]

Theosis is the goal of all human existence, at the resurrection of body and soul human beings can fully participate in the eternal life of God. This participation always has one qualifier in Torrance's theology, however: it is a participation in the eternal life of God *embodied in the incarnate Son*.[101] There is no life without the Source of Life, no resurrection without the resurrected One, and no *theosis* outside of the incarnate Son of God. Thus *theosis* is not, strictly speaking, the 'divinisation' of the human person as such but the 'personalising' of the human being in *the* Person of the incarnate Son. This is the meaning behind the words of Torrance, 'for man to live in union with God is to become fully and perfectly human'.[102] Jesus alone is the *personalising Person* while we are *personalised persons*.[103] It is from Christ alone, the one through whom creation came and the one for whom humanity was created, that men and women are radically made persons in the divine image.[104] Once again Torrance brings together the doctrines of creation and redemption, the former conditioning the latter.

In light of Torrance's understanding of the vicarious humanity of Christ, it comes as no surprise that he views *Jesus Christ himself* as the true image of God in a unique and supreme sense, for he is both the image and reality of God in his incarnate Person. Because Jesus Christ is *the* image of God it is only when we are incorporated into Christ that we realise our true personhood and so the true image of God.

Being and person Evident in the discussion so far is the deliberate distinction Torrance posits between being and person, a distinction that applies both theologically and anthropologically. Theologically, the being of God refers to *ousia*, while person, when applied to God, is described by hypostasis. Torrance applies a similar distinction to his anthropology. The human creature is created in a special sense, as Genesis 1.27 makes clear, but because the *imago Dei* is ultimately christological, soteriological and eschatological, the relational aspect of the *imago* is what makes human beings human persons, true men and women. Because Jesus Christ is the only true human, he is the true image of God, and so only in Christ

---

99 It is noteworthy that Torrance refers to the 'illuminating essays' of Georges Florovsky, the prominent Eastern Orthodox theologian who advocated a doctrine of *theosis* throughout his works. The two essays noted are: 'Creation and Creaturehood', and 'The Immortality of the Soul', in *Creation and Redemption, Collected Works*, vol. 3 (Belmont, MA.: Norland Publishing Company, 1976), pp. 43–78, and 213–40.

100 Torrance, 'The Soul and Person in Theological Perspective', p. 106.

101 Ibid.

102 Torrance, 'The Goodness and Dignity of Man in the Christian Tradition', p. 315.

103 Torrance, 'The Soul and Person in Theological Perspective', p. 116.

104 Torrance, *The Christian Frame of Mind*, p. 31.

can the human creature be fully a person.[105] The movement within the salvation of men and women is from human being, a biological fact, to human person, a moral, theological fact. Anything outside of Christ falls short of true personhood.[106] This is important for Torrance's articulation of *theosis*.

Torrance, clearly influenced by Barth, sees in the creation of men and women in the image of God an otherness and togetherness that is to be expressed in an inherent relatedness, which in turn is a creaturely reflection of a transcendent relatedness in the divine Being.[107] Torrance understands that 'this is the *personal* or *inter-personal* structure of humanity in which there is imaged the ineffable personal relations of the Holy Trinity'.[108] This means that when Torrance speaks of humanity, or his more customary appellation *man*, he does not mean an individual (even less a male!)[109] but rather a person in ontological relation with other persons.[110] This is what Torrance means by 'onto-relations' or being-constituting-relations.[111] While first applied to the intratrinitarian relations, 'onto-relations' are also applicable to intrahuman relations. This explains in many ways the creation of male and female. As the Genesis account makes clear, the creation of the woman is designed to deliver the man from his isolation. From this 'primal community' arises the family unit and in time social constructions – societies.

105 Torrance is reliant upon the seminal work of Barth who argued that in the strict sense it is God who is properly Person, and humans are persons in derivation from him. Barth, *CD*, II/1, p. 272. See Thomas F. Torrance, *God and Rationality* (Eugene, Or.: Wipf & Stock, 1997), pp. 141–2.

106 One could even say that anyone outside of Christ falls short of true human *being*. Barth himself appears to argue this in his reinterpretation of the doctrine of election in Jesus Christ. See Bruce McCormack, 'Grace and Being', in *The Cambridge Companion to Karl Barth*, ed. John Webster (Cambridge: Cambridge University Press, 2000), pp. 92–110; Colin E. Gunton, 'Karl Barth's Doctrine of Election as Part of his Doctrine of God', *Journal of Theological Studies,* ns 25 (1974): pp. 381–92; and Hans T. Goebel, *Vom freien Wählen Gottes und des Menschen: Interpretationsübungen zur 'Analogie' nach Karl Barths Lehre von der Erwählung und Bedenken ihrer Folgen für die Kirchlichen Dogmatik* (Frankfurt am Main: Peter Lang, 1990).

107 See Barth, *CD*, III/4, p. 117.

108 Torrance, 'The Soul and Person in Theological Perspective', pp. 109–10.

109 'That is to say by "man" the biblical tradition means "man-and-woman", for it is man and woman who constitute in their union the basic unit of humanity,' Torrance, 'The Goodness and Dignity of Man in the Christian Tradition', p. 311.

110 The faulty idea of *person* being equated with *individual* is attributed by Torrance, as it is by most scholars, to Boethius, *De duabus naturis et una persona Christi, adversus Eutychen et Nestorium*, 2.1–5, cf. Torrance, 'The Soul and Person in Theological Perspective', p. 117, fn. 12. Torrance's view of 'person' is partially derived from the work of Richard St Victor as opposed to that of Boethius or Aquinas, both of which are described by Torrance in his *Reality and Scientific Theology*, pp. 174–6.

111 Torrance, 'The Goodness and Dignity of Man in the Christian Tradition', p. 311.

Given Torrance's doctrine of onto-relations, the *imago Dei* is thus a dynamic and eschatological reflection that, while initiated and developed in time-space within creation, is ultimately only realised in the eschaton of which the church is currently a foretaste.[112] The onto-relations work on two levels, vertically and horizontally. Vertically, one is justified and sanctified through a relationship with the triune God; horizontally, one is formed into communion with other believers in the Body of Christ, the church. But these two levels are one integrated whole, not two separate spheres. What is clear is that *theosis*, communion with God, is a 'personal' activity and persons are defined as humans-in-relationship. The ultimate person is Jesus Christ; hence mature men and women are those who have been perfected by grace as they are united to Christ in the Holy Spirit. The church thus becomes the locus of *theosis* this side of the Parousia.

Because of sin and the Fall the onto-relations that exist between all personal beings – God-humanity, humanity-God, and humanity-humanity – have been radically 'disrupted', resulting in the breakdown of personal relationships on both the horizontal and vertical levels.[113] This disruption affects the 'transcendental determinism' of human beings. As fallen humans refuse to listen to the Spirit (of God) 'transcendental determinism' is replaced with self-determinism. As a result only through the mediation of Christ can the Holy Spirit be poured out on human beings so that they can reflect the *imago Dei* as God intended.[114]

Given this definition of the *imago Dei*, one that is restored through the vicarious humanity of Jesus Christ and mediated to us by the Spirit who unites us with Christ, we can see what Torrance means when he uses the concepts of *theosis*. As Colyer helpfully summarises:

> *Theosis* or *theopoiesis* is not the divinizing or deification of the human soul or creaturely being, Torrance contends, but rather is the Spirit of God humanizing and personalizing us by uniting us with Christ's vicarious humanity in a way that both confirms us in our creaturely reality utterly different from God, and yet also adapts us in our contingent nature for knowledge of God, for communion with God and for fellowship with one another.[115]

---

112 Torrance, 'The Soul and Person in Theological Perspective', p. 109, even maintains that the bond of union between man and woman will remain intact in eternity!

113 Torrance, 'The Goodness and Dignity of Man in the Christian Tradition', p. 313.

114 Ibid., pp. 320–21. An interesting parallel is found in Staniloae's theology of the *Logos*, whereby the human person is created with an inherent orientation toward the ontological pursuit of 'ultimate transcendence'. This ultimate transcendence is made known supremely in the person of Jesus Christ the *Logos* and it is here that *theosis* takes place. Staniloae goes beyond Torrance, however, when he makes this movement one of necessity rather than of grace. See Dumitru Staniloae, *Teologia Dogmatica Ortodoxa* (Bucuresti: EIBMBOR, 1978), 2, p. 47.

115 Colyer, *How To Read T.F. Torrance*, p. 178.

By distinguishing between grace and nature, Torrance and the Reformed tradition in general safeguard the distinction between God and creation.[116] This becomes vital when considering a doctrine of *theosis*. Because of the contingent character of the created order there is no innate 'point of contact' between God and humanity. This includes the human soul and rationality, which are also created *ex nihilo.* Torrance believes the creation can know God personally, not through any inherent *analogia entis* but rather by a 'created correspondence' between the creature and the Creator.[117] To further this distinction Torrance adopts Barth's idea of the *analogia relationis*, in contradistinction to classical Western conceptions of an *analogia entis*.[118]

The Humanisation of Humanity In a 1963 essay Torrance reminds us that:

> God does not override man but recreates, reaffirms him and stands him up before himself as his dear child, and man does not seek to use or manipulate knowledge of God for the fulfilment of his own ends in self-will and self-understanding, but loves him objectively for his own sake and is so liberated from himself that he can love his neighbour objectively also.[119]

In order to speak accurately of *theosis* Torrance introduces the themes of *objectivity* and *subjectivity*. For Torrance *theosis* involves achieving creaturely *objectivity* as opposed to sinful *subjectivity*. True objectivity is secured only in the Spirit who unites the creature to the humanity of the incarnate Son. This is important, as it guards Torrance's doctrine of *theosis* from any false view of the 'divinisation' of humanity by any mechanical, naturalistic, evolutionary means. Participation in God is achieved by *grace*, by *God alone*. As Torrance maintains:

> By coming *into* man the Holy Spirit opens him *out* for God. But at the very heart of this movement is the act of God in which he became man in order to take man's

---

116 Thomas F. Torrance, *Theological Science* (London: Oxford University Press, 1969), pp. 65–75; *Theology in Reconstruction*, pp. 64–7; 99–116; 'Introduction', *The School of Faith*, lii–lv; and *Calvin's Doctrine of Man*, pp. 23–34, argues that this is true of Reformed theology from Calvin to Barth.

117 Torrance, 'The Goodness and Dignity of Man in the Christian Tradition', p. 312; and *The Christian Doctrine of God*, pp. 219–20.

118 See especially Barth, *CD*, II/2, p. 243. For analyses of Barth's response to the *analogia entis* see: Eberhard Jüngel, 'The Possibility of Theological Anthropology on the Basis of Analogy', in *Karl Barth: A Theological Legacy*, trans. Garrett E. Paul (Philadelphia: Westminster Press, 1986); and Alan J. Torrance, 'Theological Language, Vestigiality and the Question of Continuity between the Human and Divine Realms', in *Persons in Communion: Trinitarian Description and Human Participation* (Edinburgh: T & T Clark, 1996), pp. 120–212.

119 Torrance, *Theology in Reconstruction*, p. 237.

> place, and give man a place within the communion of the divine life. It is the act of the divine love taking the way of *substitution*, and opening up the way for a corresponding act on the part of man in which he renounces himself for God's sake that the divine love may have its way with him in selfless objectivity.[120]

Torrance understands God's presence in creation as communion, a communion in correspondence to the *hypostatic union* between God and humanity in Christ, and the onto-relations that exist in the *perichoretic* union of the three divine Persons in the one being of God. In idiosyncratic language, a Patristic doctrine of *theosis* is presented. Torrance posits an immediate divine presence in creation and creation's real participation in God; however, God and humanity are never confused or mixed into one.[121] This allows Torrance to distinguish between Christian doctrines of *theosis* conceived in terms of *koinonia* from a Greek philosophical conception of '*divinisation*' in terms of *methexis* (mixture of being); he clearly affirms the first and rejects the second. Much of Torrance's thought on the doctrine of *theosis* revolves around making this distinction clear.

Torrance sees the idea of intimate communion developed masterfully in the theology of the Nicene Fathers and again in the Reformation. Torrance's positing of a dialogical relation between creation and God asserts a personal interaction that includes a clear distinction and close union in reciprocity. It was the Hellenistic notion of divine immutability, according to Torrance, that created a wedge between God and creation necessitating a realm of intermediation that was then conceptualised in the formation of causes. Torrance sees in the alternative Chalcedonian notion of participation an assertion of a direct communion without mediating causes. This same idea is presented or reclaimed by Calvin when he writes that 'all nature, and the gifts and endowments of man, depend for their being upon the immediate agency of God through His Spirit and His Word'.[122]

It is clear that Torrance does not confuse the distinction between God and creation. Rather, communion has the idea of encounter between two distinct but not separate entities. To maintain the strongly personalist force of this communion between God and human beings Torrance adopts Calvin's stress on the importance of the Holy Spirit as 'God's creative personal presence'.[123] What the Spirit creates is a real personal relation between the human person and God that 'posits us as subjects over against the divine Subject'.[124] Spjuth recounts Torrance's communion theology with the declaration, 'Communion as personal interaction means that God can be present *as* transcendent *without* being confused with creation; "union

---

120 Ibid., p. 138.

121 Ibid., p. 184.

122 Torrance, *Calvin's Doctrine of Man*, p. 63.

123 Torrance, *Theology in Reconstruction*, pp. 96–7.

124 Ibid., p. 97.

without mixture"'.[125] For this reason Torrance lays the stress on the objectivity of God over and above the subjectivity of humanity.

On more than one occasion Torrance argues against the idea of human nature being 'deified', if by 'deified' one means 'made divine' in some *non-human* way. This is why he places so much stress on *theosis* understood through the Chalcedonian doctrine of the hypostatic union. Human nature is 'reaffirmed and recreated in its essence as human nature, yet one in which the participant is really united to the Incarnate Son of God partaking in him in his own appropriate mode of the oneness of the Son and the Father and the Father and the Son, through the Holy Spirit'.[126] This participation in the Divine life (*theosis*) is an eschatological mystery that Torrance is careful not to delve into inappropriately. *Theosis* begins now as we participate in the new creation through the Spirit; it is also 'not yet' as we wait for the *Parousia* of the Lord when God in Christ will make all things new.

For Torrance the goal of *theosis* is not to become 'God' or even, technically speaking, to become 'gods'. It is not the process of transcending the confines of human nature but the process and means by which the human can achieve true personhood. *Theosis* does not do away with our creatureliness; it fulfils it. In a similar vein Staniloae suggests that *theosis* cannot be taken *literally*. One cannot *literally* become God since that would be as absurd as if we were to state that God is a creature.[127] The 'transcendental determination' inherent within each human person and realised by those united to Christ Jesus, means that men and women will be able to be and do what they were created to be and do – mirror God back to God, through Christ by the Holy Spirit. This is the goal of humanity summarised by the term *theosis* within Torrance's theology.

Through a close reading of Torrance it is evident he supports an evolutionary view of the cosmos, an expanding universe that resulted from some form of original Big Bang, along with a concomitant commitment to some form of theistic evolution.[128] When it comes to the human person, however, Torrance is ambiguous on this issue. *Theosis* is not a *natural* development but a supernatural irruption of grace initiated on the part of God, achieved in the person of the incarnate Son, and applied to believers by the Holy Spirit. Because evolution is not used by Torrance in relation to a doctrine of *theosis* we shall not pursue the question any further.[129]

---

125 Spjuth, *Creation, Contingency and Divine Presence*, pp. 36–7.

126 Torrance, *Theology in Reconstruction*, p. 186.

127 See Bartos, *Deification in Eastern Orthodoxy*, p. 145.

128 Thomas F. Torrance, *Preaching Christ Today* (Grand Rapids: Eerdmans, 1994), p. 24.

129 See Torrance, *Divine and Contingent Order*, pp. 80–81; *The Christian Frame of Mind*, p. 44; 'Torrance Responds', in *The Promise of Trinitarian Theology*, pp. 332–5; *The Doctrine of Jesus Christ*, p. 79; and Christopher B. Kaiser, 'Humanity in an Intelligible Cosmos', in *The Promise of Trinitarian Theology*, pp. 239–67.

Humanity as Priest of Creation

By means of the image 'priest of creation', Torrance brings together his cosmology and anthropology. Humanity is the 'crown of creation',[130] even the purpose for the creation of the world. As 'priest of creation', humanity has the function and privilege to assist the creation as a whole to realise and evidence its rational order and beauty and thus to express God. According to Torrance, 'through human cultivation and development nature should bring forth forms of order and beauty of which it would not be capable otherwise'.[131] It is necessary to creation that humanity realise its priestly vocation, in order to bring forth the requisite praise that God deserves. This is why humanity becomes 'an essential member of the creation'.[132] Men and women are the 'stewards' or 'keepers' of the Garden/creation, and by tending the earth are meant to bring praise to the Creator.

One specific way in which humanity exercises this priestly function is through natural science.[133] It is through the natural sciences that the order and the beauty of creation can sing forth the praise of the Creator. At one point Torrance declares that: 'man the scientist is nature's midwife'.[134] With this priestly function scientific inquiry becomes a deeply religious duty in humanity's relation to God. Torrance even declares that 'science itself is part of man's religious duty, for it is part of his faithful response to the Creator and Sustainer of the cosmos'.[135]

In an essay on humanity in an intelligible cosmos, Kaiser notes that, 'If I read him correctly, Torrance is suggesting that humanity plays a role in the universe analogous to that of light, only on a different level'. He continues:

> Light orders the cosmos in the special sense that the invariance of its speed is the basis of the equations governing space, time, and motion that Einstein discovered in 1905. In this special sense, Torrance argues, physical light is a created reflection of the uncreated Light of God. In a similar way, humanity is created in the image of God and plays a unique role in the universe, ordering it epistemically with pure science.[136]

---

130 To use Calvin's words, as Torrance himself does, *The Ground and Grammar of Theology*, p. 1; and *Calvin's Doctrine of Man*, p. 23.

131 Torrance, *Divine and Contingent Order*, p. 130.

132 Torrance, *Reality and Evangelical Theology*, pp. 25, 26. This same theme is presented by his brother James B. Torrance in *Worship, Community and the Triune God of Grace* (Downers Grove: IVP, 1996), pp. 13–15.

133 This priestly function is discussed further in Chapter 4, pp. 185–91.

134 Torrance, *Reality and Evangelical Theology*, p. 26.

135 Torrance, *Space, Time and Resurrection*, pp. 179–80. It should be noted that theological inquiry is one of the sciences; hence his own theology is a self-styled 'scientific theology'.

136 Kaiser, 'Humanity in an Intelligible Cosmos', p. 252.

The association or identification of the role of humanity with the role of light is highly significant in a discussion of *theosis*. One of the ten cognates for *theosis* used by Gregory Palamas is light. Williams explains that for Palamas, 'light stands on the border of our hierarchy of images between the lesser and the greater and reflects this status by partaking of the characteristics of both groups. He identifies light with God, and deification's source, as the agent of human sanctification, and as deification itself (αὐτοθεωσις)'.[137] We shall examine Torrance's use of light as a cognate of *theosis* further in the next chapter.[138]

Torrance's view of humanity as the priest of creation bears a striking similarity to the Eastern Orthodox teaching that understands the human creature as creation's master (*archon*).[139] For instance, Staniloae prefers to describe men and women as creation's master, its created co-creator, co-worker or continuator.[140] On some occasions Staniloae uses the same expression as Torrance when he considers the world as God's gift to humanity in order that humanity may gift it back to God. In this way, argues Staniloae, the sacrifice offered to God by men and women is a Eucharist, making every person a 'priest of God for the world'.[141] From this relationship of Creator to creature human beings derive their significance and responsibility in the formation of the world towards its final consummation.[142]

While Torrance's image of humanity acting as 'priests of creation' is compelling, it is not without its problems.[143] By tying it so closely to natural science Torrance fails to engage adequately in the wider realm and riches of what this priestly ministry may entail. In addition, Spjuth notes that if taken to its logical end this separation between the realm of grace and the realm of nature within Torrance's

---

[137] Anna N. Williams, *The Ground of Union: Deification in Aquinas and Palamas* (New York: Oxford University Press, 1999), p. 114.

[138] See Chapter 3, pp. 131–5.

[139] See for example John Meyendorff, *Christ in Eastern Christian Thought* (Crestwood, NY.: St Vladimir's Seminary Press, 1975); Elizabeth Briere, 'Creation, Incarnation and Transfiguration: Material Creation and our Understanding of It', *Sobornost* 11 (1989): pp. 31–40; Myroslaw Tataryn, 'The Eastern Tradition and the Cosmos', *Sobornost* 11 (1989): pp. 41–52; and Staniloae, *The Experience of God*, vol. 2.

[140] Staniloae, *The Experience of God*, vol. 2. pp. 21–112.

[141] Dumitru Staniloae, 'The World as Gift and Sacrament of God's Love', *Sobornost* 9 (1969): pp. 662–73, and *Teologia Dogmatica Ortodoxa*, vol. 1, p. 389.

[142] John D. Zizioulas, 'Preserving God's Creation: Three Lectures on Theology and Ecology', *King's Theological Review* 12 (1989): pp. 1–5, 41–51, 13 (1990), pp. 1–5, also takes up Torrance's phrase 'man the priest of creation' but develops it in a much broader sense than Torrance's restriction to science. See Gunton's defence of Torrance over Zizioulas at this point in Colin Gunton, *Christ and Creation* (Carlisle: Paternoster, 1992), pp. 119–22, and the critical interaction of Spjuth, *Creation, Contingency and Divine Presence*, pp. 181–3.

[143] Acknowledging the limitations of Torrance's application of anthropology to human vocation, Flett considers the cultural or concrete social implications of Torrance's theological anthropology in 'Priests of Creation, Mediators of Order', pp. 161–83, especially pp. 179–83.

theology could end up affirming the very dualism that Torrance wishes to expunge from all theology. If humanity is the priest of creation only through the field of natural science then there runs the risk of the realm of human activities becoming an autonomous reality.[144] As Chapter 4 will highlight, Torrance does consider other ways in which humanity fulfils this priestly duty. However, he reserves the language of 'priests of creation' almost exclusively for human scientific activity and this has occasioned much misunderstanding.

Conclusion

As Williams correctly points out in her survey of the Patristic doctrine of *theosis*: '[W]here we find the ideas of participation in divine life, union with God and humanity portrayed as human destiny, and a mode of articulating divine transcendence in this context, we can say we are dealing with a doctrine of deification.'[145] Torrance deals with each of these specific points and is thus engaging with a doctrine of *theosis* in his account of creation, even if the technical vocabulary is used only sparingly.

Torrance's doctrines of creation and anthropology highlight the starting point for a discussion of *theosis* within Torrance's wider theological programme. According to Torrance, *theosis* is prescriptive of a relation between God and creation which consistently holds together two distinct aspects of this relationship: first, the complete distinction between Creator and creature; second, the dynamic relationship between God and humanity in which a real – even, according to Torrance, an ontological – participation of the creature in God is affirmed to be possible. In large part this is due to the creation of humanity in the *imago Dei* and then, as will be discussed in Chapter 2, the Incarnation.

In terms of creation and anthropology specifically, *theosis* provides Torrance with a way of describing the reality of human participation in God through transformation into the image/likeness of the incarnate Son, Jesus Christ. The more believers conform to this image the more they reflect the Triune relationship of love within their human communities, and the more they show it to cosmic constituencies as well. Believers in Christ are enabled to act as priests of creation, glorifying God through bringing harmony to creation as they mediate God's presence. As they participate in the incarnate Son by the Spirit they become increasingly personalised and humanised, transformed into the likeness of the Son.

We now examine more closely Torrance's account of the Incarnation of the Son and how the life of Christ becomes both a vicarious substitute for ours and a model and paradigm into which we may enter.

---

144 Spjuth, *Creation, Contingency and Divine Presence*, p. 183. Cf. pp. 161–5.

145 Williams, *The Ground of Union*, p. 32.

Chapter 2
Incarnation: God Became Human

Incarnation and Redemption

Torrance notes that his main theological work or interest is 'in the field of Christology and Soteriology.'[1] The incarnation thus forms the central context within which Torrance works out the concept of *theosis*. The christological aspects of *theosis* in Torrance's theology highlight the fact that God in Christ has achieved reconciliation and communion between God and humanity (*theosis*), first in the person of the incarnate Son, and then through the Son (by the Holy Spirit) in the redeemed. This is highlighted through articulating the *homoousion*, the hypostatic union, the vicarious humanity of Christ, and the assumption of humanity into the life of God in, through, or by Christ. Further, when Torrance formulates a soteriology proper, he does so on the basis of his incarnational christology.[2] This is most vividly highlighted in Torrance's development of *theosis* and cognate terms, such as 'atoning exchange'. Just as Jesus Christ and his humanity are the key issue in anthropology, here it will be shown how Jesus is central to the process of

---

[1] Torrance, *Conflict and Agreement in the Church*, vol. 1: *Order and Disorder* (London: Lutterworth, 1959), p. 7. Torrance follows Barth as having the Word of God central to all dogmatic thinking. Thomas F. Torrance, Karl Barth: *An Introduction to His Early Theology 1910–1931* (1962. Edinburgh: T & T Clark, 2000), p. 132.

[2] The main sources of Torrance's christology include: *The Doctrine of Jesus Christ: Auburn Lectures 1938–39* (Eugene, Or.: Wipf & Stock, 2002); *Space, Time and Incarnation* (Edinburgh: T & T Clark, 1997), chapter 3; *God and Rationality* (Eugene, Or.: Wipf & Stock, 1997), chapter 6; *Space, Time and Resurrection* (1976. Edinburgh: T & T Clark, 1998); *Theology in Reconstruction* (Grand Rapids: Eerdmans, 1965), chapters 7, 8, 9, 10; 'Introduction', in *The Incarnation: Ecumenical Studies in the Nicene-Constantinopolitan Creed A.D. 381*, ed. Thomas F. Torrance (Edinburgh: Handsel Press, 1981), pp. xi–xxii; *Reality and Evangelical Theology* (Downers Grove: IVP, 1999), chapter 3; 'The Deposit of Faith', *Scottish Journal of Theology* 36 (1983): pp. 1–28; *The Trinitarian Faith: The Evangelical Theology of the Ancient Catholic Church* (Edinburgh: T & T Clark, 1995), chapters 4 and 5; *The Mediation of Christ*, 2nd edn (Edinburgh: T & T Clark, 1992); 'The Atonement the Singularity of Christ and the Finality of the Cross: The Atonement and the Moral Order', in *Universalism and the Doctrine of Hell*, ed. Nigel M. de S. Cameron (Carlisle: Paternoster, Grand Rapids: Baker, 1992), pp. 225–56; and 'Incarnation and Atonement: Theosis and Henosis in the Light of Modern Scientific Rejection of Dualism', *Society of Ordained Scientists*, Bulletin No. 7 (Edgeware, Middlesex, Spring 1992): pp. 8–20. Unavailable at the time of writing is Thomas F. Torrance, *The Incarnation: The Person and Life of Christ*, ed. Robert T. Walker (Grand Rapids: IVP, Carlisle: Paternoster, 2008).

theosis.[3] Christology paves the way for soteriology, incarnation for reconciliation, and only in this order may Torrance's doctrine of *theosis* be understood.[4]

On the basis of his articulation of *homoousios*, hypostatic union, and the vicarious humanity of Jesus Christ, it is clear that central to Torrance's soteriology is the articulation of Christ's incarnational redemption. He dismisses what he sees as the radical distinction between the person and work of Christ as a consequence of a dualism rejected first by the Fathers and then again at the time of the Reformation.[5] This dualism allegedly led to a cleavage between incarnation and atonement in the theologies of Arius, Augustine,[6] and those of Schleiermacher, Tillich and Bultmann that dominated immediately prior to Barth. This is what has led, in Torrance's estimation, to the doctrine of redemption being 'expounded in terms of external relations between Christ and sinful people'.[7] Torrance seeks to avoid this dualism and its resultant external, transactional notion of redemption in his incarnational model of atonement.

Torrance adopts Barth's methodology when, in his *Church Dogmatics*, he brought christology and soteriology together in the volume dedicated to reconciliation.[8]

---

3 The articulation of the saving significance of the incarnation is one of the most significant contributions Torrance has made to contemporary theology. See Gunther Pratz, 'The Relationship Between Incarnation and Atonement in the Theology of Thomas F. Torrance', *Journal for Christian Theological Research* 3 (1998): http://apu.edu/~CTRF/articles/1998_articles/pratz.html. Cf. Thomas F. Torrance, 'The Christ Who Loves Me', in *A Passion for Christ: Vision that Ignites Ministry*, eds Gerrit Dawson and Jock Stein (Edinburgh: The Handsel Press, 1999), p. 10.

4 See Torrance, *The Doctrine of Jesus Christ*, p. 115.

5 Torrance, *The Trinitarian Faith*, p. 159.

6 Augustine comes in for special critique by Torrance, particularly in 'Karl Barth and the Latin Heresy', *Scottish Journal of Theology* 39 (1986): pp. 461–82; and *Divine Meaning: Studies in Patristic Hermeneutics* (Edinburgh: T & T Clark, 1995), pp. 392; 170–228. Both Ayres and Barnes challenge such readings of Augustine given by Torrance. See Lewis Ayres: 'The Fundamental Grammar of Augustine's Trinitarian Theology', in *Augustine and His Critics: Essays in Honour of Gerald Bonner*, eds Robert Dodaro and George Lawless (London: Routledge, 2000), pp. 51–76; '"Remember That You Are Catholic" (serm. 52.2): Augustine on the Unity of the Triune God', *Journal of Early Christian Studies* 8 (2000): pp. 39–82; and Michel R. Barnes: 'Rereading Augustine's Theology of the Trinity', in *The Trinity*, eds Stephen T. Davis, Daniel Kendall and Gerald O'Collins (Oxford: Oxford University Press, 1999), pp. 145–76; and 'Augustine in Contemporary Trinitarian Theology', *Theological Studies* 56 (1995): pp. 237–50.

7 Thomas F. Torrance, *Theology in Reconciliation: Essays Towards Evangelical and Catholic Unity in East and West* (London: Geoffrey Chapman, 1975), p. 230.

8 See Barth's dissatisfaction with the traditional distinction between christology and soteriology in Barth, CD, IV/1, pp. 122–8. This dissatisfaction is what led, in part, to his construal of both categories as the doctrine of reconciliation which took up vols IV/1–IV/4 of his CD. Torrance follows a similar procedure and hence we speak of his doctrines of incarnation-and-reconciliation.

Gunton's remarks on Barth's theology are applicable to Torrance's: 'The person of Christ *is* his saving work, so that an adequately articulated Christology will also be a theology of salvation.'[9] A consequence of Torrance's basic Barthian axiom that God's being is known only through his act is the christological corollary of the doctrine that the person and work of Christ are inseparable.[10] In Torrance's own words, 'Christ is what he does, and does what he is'.[11] If the identity and mission of Jesus Christ form a coherent whole then the person no less than the work has redemptive significance. 'The Redemption is the Person of Christ in action; not the action itself thought of in an objectivist impersonal way.'[12] Quoting Emil Brunner in support, Torrance goes so far as to say that Christ's 'being is itself Redemption'.[13] This means that for Torrance '*Jesus' whole life is his vicarious Passion*'.[14] Incarnation thus provides the sphere in which reconciliation is to be examined.[15]

In his study of the relationship between incarnation and atonement in Torrance's theology Gunter Pratz writes:

> Some have understood Torrance to connect the Incarnation with redemption in a way implying that atonement is achieved simply through the hypostatic union of divine Logos and 'decaying humanity.' However, to understand the Athanasian statement, 'He became man that we might be made divine' in such a way is a serious misinterpretation for Torrance. In order to grasp his position better, it might prove beneficial to look at his understanding of the doctrine which Reformed theology has called the *Active* and *Passive Obedience* of Christ.[16]

This is wise counsel, for Torrance follows the Reformed theology of the active and passive obedience of Christ and his incarnational assumption and sanctification of our human nature.

On the basis of the solidarity between the person and work of Christ (established on such biblical passages as Heb 1.3; 2.14–18; 4.14–15.10; 9.11–10.10), Torrance argues that the incarnation is inherently redemptive, and redemption is intrinsically

[9] Colin Gunton, 'Salvation', in *The Cambridge Companion to Karl Barth*, ed. John Webster (Cambridge: Cambridge University Press, 2000), p. 144.

[10] Torrance, *The Doctrine of Jesus Christ*, p. 150.

[11] Ibid., p. 150; cf. p. 165.

[12] Ibid., p. 151. Torrance accuses Anselm of working in this objectivist way.

[13] Ibid.

[14] Ibid., p. 152 (italics in original).

[15] This is not to be thought of as diminishing the importance or place of the cross within Torrance's theology; quite the opposite: 'The Cross is, so to speak, a cross-section of the life and work of the Mediator at the most intense moment of his vicarious passion, in his death for us.' Torrance, *The Doctrine of Jesus Christ*, p. 153.

[16] Pratz, 'The Relationship Between Incarnation and Atonement in the Theology of Thomas F. Torrance', par. 15.

incarnational.[17] This makes the entire life of the incarnate Son a continuous vicarious sacrifice sanctifying all aspects of our life. This is the active obedience of Christ: the positive fulfilment of his Sonship in the whole life of Jesus.

Torrance has been accused of reducing soteriology to christology by collapsing the passive obedience of Christ into his active obedience,[18] and is thereby charged with advocating a physical theory of redemption, something that will occupy our attention in more detail later in the chapter.[19] But this is to misunderstand Torrance's logic. Torrance distances his theology of *theosis* from various forms of deification by rejecting any idea that posits a physical theory of the atonement in which humanity is literally 'divinised' or God is literally 'humanised'. The two-natures doctrine of Chalcedon and the *homoousios* doctrine of Nicaea are too strong in Torrance's work for him to allow such notions of 'divinisation' into his soteriology. However, like Athanasius, Torrance fails to adequately construct a christology that explains the functional relation between the divine and human natures of Jesus.[20]

Emphasising that both aspects are absolutely integral to an understanding of Christ's work of reconciliation, Torrance makes clear the distinction between the active and the passive obedience of Christ in Reformed theology has not served to divide or separate the two perspectives but actually to unite them. As Louis Berkhof's once-standard manual of Reformed theology states, 'But in discriminating between the two, it should be distinctly understood that they cannot be separated. The two accompany each other at every point in the Saviour's life… Christ's active and passive obedience should be regarded as complementary parts of an organic whole'.[21] As a consequence atonement cannot simply be limited to the passive obedience of Christ, the submission to death as the penalty for our sins.

---

17 Torrance, *The Mediation of Christ*, p. 65.

18 See Francis Watson, 'Did Christ Die as our Substitute? Reconsidering the Logic of Atonement', a paper presented in a seminar of the Research Institute in Systematic Theology, Kings College, London (1993), cited in Pratz, 'The Relationship Between Incarnation and Atonement in the Theology of Thomas F. Torrance', fn. 6.

19 Torrance, *The Trinitarian Faith*, p. 156. See pp. 57–9.

20 Others in the Reformed tradition have turned to pneumatology to further explicate this relationship. See Alan Spence, 'John Owen and Trinitarian Agency', *Scottish Journal of Theology* 43 (1990): pp. 157–73; and Colin E. Gunton, 'The Church: John Owen and John Zizioulas on the Church', in *Theology Through the Theologians: Selected Essays 1972–1995* (Edinburgh: T & T Clark, 1996), pp. 187–205.

21 Louis Berkhof, *Systematic Theology* (Edinburgh: Banner of Truth Trust, 1949), pp. 379–80. For a history and analysis of the work of Christ and its derivation into active and passive dimensions see Gerrit C. Berkouwer, *The Work of Christ* (Grand Rapids: Eerdmans, 1965), pp. 314–27; and Charles Hodge, *Systematic Theology*, 3 vols (Grand Rapids: Eerdmans, 1997), 3. pp. 142–50.

Torrance finds this insight is already evident within the theology of Calvin who pointed out that from birth Christ initiated the salvation of humanity.[22]

Torrance appeals to Calvin, along with Irenaeus and Athanasius, as viewing the entire incarnation as the locus of atonement – that is, he sees the active and passive obedience of Christ as two stages of one reconciling activity. In Jesus Christ, Calvin says, all parts of our salvation are complete. Every aspect of the life that God intends for humanity is fully and finally fulfilled and made real in our humanity by Jesus Christ. Calvin uses language from a variety of models of atonement and places all of them in a radically substitutionary framework (*Institutes* 2.17). Jinkins argues that 'a more helpful way of looking at the meaning of Christ's life, death and resurrection would be to see the *various aspects of atonement…in a more inclusive incarnational framework*'.[23] This is exactly what Torrance sought to do throughout his christology and soteriology.

In stressing the redemptive significance of the active and passive obedience of Christ, Torrance manages to emphasise, more forcefully than any other contemporary Reformed theologian, the twin emphases that reconciliation brings, that is, both imputed righteousness in justification and imparted righteousness through participation in his divine-human righteousness. Christ secured both in his life, death, and resurrection. To be developed later in the study, for Torrance reconciliation means declaration and 'deification'.[24] This accounts for Torrance's strong emphasis upon the active obedience of Christ and its application to believers. Present in Reformed theology is the very clear, if largely neglected, idea that the benefits of redemption go far beyond mere forgiveness of sins;[25] they actually result in blessing and promises of future grace.

Retrospective and Prospective Aspects of Atonement

Along with the distinction between the active and passive obedience of Christ in Reformed theology generally, Torrance appropriates a twofold perspective on the atonement derived from John McLeod Campbell, who, in *The Nature of the*

---

22 While Calvin did not use the terms 'active' and 'passive obedience' he did advocate what these later terms represent, see for example, *Institutes,* 2.16.5. For Torrance's understanding of Calvin's position see Thomas F. Torrance, 'Introduction', in *The School of Faith: The Catechisms of the Reformed Church*, trans. and ed. with Introduction by Thomas F. Torrance (London: James Clarke and Co, 1959), pp. lxxxiv–lxxxvii.

23 Michael Jinkins, *Invitation to Theology* (Downers Grove: IVP, 2001), p. 149 (italics in original).

24 See Chapter 3, pp. 124–6, and 135–8.

25 Torrance, *The School of Faith*, p. lxxxvi, insists that when the active obedience of Christ is diminished in theology, as he believes it was in post-Reformation Reformed dogmatics, then it becomes difficult to understand justification as anything but a forensic non-imputation of sin.

Atonement,[26] makes the terminological distinction between the 'retrospective' and the 'prospective' aspects of atonement. While the terminology was McLeod Campbell's the substance of the distinction goes back to Calvin.[27]

Campbell sought to present the atonement in filial as opposed to judicial terms, emphasising the love of God for all humanity.[28] This drove him back to the doctrine of the incarnation which, in his later theology he sought to explicate as the twofold movement of God to humanity and humanity to God in the one person of the incarnate Son, something he labelled the *retrospective* and *prospective* aspects of atonement. *Retrospectively* God has dealt with every human being's guilty past by penetrating the depths of human sin and guilt and pardoning them. However, this can not be understood apart from seeing that God *prospectively* brings people to share in Christ's Sonship, lifting them from imprisonment in their mortal existence into the new life of the risen Jesus. Campbell argued that traditional doctrines of atonement had limited themselves to the *retrospective* aspect only, resulting in a doctrine of strict penal substitution. When the *prospective* aspect is considered, not only are the necessary means of atonement taken into account but the goal of the incarnation is also set forth, namely, the Father's filial purposes for all humankind.[29]

As Redding's exposition makes clear, 'At the heart of Campbell's thinking on this matter lies a concentrated focus on one's union with Christ – a union which is the fruit of the incarnation'.[30] Christ in our humanity offers a perfect vicarious response to the love and judgement of God. Believers respond personally to this twofold movement through the Holy Spirit, who enables them to participate in Christ's own response made on their behalf. Christ's work is of no avail for believers apart from participation in his person. Hence, in the incarnation Christ unites himself with us by taking our humanity into union with himself. In our

---

26 John McLeod Campbell, *The Nature of the Atonement* (Edinburgh: Handsel Press, Grand Rapids: Eerdmans, 1996).

27 See Leanne Van Dyk, *The Desire of Divine Love: John McLeod Campbell's Doctrine of the Atonement* (New York: Peter Lang, 1995), pp. 137–66, who shows the continuity of Campbell's theology with that of Calvin.

28 See the helpful overview of Daniel P. Thimell, 'Christ in Our Place in the Theology of John McLeod Campbell', in *Christ in Our Place: The Humanity of God in Christ for the Reconciliation of the World*: Essays Presented to Professor James Torrance, eds Trevor A. Hart and Daniel P. Thimell (Exeter: Paternoster, 1981), pp. 182–206.

29 This theme is defended in Torrance, 'Review of Leanne Van Dyk, The Desire of Divine Love. John McLeod Campbell's Doctrine of the Atonement', *Scottish Journal of Theology* 49 (1996): pp. 125–7; and Torrance, 'John McLeod Campbell (1800–1872)', in *Scottish Theology from John Knox to John McLeod Campbell* (Edinburgh: T & T Clark, 1996), pp. 301–2, where Campbell's theology is compared to that of Athanasius.

30 Graham Redding, *Prayer and the Priesthood of Christ in the Reformed Tradition* (Edinburgh: T & T Clark, 2003), p. 194. For the same view see Torrance, *Scottish Theology from John Knox to John McLeod Campbell*, p. 304, where he associates Campbell's doctrine of union with Christ with that of Calvin and Cyril of Alexandria noting that all three linked justification and union with Christ closely together.

humanity he repented, believed, and died for all. By the Spirit we are united with him to participate in his vicarious response ('perfect repentance')[31] which, in turn, is a response offered in our humanity.

From this brief account of Campbell's theology we can discern some of the constituent features of Torrance's soteriology. We see the twofold movement of God to humanity and humanity to God embodied in the incarnate Person of the Son through the hypostatic union; the familiar emphasis on the dire consequences of viewing the incarnation and atonement from only one of those perspectives, the retrospective; and the integral link between incarnation and atonement worked out in the Person of the Mediator.[32] Within Torrance's soteriology all these aspects become essential to a doctrine of *theosis* and from this perspective Torrance attempts to advocate a doctrine of participation in God that amounts to a theology of *theosis* while rejecting certain misunderstandings such a doctrine often engenders.[33] This is what leads Torrance to affirm an ontological atonement.

Ontological Atonement

Torrance follows the Greek Fathers in constructing a doctrine of *theosis* around two distinct but interrelated movements. The first is the 'divinising' of the human nature of the Logos; the second is the application of this to human persons in 'deification'. The two are interrelated, albeit distinct, aspects of the one reality of reconciliation.

Torrance generally applies the English term 'divinisation' (*theopoiesis*) to the human *nature* that Jesus Christ took upon himself in his incarnate person, not to human *persons* in general (*theosis*).[34] This should not be taken to imply that he makes a formal distinction between *theosis and theopoiesis*, applying the first to believers and the second to Christ in a strictly formal way. Strictly speaking there is only *one* 'divinised' person – the man Jesus Christ. In the hypostatic union Jesus divinised human nature ontologically and subsequently worked out this *theopoiesis* through his sinless life, death, and resurrection. As a result:

---

31 Torrance, *Scottish Theology from John Knox to John McLeod Campbell*, pp. 305–8.

32 This is stressed in ibid., p. 313.

33 Campbell's views are not without their critics. According to Robert Letham, *The Work of Christ* (Leicester: IVP, 1993), p. 32, Campbell is a universalist who rejects any penal element to reconciliation. Controlling Letham's assessment is the vexed issue of the extent of the atonement. Letham's criticisms could equally be levelled at Torrance for he too considers the atonement to be universal in scope. See Paul Helm, 'The Logic of Limited Atonement', *Scottish Bulletin of Evangelical Theology* 3 (1985): pp. 37–54; and Redding, *Prayer and the Priesthood of Christ in the Reformed Tradition*, pp. 98–108. For a reply to such criticisms see Torrance, *Scottish Theology from John Knox to John McLeod Campbell*, pp. 308–9; 312.

34 See for example Torrance, *The Trinitarian Faith*, pp. 138, 139, 140, 141, 188, 189, 264, 305.

> ...the blessed exchange involved between the divine-human life of Jesus and mankind has the effect of finalising and sealing the ontological relations between every man and Jesus Christ...since in him divine and human natures are inseparably united, then the secret of every man, whether he believes or not, is bound up with Jesus for it is in him that human contingent existence has been grounded and secured.[35]

Torrance is insistent on this point. The saving act of God in Christ was internal to the incarnate Son before it could be applied externally. Redemption, reconciliation, and *theopoiesis* are not simply an external arrangement between God and humanity, or between Christ and the world. Rather, 'if the soteriological exchange takes place within the constitution of the incarnate Person of the Mediator, then it is as eternal as Jesus Christ himself, the eternal Son'.[36] Throughout the life of the incarnate Son an atoning exchange is made once and for all as human nature is taken up and given a place in God and thus grounded in his eternal unchangeable reality. By 'human nature' Torrance specifically refers, in the first instance, to the human nature of Jesus Christ the incarnate Son. In the incarnate person of the Son an ontological atonement has been perfectly accomplished – God and humanity have been reconciled once and for all. It is on this basis that believers may also be 'deified' but only in, by, or through the incarnate person of the Son.

The distinction (although not the specific terminology) between Christ's *theopoiesis* and human *theosis* is crucial to Torrance as it was for the patristic theologians from whom he derives this doctrine.[37] An example is how Athanasius bases one of his principal arguments for the perfect divinity of the Son of God upon this distinction when in *On the Councils of Ariminum and Seleucia* he writes:

> If the Logos had also been God by participation, and not consubstantial divinity and the image of the Father by Himself, He would not have been able to deify, being Himself deified. For it is not possible that one who only possesses by participation communicate to others what he has thus received, because what he does not have from himself, but from the giver, and what he has received, is barely sufficient for himself.[38]

The ascension is also in Torrance's view for 'the ascension means the exaltation of man into the life of God and on to the throne of God. In the ascension the Son

35 Ibid., pp. 182–3.

36 Ibid., pp. 183–4.

37 Ibid., pp. 179–80.

38 Athanasius, Syn. 51 (PG 26:784b) cited in Jules Gross, *The Divinization of the Christian According to the Greek Fathers*, trans. Paul A. Onica (Anaheim, CA.: A & C Press, 2002), p. 163.

of Man, New Man in Christ, is given to partake of divine nature'.[39] While the term *theopoiesis* is not used here certainly the doctrine is explicitly taught. *Theosis* was mentioned earlier in the same work when Torrance stated that 'through the Spirit Christ is nearer to us than we are to ourselves, and we who live and dwell on earth are yet made to sit with Christ "in heavenly places", partaking of the divine nature in him'.[40] These two statements clearly contrast what Torrance means by *theopoiesis* as applied to Christ on the one hand and *theosis* as applied to humans on the other. Christ's human nature is 'divinised' due to the hypostatic union and the active and passive obedience; our human nature undergoes *theosis* only by grace as we are united to Christ in, with, or by the Holy Spirit and in that relationship we partake of the divine nature.

Beyond a physical theory of redemption Given Torrance's stress on incarnational redemption it will pay us to return to the mistaken charge that Torrance presents a physical theory of redemption. Like Athanasius, Torrance understands the uniting of the divine Logos and human nature in the one person of the Son (hypostatic union) to divinise human nature.[41] If this same process were applied to men and women generally, it would amount to a 'physical theory' of redemption. However, according to the way in which Torrance adopts patristic theology, the physical theory, mistakenly first put forward by Irenaeus,[42] is not what is in mind.

According to the physical theory of *theosis* human nature is immortalised (*aphtharsia*) and thus divinised by the fact of the ultimate contact that the incarnation establishes between it and the divine nature of the Word.[43] This would make human beings indistinguishable from God and deification would be automatic. At the very least a strict adherence to a physical theory of the atonement postulates deification by contact.[44] In place of a physical theory whereby 'deification' or *theosis* occurs

---

39 Torrance, *Space, Time and Resurrection*, p. 135. See further in Chapter 2, pp. 87–91.

40 Ibid., p. 135.

41 Athanasius, *Contra Arianos*, 1.70 (NPNF, 2nd series, vol. 4. pp. 959–60). Cf., *Contra Arianos* 2.67; 3.33; 3.34; 2.61; 2.67; and *De Incarnatione*, 13; and 44.

42 See Trevor A. Hart, 'Irenaeus, Recapitulation and Physical Redemption', in *Christ in Our Place: The Humanity of God in Christ for the Reconciliation of the World*: Essays Presented to Professor James Torrance, eds Trevor A. Hart and Daniel P. Thimell (Exeter: Paternoster, 1981), pp. 152–81.

43 I am following the standard definition provided by Gross, *The Divinization of the Christian According to the Greek Fathers*, p. 125.

44 Jean Rivière, *Le dogme de la redemption: Essai d'étude historique* (Paris: Librairie Victor Lecoffre 1905), p. 147 and Adolf von Harnack, *Lehrbuch der Dormengeschichte* (Tübingen: Mohr, 1909), 2. pp. 160–61, both mistakenly present Athanasius's theology of *theosis* as a mechanical process of physical redemption. See Torrance, *The Trinitarian Faith*, p. 156; and Hart, 'Irenaeus, Recapitulation and Physical Redemption', pp. 152–70. It is correct, however, that Athanasius never clearly distinguished between the terms οὐσια and ὑποστασις, as Gross, *The Divinization of the Christian According to the Greek Fathers*,

automatically or naturally within human persons, Torrance presents an ontological theory of incarnational redemption, as we have seen. This *ontological* atonement, mediation, or redemption forms the first stage of *theosis* proper in Torrance's theology, characterised by the *theopoiesis* of Christ's own human nature. As Torrance articulates it:

> [Christ] had come, Son of God incarnate as Son of man, in order to get to grips with the powers of darkness and defeat them, but he had been sent to do that not through the manipulation of social, political or economic power-structures, but by striking beneath them all into the ontological depths of Israel's existence where man, and Israel representing all mankind, had become estranged from God, and there within those ontological depths of human being to forge a bond of union and communion between man and God in himself which can never be undone.[45]

At the cross God meets, suffers, and triumphs over the enmity entrenched in human existence once and for all in Jesus Christ. Ontological atonement has been achieved in the incarnate life and death of the Son of God, confirmed in the resurrection from the empty tomb, and in the sending of the Spirit at Pentecost.[46]

The human life of Christ contains redemptive value in the sense that it completes the efficacy of the incarnation. For full redemption and reconciliation to occur the incarnate Logos assumed our natural – fallen – human condition in order to divinise the human life in its various stages. That is to say 'he lived it personally'.[47] This does not imply that Torrance's conception of the matter has any form of mechanical *theosis* for men and women, the physical theory *simpliciter*. There are processes or stages to be followed by which human beings in general may be 'deified', including the sacraments and the Christian life. This will be considered later in the study.[48] Before that, Torrance constructs the basis for *theosis* to occur; it must first of all be a reality in the life of the incarnate Word, Jesus Christ. The work of *theosis* is supremely the work of Christ (and the Holy Spirit), to whom the initiative goes completely.

---

p. 169, notes: 'Through a lack of important a distinction as this, it was difficult for him to specify – as Saint John Damascene will do later – that the deification of the human nature does not automatically entail that of the persons. Still, the fact is that he presents individual divinization as the result of the combined action of the subject, Christ, and the Holy Spirit.'

[45] Torrance, *The Mediation of Christ*, p. 30.

[46] Ibid., p. 31.

[47] Gross, *The Divinization of the Christian According to the Greek Fathers*, p. 171, applied these words to Athanasius's doctrine of Christ's *theosis*.

[48] See Chapter 4, pp. 170–85.

Torrance repeatedly advocates the axiom of Gregory Nazianzus: 'that which has not been assumed has not been healed'.[49] Torrance uses this phrase in at least two senses: first, that Christ assumed a complete or total human nature, the sense that Gregory of Nazianzus appears to have made of it; and second, that Christ has completely healed humanity in his own incarnation. This is what Torrance means by a doctrine of *theopoiesis* applied to the hypostatic union.[50] On this basis there is a sense in which Torrance is advocating a physical theory of *theosis*: through the hypostatic union the human nature of Jesus Christ was perfected, redeemed and reconciled. This work of *theopoiesis* is what has enabled or qualified the incarnate Word to deify those who are united to himself – what Torrance would more technically term *theosis* rather than 'divinisation'. Clearly this form of physical redemption is not what his critics have in mind when making the charge.

The result of *theopoiesis* is that Christ has totally redeemed, reconciled, cleansed, lifted, restored, and recreated human nature to what God had intended it to be in the first place.[51] The consummation of deified humanity is centred upon the summing up of all things in Christ, when he transforms us in the whole of our human nature. 'When we see him we shall become like him, and when we become like him we shall see him with healed vision and recreated natures.'[52]

With his commitment to a significantly modified physical theory of the atonement we complete a major rung of Torrance's doctrine of *theosis*. The uniting of human and divine natures in the one person of the incarnate Son achieves *theopoiesis;* it divinises human nature ontologically. This has yet to be applied to other human beings but the important point is that it has been achieved in the God-man. This is what qualifies the Son to be the Mediator, Saviour and diviniser of humanity.

Because humanity is divinised in Christ through the incarnation, atonement has been perfectly achieved in his own person, that is, ontologically. However, Torrance does not imply by this ontological atonement that all men and women are thus automatically saved. Torrance does not espouse a doctrine of universalism. Instead, he seeks to work out the soteriological implications of the *homoousion* and the hypostatic union, themes to which we must now consider.

---

49 Gregory Nazianzen, *Epistle 101* (NPNF, 2nd. series, vol. 7. p. 830). See Torrance, 'Incarnation and Atonement', p. 12; 'The Atonement the Singularity of Christ', pp. 237–9; and *The Christian Doctrine of God: One Being Three Persons* (Edinburgh: T & T Clark, 1996), p. 250.

50 Torrance, *The Trinitarian Faith*, pp. 188–90.

51 See Torrance, *Space, Time and Resurrection*, p. 139.

52 Ibid., p. 140. Torrance uses the concept of 'transparency' here as a conceptual equivalent of theosis.

The *Homoousion*

The doctrine of the *homoousion* speaks to the fact that Jesus is both 'of one being with the Father' (Nicene Creed) and of one being with us in our humanity.[53] This double *homoousion* forms the hinge upon which Torrance's development of incarnation and reconciliation turns. 'The *homoousion* is the ontological and epistemological linchpin of Christian theology. With it, everything hangs together; without it, everything ultimately falls apart.'[54] Torrance's christology is thus an attempt to work out this point in detail. As Lee's study points out, 'For Torrance, the *homoousion* is not only the one-and-sameness in their being but also the "unbroken continuity" in their presence (*homopraesens*) and activity (*homoenergeia*). The consubstantial relation between Jesus Christ and God denotes the fullness of the Godhead in His *bodily* dwelling in Christ'.[55] Jesus Christ is thus *homoousios* with God in being and in act.

Lee's study on the motif of union with Christ in Torrance's theology identifies four significant implications of Torrance's use of the *homoousion.* It will be useful to note them here. First, the *homoousion* asserts that Christ's word of forgiveness is genuinely the Word and the forgiveness of God, 'for only God can forgive sins'. By extension this applies to all that Christ did in his incarnation to secure our salvation.[56] As Torrance makes abundantly clear, without the *homoousion* the Gospel collapses.[57]

Second, there is the epistemological significance of the term. Divine revelation is God himself coming to deliver his own message of reconciliation. It is only through Jesus Christ that we are able to really know this God and hence the *homoousion* is the concept that moves our thought from the economic to the immanent Trinity. The logical step beyond the assertion of Christ's oneness with God is to apply the *homoousion* to the Trinity as a whole and to see this heuristic device as stating the ontological relation between the economic and the immanent Trinity. What God reveals to us in Jesus Christ is nothing other than a *self*-revelation of his own being. The God who acts *ad extra* is the God who is *in se*. This onto-relational

---

53 Torrance, *The Trinitarian Faith*, pp. 110–45.

54 Thomas F. Torrance, *The Ground and Grammar of Theology* (Charlottesville: University of Virginia Press, 1980), pp. 160–61.

55 Kye W. Lee, *Living in Union With Christ: The Practical Theology of Thomas F. Torrance* (New York: Peter Lang, 2003), p. 140. See: Torrance, *Space, Time and Incarnation*, p. 1; *The Ground and Grammar of Theology*, pp. 41, 160; *The Mediation of Christ*, pp. 43, 54, 62, 101, 124; and *Conflict and Agreement in the Church*, vol. 1, p. 216.

56 Lee, *Living in Union With Christ*, p. 142.

57 Torrance, *The Mediation of Christ*, pp. 57–8; and *Christian Theology and Scientific Culture* (New York: Oxford University Press, 1981), pp. 102–3.

notion of the Triune Persons Torrance more specifically treats under the concept of *perichoresis*.[58]

The third significance is that the Holy Spirit is the *other Paraclete* (Jn 14.16) whom Christ sends to act in his place. In his *homoousion* with Christ in being and act the Spirit is Christ's *other self* through whose presence in us Christ makes himself present to us. 'Thus it is by the Spirit that our adoption in Christ through atoning propitiation is sealed so that we are united to Christ and freely given to share in the Son's filial relation with the Father.'[59]

Finally, Torrance applies the *homoousion* to the doctrine of grace. Working under a Reformed notion that grace is God's personal self-impartation Torrance makes much of the fact that 'God is really like Jesus'. From his pastoral experiences in Scottish parishes and on the battlefield in World War II, Torrance finds in this doctrine great comfort for people lacking assurance:

> Fearful anxiety arises in the human heart when people cannot connect Jesus up in their faith or understanding with the ultimate Being of God, for then the ultimate Being of God can be to them only a dark, inscrutable, arbitrary Deity whom they inevitably think of with terror…[60]

Grace *is* Jesus Christ for there is no other gift from the Father besides his Son.

Because of the oneness in being and act between Christ and God; salvation, knowledge, union, communion, and *theosis* are possible. Before this can be applied to human persons it first of all becomes a reality in the person of the Mediator, Jesus Christ. The *homoousion* thus necessitates the hypostatic union, the distinct instantiation of communion between God and humanity in the person of the Son.

Hypostatic Union

'Christ is of one and the same being as God, as well as of one and the same being as ourselves.'[61] Torrance treats this theme properly under the concept of the hypostatic union between the divine and human natures in the one person of Christ. The communion between God and humanity is made possible by the incarnation, hence retaining the christocentric nature of Torrance's theology. Torrance believes 'the one supreme relation is the hypostatic union, the unique relation of divine and human natures in the One Person of the Son, but by reference to that personal relation, all other personal relations are to be understood in their likeness and in

---

[58] See Torrance, *The Ground and Grammar of Theology*, pp. 39–40; 172–5; and *Reality and Evangelical Theology*, pp. 14–15, 112.

[59] Lee, *Living in Union With Christ*, p. 143. Lee then cites Torrance, *The Mediation of Christ*, pp. 117–18.

[60] Torrance, *The Mediation of Christ*, p. 59.

[61] Ibid., p. 124.

their difference to it.'[62] This has profound consequences for the development of Torrance's doctrine of *theosis*.

The hypostatic union functions within Torrance's theology in an epistemological way: personal knowledge of the Father is commensurate with personal knowledge of the Son; the two are inseparable. We do not know the Father apart from the Son, or the Son apart from the Father.[63] It is this trinitarian 'knowledge' that constitutes the *ground and grammar* of Torrance's theology. He explains:

> To know this God, who both condescends to share all that we are and makes us share in all that he is in Jesus Christ, is to be lifted up in his Spirit to share in God's own self-knowing and self-loving until we are enabled to apprehend him in some real measure in himself beyond anything that we are capable of in ourselves. It is to be lifted out of ourselves, as it were, into God, until we know him and love him and enjoy him in his eternal Reality as Father, Son, and Holy Spirit, in such a way that the Trinity enters into the fundamental fabric of our thinking of him and constitutes the basic grammar of our worship and knowledge of the One God.[64]

Here we have a window into Torrance's meaning behind the term 'knowing' and through it into his conception of *theosis*. To 'know' God is to transcend our creaturely boundaries and to be 'lifted out of ourselves…into God', to 'apprehend him', 'love him', and 'enjoy him' forever as Father, Son, and Holy Spirit. It is, as advocates of *theosis* consistently state, to participate in the Triune communion.[65] This is the supreme *telos* of *theosis*. In the person of Jesus Christ we see true humanity partaking of true Divinity *by nature* in such a way that by union, communion, and *theosis* with Christ by the Spirit we too, *by grace*, can participate in the divine nature. This is worked out in a thoroughly christological fashion. Union of the two natures *in Christ* is the key to understanding *our* union with Christ.[66] The former is by nature and substantial; the latter is by grace and is relational.

Torrance's earliest mention of *theosis* occurs amidst a discussion of christology, when, commenting on the relevance of the hypostatic union for men and women he writes, 'And in this God-Man we partake in grace, as members of his body, reconciled to God through him and in him, and even it is said, are incomprehensibly partakers of Divine nature!'[67] Here as early as 1938–39 we have a bold statement

[62] Thomas F. Torrance, *Theological Science* (London: Oxford University Press, 1969), p. 217.

[63] This is made clear in Torrance, 'Access to the Father', in *The Trinitarian Faith*, pp. 47–75.

[64] Torrance, *The Ground and Grammar of Theology*, p. 155.

[65] Yeung contrasts this type of 'knowing' to that of Tillich who argued for 'knowing' as mere ecstasy, Yeung, Being and Knowing, pp. 103–5.

[66] Cf. Barth, *CD*, IV/1, pp. 67–78, 123–8, who makes this point strongly.

[67] Torrance, *The Doctrine of Jesus Christ*, p. 121.

on the orthodoxy of *theosis* and how it functions within Torrance's theology. As Yeung observes:

> When God became man He was no less God, for He was not diminished by the development of the body, but rather 'deified' the body and rendered it immortal. 'Deification' did not mean any change of human essence, but that without being less human we are by grace made to participate in divine Sonship.[68]

Because of Christ's hypostatic union a trinitarian movement is accomplished in his life from the Father through the Son in the Spirit, along with a doxological 'return' in the Spirit through the Son to the Father. This movement takes place first in the Son and then in believers by the Spirit of the Son. We share in the love of God through the grace of Christ in the communion of the Holy Spirit. This is what Torrance calls the evangelical, doxological theology of the trinitarian life and love that God is.[69] This constitutes an internal relation as the Son is *homoousios* with the Father and the Spirit and hence this trinitarian structure is at the same time christocentric, 'for it is only through Jesus Christ that we know the Father and only through him that we receive the Holy Spirit. Everything depends on the indivisible inner relation in being of the Son and the Spirit to the Father…'.[70]

How is this 'return' made possible? Torrance answers: exclusively by the incarnate Son, Jesus Christ. In line with Athanasius and other patristic theologians, Torrance is careful to explain *theosis* as it occurs ontologically in the one person of Christ, via the hypostatic union, before going on to consider *theosis* as it relates to men and women. In this way false notions of *theosis* are explicitly ruled out, such as pantheism or varieties of post-Kantian, neo-Protestant theologies, which are based on a non-conceptual relation to God.[71]

Torrance appreciatively cites the work of Martin Buber who saw through the problem of modern Protestant thought when he attacked it for what he called its 'conceptual letting go of God'. Torrance imagines a mountain climber trying to climb the face of a rock cliff: If it is utterly smooth, without any cracks in it, it is impossible. Unless he can get his fingers or spikes into the rock, and thus make use of the interstices or intrinsic relations on the rock, he cannot grasp hold of it. Against notions of mysticism and liberalism Torrance argues the fact that God is

---

68 Yeung, *Being and Knowing*, p. 113.

69 Torrance, 'Karl Barth and the Latin Heresy', pp. 461–2. Against Apollinaris, Torrance sides with Athanasius who stressed the redemption of the mind and the inner-man no less than the redemption of the flesh. This is the teaching about the redemption of the 'whole man in the whole Christ' which Torrance sees developed so powerfully in Athanasius's two books *Contra Apollinarem*, and it is precisely from this work that Torrance derives his emphasis on the 'reconciling exchange' achieved by Christ. See Torrance, *The Trinitarian Faith*, pp. 164–8.

70 Torrance, 'Karl Barth and the Latin Heresy', p. 462.

71 Torrance, *The Ground and Grammar of Theology*, p. 150.

a triunity means that there are relations of love inherent to God which allow us to know this God as he is in his inherent relations (onto-relations). 'There is a kind of meeting of love, a profound reciprocity, within God, and it is when our knowledge of God latches on to that internal relationship deep in God that we can really conceive him and know him in accordance with his intrinsic nature. And that is the ground, as Buber showed, for a conceptual grasp of God.'[72]

A related idea is the Pauline concept of being 'in' Christ, an analogical motif discussed by Torrance along with the wider special issues of time-space itself. Drawing on Athanasius, Torrance takes issue with the 'container' notion of space that he alleges dominated scientific, philosophical, and theological thinking up to the time of Einstein and beyond.[73] Athanasius employed the concept of 'in' to illustrate the concept of space. Christ is 'in' us and he is 'in' the Father, according to Scripture, especially the Pauline corpus.[74] But how are we to work out the relation between these two 'in's? According to Athanasius, by means of an analogical account. By respecting both the divine and the human nature we can see that to be 'in' the other (Christ *in* the Father and men and women *in* Christ), applies not to *place* but to *nature*. For in place (spatially) nothing is far from God. Therefore the phrase, 'we are in Christ Jesus' does not signify that we are located somewhere within the physical confines of the incarnate Christ, but points analogically to the fact that we are in a relationship with him. This applies to Christ being in the Father and to men and women being in the Son. As Athanasius and the tradition puts it, the 'inter-relations of the Father and the Son must be thought out in terms of "abiding" and "dwelling" in which each wholly rests in the other. This is the doctrine of *perichoresis* (περιχωρησις) in which we are to think of the whole being of the Son as proper to the Father's essence, as God from God, Light from Light'.[75]

Getting back to *theosis* as it occurs first to the human nature of Jesus Christ we read, 'The *hypostatic union* carries with it the realisation that the atoning exchange whereby we are reconciled to God takes place within the incarnate constitution of

---

72 Ibid.

73 Torrance works out issues of space-time in his companion volumes, *Space, Time and Incarnation*; and *Space, Time and Resurrection*. Also see his 'The Relation of the Incarnation to Space in Nicene Theology', in *The Ecumenical World of Orthodox Civilisation. III. Russia and Orthodoxy: Essays in Honor of Georges Florovsky*, ed. A. Blane (The Hague: Mouton, 1973), pp. 43–70.

74 The themes of incorporation and participation are strong within the Pauline literature, 'in Christ' appearing 170 times alone. On Pauline participation see: A.J.M. Wedderburn, 'Some Observations on Paul's Use of the Phrases "in Christ" and "with Christ"', *Journal for the Study of the New Testament* 25 (1985): pp. 83–97; and Michel Bouttier, *En Christ: Étude d'exégèse et de théologie pauliniennes* (Paris: Universitaires de France, 1962).

75 Torrance, *Space, Time and Incarnation*, p. 15. For a history of the term and some cautions as to its modern use see Randall E. Otto, 'The Use and Abuse of Perichoresis in Recent Theology', *Scottish Journal of Theology* 54 (2001): pp. 366–84.

the Lord Jesus Christ as the one Mediator between God and man'.[76] Torrance has consistently rejected any and all suggestions that the humanity of Jesus Christ, the human nature he partook of in the incarnation, was anything other than a particular humanity – that of this person, Jesus of Nazareth. It was not simply some Platonically 'ideal' humanity. In this regard any notion that the human nature of Jesus Christ was deified 'in itself apart from the fact that it is united to the eternal Word or Son of God'[77] is rejected. That is to say, the work of Christ did not divinise human nature in an automatic or mechanistic sense. Rather, it was a specific, personal, and real divinisation of a human nature. This leads Torrance into evangelical praise:

> The supreme truth that lies behind everything else in the Gospel and gives it its decisive import and redemptive power is the love of God the Father for mankind – the divine *philanthropia* manifested in the astonishing event in which God the Son became man, not 'man' in some ideal or abstract sense, but actual historical man.[78]

The *homoousion* and the hypostatic union are thus central to a construction of *theosis* within Torrance's theology.

Antiochene or Alexandrian Christology?

In order to understand his articulation of Christ's divinisation Torrance must be situated with the wider Christian tradition. According to standard textbook accounts, two 'schools' of thought emerged in the fourth and fifth centuries – the Alexandrian and the Antiochene – with differing proposals on how to explain the precise nature of the divinity of Jesus Christ.[79] While the 'two-schools' theory is now thought to be radically simplistic it does draw attention to some of the general positions inherent in the early church.[80] On the one hand the Antiochene 'school' with its so-called 'Logos-anthropos' christology found its most radical

---

76 Torrance, 'Incarnation and Atonement', p. 12.

77 Torrance, *The Doctrine of Jesus Christ*, p. 132.

78 Torrance, *The Trinitarian Faith*, p. 147.

79 Alloys Grillmeier, *Christ in Christian Tradition. vol. 1: From the Apostolic Age to Chalcedon* (451), trans. John Bowden (London: Mowbrays, 1975), in particular popularised the Logos-sarx/Logos-anthropos distinction. See David F. Wells, *The Person of Christ: A Biblical and Historical Analysis of the Incarnation* (Illinois: Crossway, 1984), pp. 98–109; John N.D. Kelly, *Early Christian Doctrines*, 4th edn (London: A & C Black, 1968), pp. 153–8; 301–2; and Robert V. Sellers, *Two Ancient Christologies: A Study in the Christological Thought of the Schools of Alexandrian and Antioch in the Early History of Christian Doctrine* (London: SPCK, 1954).

80 While two streams of theology did exist they were by no means separate or so well defined. Recent scholarship, especially on Athanasius, has challenged the readings of Grillmeier, Kelly, and others on the Logos-sarx model of Alexandrian christology. See

exponents articulating Nestorianism.[81] The other 'school', the Alexandrian, and its so-called 'Logos-sarx' christology found its most radical exponents articulating Apollinarianism or Eutychianism.[82] Apollinaris and his followers claimed that the Logos replaced the soul of Jesus, something refuted by the pro-Nicene tradition. Eutychianism held that Christ had only one nature, hence this tended to be Docetic, something rejected by the Chalcedonian Formula and its theology.

Rejecting a simplistic two-schools approach to the issues, Torrance's theology, like Barth's, reflects both christologies.[83] According to an Antiochene christology, finite realities can be said to be divine; this applies to the Bible, to the bread and wine of the Eucharist, to the water of baptism, and to the words of gospel proclamation.

> According to the Antiochene understanding of Torrance, the grounds for affirming Christ's deity are essentially the same as those used to establish the divinity of other creaturely media. These creatures are said to be divine because of their relation to God, their roles in revelation, not because of their inherent nature.[84]

Khaled Anatolios, *Athanasius: The Coherence of his Thought* (London: Routledge, 1998), pp. 70–73; 138–46, especially.

81 Nestorius's theology has not escaped the criticism of the 'pantomime horse', the theory that while Christ appears to be one, at the deepest level Christ remains two. His views were condemned at Ephesus in A.D 431. Grillmeier, *Christ in Christian Tradition*, vol. 1. pp. 447–72.

82 For a more critical evaluation of the two 'schools' see Francis Young, *Biblical Exegesis and the Formation of Christian Culture* (Cambridge: Cambridge University Press, 1997), pp. 202–12.

83 The debate over Barth's commitment to either 'school' can be followed in: Charles T. Waldrop, *Karl Barth's Christology: Its Basic Alexandrian Character* (Amsterdam: Mouton, 1984); Richard A. Muller, 'Directions in the Study of Barth's Christology', *Westminster Theological Journal* 48 (1986): pp. 125–31; and Hans Boersma, 'Alexandrian or Antiochian? A Dilemma in Barth's Christology', *Westminster Theological Journal* 52 (1990): pp. 263–80. George Hunsinger, 'Karl Barth's Christology: Its Basic Chalcedonian Character', in *The Cambridge Companion to Karl Barth*, ed. John Webster (Cambridge: Cambridge University Press, 2000), pp. 127–42, argues that Barth 'offers one of the most fully elaborated Chalcedonian Christologies ever to have appeared in Christian doctrine', and when his theology is categorised as other than Chalcedonian, that is either Alexandrian or Antiochian, it is normally done so as to allege that he has succumbed to one or another of the inherent extremes each 'school' veers towards (p. 129). Hunsinger concludes that 'Barth is probably the first theologian in the history of Christian doctrine who alternates back and forth, deliberately between an 'Alexandrian' and an 'Antiochian' idiom' (p. 130).

84 Yeung, *Being and Knowing*, p. 134; cf. Torrance, *Reality and Evangelical Theology*, pp. 85, 86–7. Jesus can be said to be divine because he reveals the Father. Israel can be said to be divine (holy) because she reveals the Father. By implication, men and women in Christ can be said to be divine (*theosis*) as they know and reveal the Father. Other examples provided by Yeung include a discussion on the Lord's Supper based on Thomas F. Torrance,

While Yeung applies this only to Scripture, the sacraments, and preaching, we can also see how it may apply to a doctrine of *theosis*. Men and women can be said to be *divine* in so far as they are related to Jesus Christ and through that relation are able both to know God and make him known. Creatures are not divine in the absolute sense but can be said to be 'divine' when they are relationally united through Christ and the Holy Spirit to the Father and in turn are witnesses to that relationship in the world. Such an 'Antiochene' approach is at least a possibility in Torrance's theology, although he never speaks of humans as 'divine'.

However, there is a decided propensity in Torrance's christology towards the Alexandrian understanding and its 'Logos-sarx' christology.[85] Jesus Christ is not only divine by relation but also uniquely divine in nature. This is what separates him from the rest of creaturely being. According to Torrance, Jesus Christ is the Word Incarnate, God in the flesh, Emmanuel – and the hypostatic union explains this: two natures, but one person, the God-man Jesus Christ. 'For Torrance, there is no tension between the divinity of Jesus Christ and the divinity of God. The act of God is the divine being of God, and this act is Jesus Christ as the deity of God.'[86]

This suggests that when he speaks about men and women and their 'deification', Torrance considers this under a Logos-anthropos construction similar to an Antiochene christology. This means that by adoption, men and women are made to partake of the divine nature (*theosis*). Adoption is a metaphor applicable to believers and has biblical sanction (Rom 8.15, 23, Gal 4.5, Eph 1.5); however, it is inadequate when applied to the incarnate Logos, the Son of God. Thus, when speaking of Christ, Torrance vigorously asserts that there is no indication that Christ is divine only by association or adoption: he is so by nature, because he is the act of God and hence the being of God in his act.

According to some commentators Torrance adopts a synthesis between the Antiochene and Alexandrian paths, or he maintains a dialogical relation between these two traditions. In Yeung's opinion, 'Torrance is not inconsistent because the Antiochian [sic] Christology makes claims consistent with an Alexandrian christology foundation. The important Antiochian [sic] elements fit within a framework that is basically Alexandrian'.[87] Yeung concludes:

> The Antiochian Christological conceptualization is based upon the Alexandrian claim that Jesus Christ is fully and absolutely identical with the Word of God who speaks through the human nature. The human nature of Christ can be said to be divine only because the essentially and originally divine Christ decided to assume the human nature and become man.[88]

Conflict and Agreement in the Church. vol. 2. The Ministry and the Sacraments of the Gospel (London: Lutterworth, 1960), pp. 141, 178.

[85] This conclusion is supported by Yeung, *Being and Knowing*, p. 134.

[86] Ibid., p. 136. See Torrance, *The Ground and Grammar of Theology*, pp. 157–9.

[87] Ibid., p. 139.

[88] Yeung, *Being and Knowing*, p. 139.

While a dialogical relation to the 'two schools' appears to be the most natural reading of Torrance's method it is not the way he sees it himself. Because the 'two schools' typology often creates an artificial distinction between Antiochene and Alexandrian thought, Torrance argues, there was a third 'school' of thought operative in the early church: one that gave priority to the vicarious humanity of Jesus, and emphasised the deity and lordship of Christ.[89] According to Torrance, patristic thought plotted this middle path between the other two 'schools', and Athanasius is held up as the supreme model.[90] Athanasius understood the incarnation to be God *as* man in Jesus Christ. Understanding God *as* man meant that he had to understand the humanity of Jesus in a profoundly vicarious manner. From this came his advocacy of the doctrine of *theosis*, the exchange wrought by Jesus Christ for men and women.

Further support is found for this in Torrance's christology of explicit double objectivity – the human and divine. When treating the human nature of Christ, Torrance can be very Antiochene, but when treating the divine nature or the person of Christ he is very Alexandrian. In so doing Torrance believes he is following a third path.[91]

Though the issue underscores the over-simplification of the 'two schools' account in general, the supposition of a 'third school' is improbable. Rather than enlightening the somewhat fluid categories in which the early church worked, this suggestion merely posits another artificial 'school' of thought into which each thinker is made to fit. However, it does explain how Torrance reads patristic theology by adopting an Athanasian christology as his own.[92]

It is more correct to describe Torrance's theology as neither strictly Alexandrian nor Antiochene, but as pro-Nicene and pro-Chalcedonian, or, in J.B. Torrance's categorisation, a 'Nicene Incarnational Model'.[93] While this was not a discrete 'school' it was an approach to the issues of the day that Torrance adopts in his own work.

---

[89] Thomas F. Torrance, 'The Place of the Humanity of Christ in the Sacramental Life of the Church', *Church Service Society Annual* 26 (1956): pp. 3–10. Redding assesses this claim in *Prayer and the Priesthood of Christ in the Reformed Tradition*, pp. 34–40.

[90] This is made clear in the unpublished lectures of Thomas F. Torrance, 'Christology and Soteriology', Chapter 3, Section 4 (c), cited in Joannes Guthridge, 'The Christology of T.F. Torrance: Revelation and Reconciliation in Christ', *Excerpta ex dissertation ad Lauream* (Melbourne: Pontificia Universitas Gregoriana, 1967), p. 13. Torrance considers Irenaeus, Athanasius, Euchologion of Serapion, the liturgy of the Apostolic Constitutions, Cyril of Alexandria, and John Calvin as epitomising this approach. See Torrance, *Theology in Reconciliation*, pp. 115; 225–6; and for Calvin specifically see *Conflict and Agreement in the Church*, vol. 1, 91; *Conflict and Agreement in the Church*, vol. 2, p. 144.

[91] Torrance, *The Mediation of Christ*, p. 63.

[92] Redding, *Prayer and the Priesthood of Christ in the Reformed Tradition*, p. 44, agrees with Torrance's reading of Athanasius over that of Wiles and Grillmeier.

[93] James B. Torrance, 'The Vicarious Humanity of Christ', in *The Incarnation: Ecumenical Studies in the Nicene-Constantinopolitan Creed A.D. 381*, ed. Thomas F. Torrance (Edinburgh: Handsel Press, 1981), pp. 135–7.

The an- and en-hypostatic Christ Having established how Torrance endeavours to read patristic theology through the eyes of a 'third school' the *theologoumenon* that Christ is *an-* and *en-hypostatic* comes into focus.[94] Torrance informs us that between the years 1945–55 Barth's christology, especially the couplet *an-* and *en-hypostasia*, gripped him.[95] Torrance takes these two correlative terms in their classical definitions: *anhypostasia* asserts that in the *assumptio carnis* the human nature of Christ has no independent subsistence apart from the event of the incarnation, and the hypostatic union; by *enhypostasia* it is asserted that in the *assumptio carnis* the human nature of Christ is given a real and concrete subsistence within the hypostatic union – it is *enhypostatic* in the Word.[96] While the terms themselves are patristic, the couplet as such is not: it developed later, not least through the influence of John of Damascus.[97] By adopting this couplet Torrance keeps together the two natures of Christ within the one person. Why is this so important? As Torrance writes:

> This is of supreme importance in application to the atonement. When we interpret a term like ἱλασκεσθαι in this light we must say on the one hand that God is the Subject of the whole atoning action: 'GOD was in Christ reconciling the world unto Himself,' and yet on the other hand Jesus Christ is Himself the ἱλασμος, for within the divine act of atonement Jesus as Man has a particular place in obedience. Reconciliation is God's supreme action, but within it, it is the concrete action of Jesus Christ that reconciles us. It is appropriate therefore that the middle voice should be used: ἱλασκεσθαι. Because *anhypostasia* and

94 See for example Thomas F. Torrance, 'The Atonement and the Oneness of the Church', *Scottish Journal of Theology* 7 (1954): pp. 249–52; 'The Atonement the Singularity of Christ', pp. 229–30; and *Karl Barth: Biblical and Evangelical Theologian* (Edinburgh: T & T Clark, 1990), pp. 199–201.

95 Thomas F. Torrance, 'My Interaction with Karl Barth', in *How Karl Barth Changed My Mind*, ed. Donald K. McKim (Grand Rapids: Eerdmans, 1986), p. 55. Barth was a champion of the couplet, see Barth, *CD*, I/2, pp. 163–5; III/2, p. 70; IV/2, pp. 49–50, 91. For a survey of Barth's use of the terms see Ivor Davidson, 'Theologizing the Human Jesus: An Ancient (and Modern) Approach to Christology Reassessed', *International Journal of Systematic Theology*, 3 (2001): pp. 141–6, and Bruce L. McCormack, *Karl Barth's Critically Realistic Dialectical Theology: Its Genesis and Development 1909–1936* (Oxford: Clarendon Press, 1995), pp. 327–67.

96 Torrance, 'The Atonement and the Oneness of the Church', p. 249. In 'The Atonement the Singularity of Christ', 230, we find that it is this construction that gives meaning to the 'logic of grace' embodied in the incarnation – 'all of grace' involves 'all of man'.

97 Torrance, *Karl Barth: Biblical and Evangelical Theologian*, p. 200, suggests that the genesis of the doctrine is to be found in Cyril of Alexandria, and also in Hippolytus. Davidson, 'Theologizing the Human Jesus', p. 135, and 'Reappropriating Patristic Christology: One Doctrine, Two Styles', *Irish Theological Quarterly* 67 (2002), pp. 225–39, argues that while Cyril did not use the an/enhypostasis as a theologoumenon as such his theology paved the way for a more comprehensive development of the couplet.

> *enhypostasia* are inseparable we cannot speak of two actions in the Cross, but of the act of the God-man.[98]

Torrance adopts the couplet in order to elaborate several dimensions of atonement. While this usage, according to Davidson, 'presses the patristic logic to lengths not obviously legitimated by its original use',[99] this is the way Torrance sees the terms working in any fully-fledged christology. From this theological construction two contrasting formulations of the atonement are ruled out by Torrance: first, Gustaf Aulén's celebrated 1983 work *Christus Victor* is dismissed for applying to the incarnation the *anhypostasia* alone, by which the cross is a pure act of God 'over the head of' humanity, and not involving an atoning act involving incorporation; and second, any Pelagianising tendencies which understand the cross to have God placated by human sacrifice are dismissed for applying the *enhypostasia* alone to the atonement.[100]

The result of keeping together the doctrines of *anhypostasia* and *enhypostasia* is, according to Torrance, that we must give greater place in our understanding of atonement to the concrete conception of substitution together with incorporation. The Word did not enter history as a third party but as an historical individual, Jesus Christ. Christ entered our state of alienation from God and stood under the curse of the Law, he 'stepped into the conflict between the covenant faithfulness of God and the unfaithfulness of man and took that conflict into His own flesh as the Incarnate Son and bore it to the end'.[101] Torrance speaks of the act of atonement as substitution and incorporation in the following way,

> Within our flesh He was thus act of God the Judge condemning sin in the flesh, and within our flesh where man has no justification before God, He the Just in the place of the unjust stood under judgment and rendered to God the answer of complete obedience even to the death of the Cross.[102]

Davidson argues that *an-* and *en-hypostatic* christology offers a helpful way of understanding the theological significance of the humanity of Jesus.[103] The christology of Torrance, with his utilisation of the *theologoumenon*, anticipates Davidson's call, for he presents a fully human Jesus Christ who is 'most definitely *a* man, with a particular human consciousness and a particular assemblage of experiences, choices, emotions, traits and temptations which were his alone'.[104] And yet, in his articulation of the full humanity of Jesus Christ, Torrance never loses

---

98 Torrance, 'The Atonement and the Oneness of the Church', p. 250.

99 Davidson, 'Theologizing the Human Jesus', p. 144.

100 Torrance, 'The Atonement and the Oneness of the Church', p. 250.

101 Ibid., p. 251.

102 Ibid., p. 252.

103 Davidson, 'Theologizing the Human Jesus', pp. 129–53.

104 Ibid., p. 138.

sight of the equally important divinity of the Son who assumed human nature. By means of *enhypostasia* and *anhypostasia* Torrance is able to state clearly what it means for Jesus to be one person, albeit acknowledged in two natures. Davidson's description of Barth's christology could equally be applied to Torrance's: 'it sets out the basic terms of reference: *vere homo*, particular, individual, historical, but never independent or generated by that which is contingent and finite – always *vere Deus* also'.[105]

Davidson maintains that any reclamation of the theological couplet must be supplemented with a robust pneumatology in order to specify the relevance of the human Jesus for revelation, salvation, anthropology, ethics and ecclesiology. Davidson is surely correct in this assessment and it is at this point that Torrance's theology is somewhat lacking. In his discussion of *enhypostasia* and *anhypostasia*, and other christological themes, Torrance speaks of the Holy Spirit regularly but fails adequately to incorporate a pneumatological discourse. By positing too great an emphasis on the agency of the divine Word on the human nature of Jesus, as opposed to a relation mediated by the Holy Spirit, Torrance implicitly makes the human nature of Christ merely instrumental. It would be too much to suggest that Torrance's christology is docetic or Apollinarian, but his lack of pneumatology in this area does risk bringing him to the brink of such a failing, a criticism which will be examined in more detail in Chapter 4.

In a concluding critical comment on Barth's christology Davidson reminds us of features of Torrance's own theology that need correcting:

> If it is in the Spirit that Jesus lives his dedication to the Father as incarnate Son, a commitment in which he is most fully himself as a man, it is by the same Spirit that we too are enabled to address the God of Jesus as *Abba*, and find our deepest human fulfilment and freedom in living towards this God. Indeed, by the Spirit's action we are privileged to live not only *towards* God, but *in* God: not simply regarding God as an example of relationship...but participating within the triune communion of God's own life.[106]

This triune participation amounts to a doctrine of *theosis* within Torrance's theology, and yet, in working out the theological implications of Christ's theandric nature, Torrance fails to adequately develop the pneumatological bond of union that is so important for the triune Persons, for the hypostatic union, and for *theosis* as a whole. Torrance is more concerned at this point with the epistemological bond of union – or with a doctrine of revelation, as we shall develop more fully in the next chapter.

---

105 Ibid., p. 147.

106 Ibid., pp. 152–3.

Vicarious Humanity

As a direct consequence of his doctrines of the *homoousion* and the hypostatic union Torrance makes significant room in his theology for the concept of the vicarious humanity of Christ whereby Christ becomes the last Adam and New Man to whom all humanity is ontologically related and must participate in for communion with God to be realised. This further clarifies what Torrance means by a doctrine of *theosis*.

Of great importance to Torrance is the issue of Christ's humanity; specifically the question: Was Christ's humanity of the fallen stock of Adam or was it untouched by Adam's sin? Throughout the history of Christian thinking the normative status of humanity has most often been ascribed to Adam and Eve in their pre-lapsarian condition rather than to the humanity of Jesus Christ in his incarnation, resulting in a general affirmation that Christ did not assume a fallen human nature. Torrance has consistently adopted the contrary position: that the eternal Son assumed a *fallen* human nature, and he argues that this is essential in a full articulation of the gospel.

> If the incarnate Son through his birth of the Virgin Mary actually assumed our flesh of sin, the fallen, corrupt and enslaved human nature which we have all inherited from Adam, then the redeeming activity of Christ took place within the ontological depths of his humanity in such a way that far from sinning himself, he condemned sin in the flesh and sanctified what he assumed, so that incarnating and redeeming events were one and indivisible, from the very beginning of his earthly existence to its end in his death and resurrection.[107]

Torrance's argument hangs on the concept of a *vicarious* assumption of human nature in its fallenness and sin. Christ did not, according to this logic, inherit sin naturally and so, unlike all other children of Adam, he had no sin-nature or stain of original sin. However, through an assumption of human nature in its post-lapsarian condition, Christ could remain guilt-free while still assuming a vicarious and fallen human nature. Torrance is thoroughly patristic when he attributes sin to the person-*hypostasis*, not as Augustine (and the West) did, to essence or nature. This accounts for why Christ could assume the likeness of sinful flesh (nature) and yet remain sinless (person). Again the *an/enhypostatic* couplet is playing its part in Torrance's christology. Considered *anhypostatically*, Christ has a sin-*nature*, albeit vicariously. Considered *enhypostatically*, Christ is sinless for his *person* is consonant with that of the eternal Son of God.[108]

Macleod claims that Torrance 'went on to reintroduce to Scotland the peculiar Christology of Edward Irving', and so Macleod calls this the 'Irving-Torrance

---

[107] Torrance, 'Incarnation and Atonement', p. 12.

[108] Torrance, The Doctrine of Jesus Christ, pp. 121–30; and 'The Atonement the Singularity of Christ', pp. 237–9.

theory'.[109] This conclusion is far too simplistic, however. According to Irving, in the incarnation the Son assumed a fallen human nature but did not become a sinner due to the influence of the Holy Spirit, active in the life of Christ from conception to resurrection. The soul of Christ was anointed with the Holy Spirit and it was this union that enabled Jesus to resist the devil and live a sinless life.[110] 'Irving believed that to rely on the Son's divinity as the solitary source of holiness within the humanity of Jesus bordered on Docetism or Monophysitism.'[111]

Torrance does speak of Irving as providing some useful resources showing that the Son assumed a fallen human nature and so in this, Irving and Torrance are at one. However, Torrance is at odds with how Irving sought to account for this assumed nature. For instance, Torrance wishes to avoid the two extremes that could result from a consideration of the vicarious humanity of Christ: on the one hand Ebionite (not Monophysitism as Weinandy mentions above), and on the other hand docetic views. Torrance believes Irving espoused an Ebionite christology because he held that the sinlessness of Christ was due to the indwelling Holy Spirit not to his own nature. On the docetic side Torrance suggests that certain notions of the 'deification' of Christ's human nature are to be ruled out; notions which would mix or confuse the human and divine natures in such a way that the human nature disappears.[112]

Torrance's problem with Irving's christology is that he makes the Holy Spirit the decisive factor to the relative neglect of the hypostatic union. While the Holy Spirit is, according to Torrance, integral to Jesus' life and especially here, to his sinlessness, it is also due to the fact of the hypostatic union that Jesus was sinless and so did not have any need to atone for his own sins. While Christ's humanity was capable of sin and rebellion, Christ did not possess a single (human) nature, as humans do. Christ had another (divine) nature which was not only sinless but also incapable of sinning.[113] Torrance realises this essential problem with Irving's christology and seeks to counter it with a stress on the vicarious assumption of

---

109 Donald Macleod, 'Christology', in *Dictionary of Scottish Chruch History and Theology*, eds Nigel D. de S. Cameron, David F. Wright, David C. Lachman and Donald E. Meek (Edinburgh: T & T Clark, 1993), p. 175. See the longer discussions in his, *Jesus is Lord: Christology Yesterday and Today* (Fearn: Mentor, 2000), pp. 125–34; and *The Person of Christ* (Leicester: IVP, 1998), pp. 221–30.

110 Edward Irving, *The Collected Writings of Edward Irving*, ed. G. Carlyle (London: Alexander Strachan, 1865). See Colin E. Gunton, 'Two Dogmas Revisited: Edward Irving's Christology', *Scottish Journal of Theology* 41 (1988): pp. 359–76; and Graham W.P. McFarlane, *Christ and the Spirit: The Doctrine of the Incarnation According to Edward Irving* (Carlisle: Paternoster, 1996).

111 Thomas G. Weinandy, *In the Likeness of Sinful Flesh. An Essay on the Humanity of Christ* (Edinburgh: T & T Clark, 1993), p. 59.

112 Torrance, *The Doctrine of Jesus Christ*, pp. 121–3.

113 See the helpful analogy provided by Thomas V. Morris, *The Logic of God Incarnate* (Ithaca: Cornell University Press, 1986), p. 15, cited in Oliver D. Crisp, 'Did Christ have a Fallen Human Nature?' *International Journal of Systematic Theology* 6 (2004): p. 285.

a fallen human nature in the incarnation. However, it appears Torrance goes too far in the direction of Alexandrian christology and under-emphasises the atoning work of the Holy Spirit in the entire life of Christ.[114]

In *Space, Time and Resurrection* Torrance further articulates how Christ remains sinless despite vicariously assuming a fallen human nature:

> Although he assumed our fallen and corrupt humanity when he became flesh, in assuming it he sanctified it in himself, and all through his earthly life he overcame our sin through his righteousness, our impurity through his purity, condemning sin in our flesh by the sheer holiness of his life within it.[115]

Torrance goes on to say that this is precisely why death could not hold Christ (cf. Acts 2.24) for there was no sin in him that allowed it to subject him to corruption. Death had nothing in him, for he had already passed through its clutches by the perfection of his holiness. In short, 'He triumphed over the grave through his sheer sinlessness'.[116] He then concludes with the statement that, 'The resurrection is thus the resurrection of the union forged between man and God in Jesus out of the damned and lost condition of men into which Christ entered in order to share their lot and redeem them from doom'.[117]

Such a focus on Christ's assumption of a fallen human nature, despite its attendant difficulties, clearly highlights the role Torrance ascribes to the vicarious humanity of Christ. Torrance goes to such extremes in order to underline the lengths to which the Word went in becoming human in order to enable humans to participate in the divine nature.

In one of his clearest statements on the issue Torrance states:

> In that life-act of the historical Jesus the Son of God so clothed Himself with our humanity and so subdued it in Himself that He converted it back from its resentment and rebellion to glad surrender to the Holy Will of God, and so lifted humanity up in himself to communion with the Father, setting it again within the divine peace, drawing it within the Divine holiness and placing it within the direction of the divine love.[118]

---

114 Bruce L. McCormack, 'For Us and Our Salvation: Incarnation and Atonement in the Reformed Tradition', *The Greek Orthodox Theological Review* 43 (1998), p. 314, fn. 53, concludes his survey of these issues within sixteenth and seventeenth century Reformed theology by affirming the need for an account of Christ's theandric nature which includes both the hypostatic union and the constitutive role of the Holy Spirit.

115 Torrance, *Space, Time and Resurrection*, p. 53.

116 Ibid., pp. 53–4.

117 Ibid., p. 54.

118 Thomas F. Torrance, 'The Atoning Obedience of Christ', *Moravian Theological Seminary Bulletin* (1959), p. 66.

This is a profound statement of *theosis* that speaks forcefully of an internal work of God for humanity rather than simply an external or transactional relation between a transcendent Creator and creatures. Once more Torrance reminds us that the work of *theosis* is first of all a work of God in Jesus Christ and only then a reality applied to human beings in general. In order to clarify this reality Torrance insists there is an indissoluble connection between substitution and incorporation. Summarising Torrance's position, Colyer writes:

> Torrance contends that when Christ's atoning reconciliation on the cross is not understood in close relation to the incarnational assumption of our fallen humanity, the atonement is inevitably interpreted in terms of external forensic relations. In addition, without a unifying center in the incarnation, the various aspects of the atonement in the biblical witness break up into various theories of the atonement, each stressing one element or another found within Scripture.[119]

Torrance distils much of this theology into the assertion that Jesus Christ is God's exclusive language to humanity as well as humanity's exclusive language to God.[120] Fallen humanity is unable to respond to God as it should, making reconciliation impossible; the Fall has affected the very core of our being. In this light, Christ is the divinely provided human through whom reconciliation is made available. To explain this Torrance enters into a sustained treatment of what the vicarious humanity of Christ means for the mediation of *our* human response to God, something he terms the 'total substitution of Christ'.

On this point Torrance has been most open to criticism as many consider his application of the vicarious humanity of Christ goes too far.[121] For Torrance faith is only properly exercised by Christ, not by the human person, and he sees conversion, worship, and even evangelism in the same way.[122] For many the natural implication is that human action is undermined. But, Torrance argues, this is to misunderstand 'the logic of grace' – all of grace does not mean to imply nothing of humanity.[123] While we shall look at how our response is incorporated into Christ's response for us in his vicarious humanity more in Chapter 3, we will take some space now to look at Christ's side of this response, his vicarious humanity.

---

119 Elmer M. Colyer, *How To Read T.F. Torrance: Understanding his Trinitarian and Scientific Theology* (Downers Grove: IVP, 2001), p. 89.

120 Torrance, *Reality and Evangelical Theology*, p. 88.

121 For instance, Tom Smail, *The Giving Gift: The Holy Spirit in Person* (London: Hodder and Stoughton, 1988), pp. 109–12, and Christian D. Kettler, *The Vicarious Humanity of Christ and the Reality of Salvation* (Lanham, MD.: University Press of America, 1991), pp. 139–42.

122 Torrance, *The Mediation of Christ*, pp. 82–3. For an illustration of this theology see Christian D. Kettler, *The God Who Believes: Faith, Doubt, and the Vicarious Humanity of Christ* (Eugene, Or.: Wipf & Stock, 2005).

123 See Colyer, *How To Read T.F. Torrance*, pp. 118–23.

According to Torrance the vicarious humanity of Christ means that only Christ's response is ultimately valid. All other responses to God are excluded because Christ is the ground and the norm of our response to God. Torrance makes this clear throughout his essay 'The Word of God and the Response of Man' where we read, 'In the Gospels we do not have to do simply with the Word of God and the response of man, but with the all-significant middle term, the divinely provided response in the vicarious humanity of Jesus Christ'.[124] The humanity of Christ occupies a unique place in which he is the exclusive representative and substitute in all our relations with God, 'including every aspect of human response to Him; such as trusting and obeying, understanding and knowing, loving and worshipping'.[125] Indeed, this is what it means for Christ to be divinised and for believers to experience *theosis* in him.

Because the incarnate Son of God is fully human (*enhypostasis*), his response personalises ours.[126] In all of his soteriological activity: 'Jesus Christ is engaged in personalising and humanising (never depersonalising and dehumanising) activity, so that in all our relations with him we are made more truly and fully human in our personal response of faith than ever before.'[127] As Colyer describes it:

> Our *telos* in Torrance's theology is *personal* sharing in union and communion with God the Father through Jesus Christ and in the Holy Spirit in which we become ever more fully human and free, and respond in thanksgiving, faith and joyous freedom, as children of God, in the Spirit through the Son to the Father. It is a personal sharing of our humanity in union and communion with God, first in Jesus Christ through *his* vicarious humanity, and then in *our* humanity as we are incorporated by the Spirit into Christ and his union with our humanity in the incarnation.[128]

Christ is the exclusive response of God to humanity and the exclusive response of humanity to God. Thus *theosis* is achieved not only *by* Christ but, importantly, also *in* Christ.

In a manner reminiscent of John McLeod Campbell and Karl Barth, Torrance argues in his presidential address delivered to the Scottish Church Theology Society in 1960 that in Jesus Christ we have God's 'yes' and 'no' to humanity.

---

[124] Torrance, *God and Rationality*, p. 145.

[125] Ibid.

[126] Torrance, *The Mediation of Christ*, pp. 64–6.

[127] Ibid., p. 92.

[128] Colyer, *How To Read T.F. Torrance*, p. 122. Colyer rightly emphasises the twofold activity of the Son and the Spirit in our human response to God. A weakness of Torrance's ontological atonement is the lack of rigorous integration of the work of the Spirit alongside that of the Son.

> Jesus Christ was not only the fulfilment and embodiment of God's righteous and holy Act or *dikaioma*, but also the embodiment of our act of faith and trust and obedience toward God. He stood in our place, taking our cause upon him, also as Believer, as the Obedient One who was himself justified before God as his beloved Son in whom he was well pleased. He offered to God a perfect confidence and trust, a perfect faith and response which we are unable to offer, and he appropriated all God's blessings which we are unable to appropriate. Through union with him we share in his faith, in his obedience, in his trust and his appropriation of the Father's blessing; we share in his justification before God.[129]

Torrance continues: 'therefore when we are justified by faith, this does not mean that it is *our* faith that justifies us, far from it – it is the faith of Christ alone that justifies us...'.[130] The incarnate Son of God is the only proper response of humanity to God and God to humanity. In short, 'We have no speech or language with which to address God but the speech and language called Jesus Christ'.[131] Only through a participation in his person and work can men and women achieve union and communion – *theosis* – with God.[132]

Torrance is open for criticism because his version of vicarious humanity is understood exclusively as the union of Christ in terms of nature (ontological), not of a union with Christ that is also spiritual (through the Holy Spirit). One appreciative critic of Torrance, Donald Macleod, speaks on behalf of many when he expresses concern with Torrance's theology of vicarious mediation: 'At first sight Torrance's exposition of this theme appears to involve a thorough-going Christo-monism in which the work of Christ is everything and that of the believer is insignificant and even needless.'[133] Macleod then develops a three-point critique of Torrance's position, of which points two and three are of interest here.

While acknowledging the work of the Son is vicarious, Macleod's first criticism is to remind us that the work of the Holy Spirit is not: 'Christ died in our place, but the Spirit does not believe in our place.'[134] The Spirit enables us to believe but it is the human subject who must finally repent, believe, and worship. In reply, Torrance, while not emphasising sufficiently the pneumatological aspects of the human response to God, may not be opposed to what Macleod presents here. Torrance does allow for a real human response to God but argues that such a response is only possible in the Spirit *of Christ* who unites the believer to the incarnate Son. Our obedient response in faith, conversion, repentance, worship and so on are free acts of our own, but free acts that are only enabled through union

---

129 Torrance, *Theology in Reconstruction*, p. 159.

130 Ibid., pp. 159–60.

131 Torrance, *The Mediation of Christ*, pp. 78–9.

132 Torrance, *God and Rationality*, pp. 145; 153–64; and *Reality and Evangelical Theology*, pp. 88–9.

133 Macleod, *Jesus is Lord: Christology*, p. 133.

134 Ibid., p. 134.

with Christ in the Spirit. It is this ontological and spiritual union that personalises humanity.[135] Macleod's argument here would appear to lack any real substance and may be passed over.[136]

The more important criticism of Macleod's is his demand for terminological clarification. What does Torrance mean by the use of the term *vicarious*? The word may mean, in differing contexts, *substituting*, *representing*, or acting in *solidarity with*. Macleod believes that when Torrance speaks of the vicarious humanity of Christ he is using the word in the last of these senses, yet most readers instinctively take it in the first. If this is correct, then what Torrance means is that Christ is a believer *with* us (Heb 12.2), but not *instead* of us.[137]

If Torrance's use of 'vicarious' were to be understood in the sense of acting in *solidarity with* he would not be too far removed from John Calvin when he speaks of Christ as our *example*. In the *Institutes* Calvin writes that 'Christ through whom we return to favour with God, has been set before us as a model [example], the image of which our lives should express'.[138] Through Calvin's exposition of the example of Christ two things stand out: first, Christ is our vicarious *substitute* on the cross in that he became a curse while we shall never be accursed (Gal 3.13);[139] and second, that the rest of the incarnate life and death was an *example* for us to follow (*imitatio Christi*).[140] It should not be inferred that this implies a simple external compulsion to imitate Christ as Latin theology has often asserted, but borrows extensively from the Eastern Orthodox view of cooperation between God and humanity made possible by the work of God in Christ.[141] Torrance's ambiguous and sometimes misleading terminology includes within it the profound mystery of

---

[135] Thomas F. Torrance, *Transformation and Convergence in the Frame of Knowledge: Explorations in the Interrelations of Scientific and Theological Enterprise* (Grand Rapids: Eerdmans, 1984), p. 345; *Theology in Reconstruction*, p. 210; and *The Mediation of Christ*, pp. 88–98.

[136] Macleod's argument could be appropriately levelled at Barth but not Torrance. By utilising the theme of *theosis* Torrance incorporates a significant space for the operation of the Spirit in a way that Barth never quite achieved, even if Torrance did not go far enough in this direction.

[137] See the helpful discussion in Lee, *Living in Union With Christ*, pp. 159–77.

[138] John Calvin, *The Institutes of the Christian Religion*, trans. H. Beveridge (London: Clarke & Co, 1953), 3.6.3. (The Beveridge translation being preferred over the Battles here.)

[139] See Trevor Hart, 'Humankind in Christ and Christ in Humankind: Salvation as Participation in Our Substitute in the Theology of John Calvin', *Scottish Journal of Theology* 42 (1989): pp. 67–84.

[140] See John Calvin's commentary on 1 Peter 2.23 in *Calvin's [New Testament] Commentaries. vol. 12: The Epistle of Paul the Apostle to the Hebrews and the First and Second Epistles of St Peter*, trans. David W. and Thomas F. Torrance (Grand Rapids: Eerdmans, 1963), pp. 275–6.

[141] See Torrance, *Space, Time and Incarnation*, 16; and *The Mediation of Christ*, pp. 67, 92–8.

godliness that the New Testament presents: that it is only through, in, and with Christ that true sanctification is achieved.

Macleod and others would have us believe that the only way in which Torrance's theology is comprehensible is if faith is understood to be an act of solidarity (or cooperation) with Christ, so that his faith is our faith, his worship is our worship, his repentance is our repentance, and so forth. But is this actually what Torrance intends? Macleod is partly correct in his conclusion about Torrance's use of vicarious mediation and vicarious humanity in this context. Torrance does not mean that humans do not believe or do not respond to grace.[142] Clearly they do. What he does retain is the priority of the response of God in Christ that allows a genuine human response. Reminiscent of the teaching of John McLeod Campbell, Torrance believes there is no human response that is *independent* of the response of Jesus Christ.[143]

The only way to correctly understand Torrance's theology of vicarious mediation is to understand it is not representative *or* substitutionary – it is *both*, and it is this fact that Macleod and others have overlooked. As Lee's study highlights, 'If Christ acts for us only as our representative, then this would mean that Jesus is only our leader representing our act of response to God. If Jesus simply acts as a Substitute in our place in an external-formal-forensic way, then his response would be "an empty transaction over our heads" with no ontological relation with us'.[144] So to posit 'solidarity' as the key to Torrance's doctrine of vicarious mediation is to undermine the point he is actually making. Representation and substitution go together in Torrance's theology and both explicate what a true human response to God actually entails. Accordingly, for Torrance, our faith in Christ is not just ours, but is the faith of Christ himself who, in his vicarious *and* substitutionary role, believes for us.

While such explanations as these are important they do not yet fully account for Torrance's theology of the vicarious humanity of Christ. What Macleod, Lee, and others have not observed is the uniquely Athanasian insight into the

---

142 Torrance, *Conflict and Agreement in the Church*. vol. 2. pp. 74–82; and *Christian Theology and Scientific Culture*, pp. 67–72. In *The Mediation of Christ*, pp. 81–98, he specifically looks at what believers do in their response of faith, conversion, worship, sacraments and evangelism, and in *God and Rationality*, pp. 153–64, he deals with faith, worship, sacraments and Christian service.

143 For defences of Campbell's theology see Christian D. Kettler, 'The Vicarious Repentance of Christ in the Theology of John McLeod Campbell and R C Moberly', *Scottish Journal of Theology* 38 (1985): pp. 529–43 and James B. Torrance, 'The Contribution of McLeod Campbell to Scottish Theology', *Scottish Journal of Theology* 26 (1973): pp. 295–311. Within Campbell's theology only 'representation' was used. Torrance is thus going beyond Campbell and in the process refuting objections such as those levelled at his theology by D. Macleod.

144 Lee, *Living in Union With Christ*, p. 163. Lee cites Torrance, *The Mediation of Christ*, pp. 79–98.

vicarious 'response' of Christ that Torrance adopts, and it is this that accounts for Torrance's real interest in the vicarious humanity of Christ. According to the logic of Athanasian christology, Christ had to be both divine and human in order to unite humanity to God. *Theosis*, the union of humanity with God, is made possible only through the incarnation of God in man, what Athanasius calls the 'double proclamation' (διπλην ἐπαγγελιαν).[145] In *Contra Arianos* 2.70, salvation is defined as being 'joined to God'. Because Christ is joined to God the Father by nature and joined to our humanity through the true human flesh that he put on, it is by being joined to both God and humanity that Christ can effectively join us to God. This is the dynamic behind Athanasius' dictum: 'Christ became human so we may become divine',[146] that is, Christ's inhominisation was the means to our deification. Of utmost importance in our present context is not simply Christ's revelation of the Father's will but more precisely the reconciliation this engenders. Christ is not only the exclusive revelation of God to humanity but he is also, by the same logic, the exclusive response (reconciliation) of humanity back to God.

According to Torrance, Christ secures our receptivity through the incarnation. In the incarnation the Word himself received grace humanly on our behalf and this granted us the definitive ability to 'remain' in grace, which, as the *De Incarnatione* demonstrates, had been the barrier in human-divine communion.[147] Anatolios summarises Athanasian christology as follows, 'Athanasius says categorically that our own reception of the Spirit, on which hangs our salvation and deification, is impossible except as derivative of Christ's human reception of it in the incarnation'.[148] Deification is understood by Torrance, as it was by Athanasius, to include all aspects of the believer's union and communion with God, not simply the inauguration of salvation in justification or adoption but the entire sanctifying and glorifying aspects which include in their scope faith, repentance, worship, and the sacraments. This is clearly the sort of receptivity and vicarious representative/substitutionary activity that the Son exercises on our behalf that Torrance has in view when he comes to speak of the activity of the believer. As Anatolios expresses it:

> Our deifying reception of the Spirit is thus derived from Christ's human receptivity. As long as the Word's activity was confined to the realm of divine 'giving,' we were not able to receive the Spirit in him. But if Christ's humanity enables us to receive the Spirit in him, this reception is rendered perfectly secure, βεβαιος, precisely because it is indivisibly united to the unalterable divine Word, who is one in being with the Father.[149]

---

145 *Contra Arianos*, 3.29 (NPNF, 2nd series, vol. 4. pp. 1002–3).

146 Athanasius, *Letter 60, to Adelphus*, 4 (NPNF, 2nd series, vol. 4. pp. 1334–40); and *On the Incarnation*, 54 (NPNF, 2nd series, vol. 4. pp. 340–41).

147 See Athanasius, *Contra Arianos* 1.50 (NPNF, 2nd series, vol. 4. pp. 863–4).

148 Anatolios, *Athanasius: The Coherence of his Thought*, p. 158.

149 Ibid., p. 159.

Behind this logic is Athanasius's argument that in Christ God is both the 'Gift and the Giver', the only bridge between humanity and divinity.[150] Thus Christ both gives and receives and it is this dialectic of redemption and deification that corresponds to the radical ontological dissimilarity between God and creation. Because Jesus is the 'Gift of the Giver', in the incarnation, God not only gives but his giving reaches the point of receiving on our behalf (we do not naturally receive due to our sinfulness), thus perfecting our capacity to receive, which is our only access to the divine. 'In this way, divine giving and human receiving continue to be irreducibly distinct, but they are now united in the unity of Christ himself, who becomes the source of our receptivity by virtue of his humanity, and the perfector and securer of this receptivity, as well as the giver of the Gift itself, by virtue of his divinity.'[151] Because of the stress on the activity of God in Christ as both Gift and Giver, Athanasius views Christ as the only legitimate human response to God.

In his adoption of 'Athanasian' theology Torrance's doctrine of the vicarious humanity applied to our faith and response makes complete sense. An ontological atonement wedded to a robust doctrine of Christ's vicarious humanity allows Torrance to argue that Christ is the *only* human response to God that is accepted. Therefore, the believer must be incorporated into Christ's human response for *theosis* to be realised in the believer. This is in line with the logic of Torrance's total argument. Identification with Christ is only made possible through Christ's prior identification with fallen humanity in the incarnation. Identification equals participation in Torrance's theology. The first movement, identification, is humanward – the movement of God into humanity in Jesus Christ. The second movement, participation, is Godward – the participation of humanity in the humanity of Christ. Christ perfectly fulfils both movements in the incarnation.[152] To miss this Athanasian strand in his christology is to misinterpret what he means by the vicarious response of Christ based upon the vicarious humanity of Christ.

The Mediation of Christ

Due to his insistence on the vicarious humanity of Christ, Torrance considers the theme of Christ's mediation as integral to his christology and soteriology. In a 1954 essay, 'The Atonement and the Oneness of the Church', Torrance examines the meaning and implications of the Chalcedonian doctrine of the hypostatic union. To do this he considers the distinct 'moments' in the incarnate life that especially

150 Athanasius, *Contra Arianos* 3.38 (NPNF, 2nd series, vol. 4. pp. 1010–11).

151 Anatolios, *Athanasius: The Coherence of his Thought*, p. 161.

152 Kettler 'The Vicarious Repentance of Christ in the Theology of John McLeod Campbell and R C Moberly', p. 539, draws these same conclusions in relation to the theology of McLeod Campbell, adding the crucial insight that 'to participate in the humanity of Christ is to participate in the filial relationship of love and trust between the Father and the Son'.

focus the process of reconciliation, incorporation, atonement and redemption.[153] Torrance uses these 'moments' to structure the correlation he draws between incarnation and reconciliation. The specific 'moments' considered include the baptism (Matt 3.13–17), the choosing of the Twelve (Mk 3.14–19), the confession of Peter at Caesarea Philippi (Mk 8.27–9), the Last Supper (Lk 22.1–23), and Pentecost (Acts 2). We would be mistaken, however, to conclude that these are the only 'moments' Torrance thinks are important christologically or the only 'moments' he discusses in his writing as a whole.[154]

Torrance asserts that throughout the life of Christ 'the immediate focus is undoubtedly centred on the *human agency* of the incarnate Son within the essential conditions of actual historical human existence, and therefore on the undiminished actuality of the whole historical Jesus Christ who was born of the Virgin Mary, suffered under Pontius Pilate, was crucified and buried, and rose again from the dead'.[155] In a summary statement we read:

> The incarnation is to be understood, then, as a real becoming on the part of God, in which God comes *as man* and acts *as man*, all for our sake – from beginning to end God the Son acts among us in a human way (ἀνθρωπινως), 'within the measures of our humanity,' as Cyril of Alexandria expressed it.[156]

From birth to baptism, cross to resurrection, Torrance sees the life of Christ as redemptive: 'The whole life of Christ is understood as a continuous vicarious sacrifice and oblation which, as such, is indivisible, for everything he assumed from us is organically united in his one Person and work as Saviour and Mediator.'[157] This is what Torrance means in the first instance by the term 'the Mediation of Christ'.

In a form of summary of the life of Christ, Torrance states, 'The first thing he did as he entered upon His active ministry was to be baptised in a crowd of sinners – that was His identification in the body of His flesh with the whole mass of sin and death.

---

153 Torrance, 'The Atonement and the Oneness of the Church', pp. 248–9.

154 In Torrance, *The Doctrine of Jesus Christ* (pp. 117–32), the virgin conception, and sinlessness of Christ are investigated; in 'The Atoning Obedience of Christ', pp. 65–81, he discusses Christ's life of prayer (pp. 68–73); his life of perfect human obedience as a Son including his words, baptism, temptation (pp. 73–8); and the perfect two-fold revelation of God to humanity and humanity to God (pp. 78–81); and in *Space, Time and Resurrection*, the resurrection, ascension (pp. 106–22), and *Parousia* (pp. 143–58) are examined. It would appear that Torrance's earlier work was more concerned to elaborate the specific life of Christ whilst in his latter work (since the late 1970's), he glossed over the specific historical life of Christ in favour of explicating the theological significance of this life.

155 Torrance, *The Trinitarian Faith*, p. 151.

156 Ibid., p. 150, citing Cyril of Alexandria, Ep. Ad Nest. (MPG, 77.3, 116BC); Adv. Nest., (MPG, 76.1; 17B; 20D; 21AB; 28C; 35A), etc.

157 Torrance, *The Trinitarian Faith*, p. 152.

By Baptism He made Himself one with us all'.[158] Jesus linked this baptism to the cross when he spoke of that 'baptism of blood' (Mk 10.38–9); by crucifixion he was incorporated wholly with us in judgement. By identifying with fallen humanity in this personal way, Christ brought about communion between the One and the many. Communion was initiated and *theosis* inaugurated. This identification, initiation and inauguration were consummated on the cross when Christ died for sin. Then came the resurrection to life and the sending of the Spirit at Pentecost. It was then that the hypostatic union carried through crucifixion to its *telos* in the Risen Christ. 'In other language, through *koinonia* the Church, for which Christ died and rose again, was given to participate in the hypostatic union, in the mystery of Christ.'[159] *Koinonia* functions as an important cognate for *theosis*; not only within Torrance's theology but also in the history of the doctrine in general.[160]

While the christological 'moments' that Torrance mentions do bring out the mediatorial significance of the life of Christ, the comprehensive treatment one would expect is absent from any of his published works.[161] The result of this lack of detailed attention to the actual historical life of Christ and its significance tends to detract from the case Torrance wants to adduce.[162] A fuller treatment of the redemptive significance of specific aspects of Christ's life might have contributed to Torrance's appeal for Western theology to reappropriate the doctrine of *theosis.*

Having made that criticism we must take explicit note of the fact that for Torrance '...the work of atoning salvation does *not* take place *outside* of Christ, as something external to him, but takes place *within* him, *within* the incarnate constitution of his Person as Mediator'.[163] This phrase functions as a theological axiom of Torrance's argument. This is what Torrance means by 'incarnational redemption' and 'ontological atonement'.[164] Especially important in Torrance's

---

158 Torrance, 'The Atonement and the Oneness of the Church', p. 248.

159 Ibid., p. 249.

160 See Gross, *The Divinization of the Christian According to the Greek Fathers*, p. 245.

161 In an Eastern Orthodox context the christological 'moments' become important stages in the imitation of Christ and form the prokope or way of *theosis* for those united to Christ by the Spirit. See for example *Panayiotis Nellas, Deification in Christ*, trans. Norman Russell (1979. Crestwood, NY.: St Vladimir's Seminary Press, 1987), pp. 121–39; and Anthony M. Coniaris, *Achieving Your Potential in Christ: Theosis: Plain Talks on a Major Christian Doctrine* (Minneapolis: Light and Life Publishing Company, 1993), pp. 45–65.

162 The same criticism has been levelled at Athanasius and the Alexandrian theologians and at Anselm's *Cur Deus Homo*, see Colin Brown, 'Christology and the Quest of the Historical Jesus', in *Doing Theology for the People of God: Studies in Honour of J.I. Packer*, eds Donald Lewis and Alister E. McGrath (Leicester: Apollos, 1996), pp. 68–70. Davidson, 'Theologizing the Human Jesus', pp. 147–51, notes a similar tendency in Karl Barth and some of his followers, including Torrance.

163 Torrance, *The Trinitarian Faith*, p. 155 (italics in original), p. 185.

164 For an overview of further aspects of this Mediation see Torrance, *The Mediation of Christ*; and in the secondary literature Colyer, *How To Read T.F. Torrance*, pp. 55–126.

doctrine of *theosis* are the place of the cross and the role of the ascended Christ. We shall consider each of these in turn.

The cross of Christ Torrance has continually stressed the redemptive significance of the incarnation because he perceives a neglect of this theme as a particular weakness of Western theology. This accounts for his sustained polemic against any form of dualistic christology that would split the person of Christ from his work.[165] For this reason Torrance has written less on the cross and its redemptive significance than he has on the atoning aspects of the life of Christ. This is certainly not to imply that Torrance does this at the expense of the cross-work of Christ. Torrance is insistent that without the cross we are not saved and the work of Christ would be incomplete. He is as respectful of the mystery of the cross as he is of the person of Christ.[166]

According to Torrance atonement cannot be confined simply to what Christ achieved on the cross (his passive obedience), nor can the incarnation (his active obedience) be regarded simply as the prelude to the cross. As Lee's study shows, 'Atonement is inseparable from the Incarnation, for what constitutes atonement is not the death of Jesus Christ, but Jesus Christ *per se*'.[167] As with his doctrine of union with Christ, it is not union that is most important but Christ. So too with the cross: what is of utmost importance is the *Christ* of the cross, but this does not entail a diminution of the centrality of the cross as the determinative climax of Christ's saving work.

Torrance speaks of the cross as the 'most astonishing part of the Christian message',[168] because it reveals nothing short of 'God crucified', as Gregory Nazianzen expressed it.[169] Indeed, in language borrowed from H.R. Mackintosh, Torrance reminds us that the cross is 'a window into the heart of God'.[170] In order to express the magnitude of the cross event there is, running like a red thread throughout Torrance's theology, the phrase – 'God loves us better than he loves himself!'[171]

---

165 Torrance refers to this as the 'Latin heresy' on a number of occasions. See Torrance, 'Karl Barth and the Latin Heresy', pp. 461–82.

166 This is clearly evident in Torrance, 'The Atonement the Singularity of Christ', pp. 255–6.

167 Lee, *Living in Union With Christ*, p. 103.

168 Thomas F. Torrance, *Preaching Christ Today* (Grand Rapids: Eerdmans, 1994), p. 27.

169 Torrance, *The Christian Doctrine of God*, p. 247, citing Gregory Nazianzen, *Orationes*, 45.28f.

170 Torrance, *Preaching Christ Today*, p. 27.

171 A typical example of his use of the phrase is Thomas F. Torrance, 'The Christ Who Loves Me', in *A Passion for Christ: Vision that Ignites Ministry*, eds Gerrit S. Dawson and Jock Stein (Edinburgh: The Handsel Press, 1999), p. 9, where four times he repeats the phrase 'God loves us more than he loves himself'.

What does Torrance mean by this phrase and where did it originate? In an article on H.R. Mackintosh, Torrance recounts that for his former professor the concept of *kenosis* did not provide an explanation of how the incarnation took place, but an account of the almighty act of God in surrendering himself to humiliation and death in order to forgive sins. In short, Mackintosh taught that the cross was a revelation of the inexhaustible power of God's love. 'It was in fact another way of expressing the grace of the Lord Jesus Christ who for our sakes became poor that we through his poverty might become rich…God loves us better than he loves himself!'[172] The phrase functions within Torrance's theology as an indication of *theosis*. It is meant to imply the same reality – that the reconciling exchange wrought by Christ on the cross, which amounts to God becoming human so that humanity may participate in divinity, can only really be explained by the divine love – a love for humanity that is *ecstatic* to the divine nature and thus 'God loves us more than he loves himself'.

By this phrase Torrance means that as God gives himself over to death in the person of the incarnate Son, so God chooses his own death in his Son over our death in sin. This is what the cross attests. Citing Rom 8.32: 'He who spared not his own Son, but delivered him up for us all, how shall he not with him also freely give us all things?' Torrance sees at the back of Paul's mind the readiness of Abraham to sacrifice his 'only son Isaac, whom he loved' (Gen 22.2, 16), thereby demonstrating that Abraham loved God more than he loved himself.[173] In giving his Son to die for us in atoning sacrifice God the Father has revealed that he loves us more than he loves himself.[174] Accordingly it is in the cross of Jesus Christ above all that God has exhibited the nature of his being as love and has irrevocably committed his being to relationship with us in unconditional love.[175] On this basis Torrance affirms that in giving to us his beloved Son God does not give us something of his love but his self and in this self-giving he gives us everything. While the language is somewhat startling it is one of Torrance's preferred ways to express the profound truth of *theosis*.

Not only is the depth of God's love for us exemplified in the Father's sending the Son to die for us; even more than that: the death of the Son implies that death is no longer foreign to God himself. 'The fact that the Lord Jesus Christ is God's Son means that in him God the Father himself was actively and personally present in

---

[172] Thomas F. Torrance, 'Hugh Ross Mackintosh: Theologian of the Cross', *Scottish Bulletin of Evangelical Theology* 5 (1987), p. 165. The phrase is also found in H.R. Mackintosh, *The Person of Jesus Christ*, cited in Torrance, *The Christian Doctrine of God*, pp. 209–10. In a later work Torrance, *Scottish Theology from John Knox to John McLeod Campbell*, p. 96, notes that Samuel Rutherford (1600–61) would often preach, 'Christ loves you better than His life, for He gave His life to get your love'.

[173] Torrance, *Preaching Christ Today*, pp. 27–8, and *The Christian Doctrine of God*, pp. 5, 210, 215, 244.

[174] Torrance, *The Christian Doctrine of God*, p. 215.

[175] Ibid., p. 5.

the crucifixion of Christ, intervening redemptively in our lostness and darkness.'[176] The emphasis is that in Christ God suffers. 'Indeed in and behind the cross, as Karl Barth once said, it was primarily God the Father who paid the cost of our salvation: *God* was in Christ reconciling the world to himself.'[177] Torrance advances the logic of the hypostatic union further to conclude that 'since it was God and Man in one indivisible Person who was crucified, God himself was crucified for us in Christ'.[178] It is this aspect of the cross that powerfully testifies to its sufficiency and completeness to which nothing can be added.[179]

What are we to make of this phrase? It would seem to imply that the greatest object, or better, subject, in existence is humanity and not God, since humanity is the object of God's greatest love. But this is not consonant with the tenor of Torrance's theology and so it would appear unlikely this is what he has in mind. Torrance maintains that God remains impassible and explains this with recourse to the *extra Calvinisticum*. It is logical then to assume that the phrase examined here is functioning at the economic level only. We also know that Torrance adopts patristic theology which understands God's suffering soteriologically, not logically, hence, God the impassable suffers.[180]

The phrase as Torrance uses it does not indicate that men and women are the supreme beings of worth in existence, even above God, but that God would go to such great lengths, even to death on a cross, in order to save men and women from eternal separation from himself because *Jesus Christ* the God-man is the supreme being. It is likely that Torrance meant to espouse Paul's remark that Jesus did not consider equality with God a thing to be grasped and so emptied himself for our sake (Phil 2.6–7). In going to the cross God shows his magnificent love, grace, and mercy in such a profound way that men and women are left with no doubt but that God is for them *in Christ Jesus*. Because God is the Supreme Being this phrase 'God loves us more than he loves himself' takes on such alarming force.

By adopting such radical language Torrance's theology is open to question. While he wants to restrict the use of this phrase to the economic level it is difficult not to include at least some ontological significance in it. This phrase becomes a relatively clumsy rhetorical device as it risks identifying God's love for sinners as greater than the Father's love for the Son. Serious concerns are also raised over the propriety of Torrance's use and endorsement of 'death of God' motifs in a *theologia crucis*. By adopting such language in the contemporary climate of

176 Torrance, 'The Atonement the Singularity of Christ', p. 235.

177 Ibid. No reference to the Barth citation is provided by Torrance; however, elsewhere he does refer to *CD*, IV/2, p. 357, for this type of thinking in Barth. I am grateful to Paul Molnar for drawing my attention to this.

178 Torrance, 'The Atonement the Singularity of Christ', p. 235.

179 Torrance, *Preaching Christ Today*, pp. 27–8.

180 See Torrance, *Space, Time and Incarnation*, pp. 40–51; *God and Rationality*, p. 126; *Space, Time and Resurrection*, pp. 123–30; *The Ground and Grammar of Theology*, p. 24; *Christian Theology and Scientific Culture*, p. 18; and *The Trinitarian Faith*, pp. 184–6.

soteriological discussion[181] Torrance unwittingly aligns himself with a theology of a suffering God along with aspects many would argue this must entail such as: a rejection of Chalcedonian christology, a reinterpretation of the Trinity, and the affirmation of a 'terminal rupture' within God on the cross.[182] If Torrance's intent was, as I have argued, merely to expose by provocative language the love of God exhibited at the cross, then he could have done so in less ambiguous terms that would not have the potential to implicitly undermine his own theology.

Despite these criticisms it is clear that Torrance considers the cross-work of Christ as central to an evangelical soteriology. What is equally clear is that the cross does not exist in a vacuum. Rather, the power of the cross is evident when viewed in the context of the action of the vicarious humanity of Christ who lived, died, and rose again. As such the nature of Christ's ascended humanity is equally important for Torrance's theology of the incarnation as it is for his use of *theosis*.

The ascended humanity of Christ While the ascension is an often-overlooked doctrine in contemporary theology Torrance returns to its central significance in constructing a doctrine of theosis. Burgess helpfully points out that: 'A theology of the ascension belongs with and informs a theology of Jesus Christ's "heavenly session"...so that together these two form more or less one locus of theology.'[183] This is true in relation to Torrance's ascension theology which covers far more than the bare act of ascension recorded in Lk 24.50–53 and Acts 1.9–11.[184] Given Torrance's commitment to explicating the incarnation it is not surprising that the ascension is considered as integral to the atoning redemption of Christ; it too has saving significance.[185]

Drawing upon John Knox, Torrance asserts: 'Ascension is not just an addendum to the story of Jesus, a bringing down of the curtain on his earthly life, but it is

181 For a survey of current thought see Paul S. Fiddes, *The Creative Suffering of God* (Oxford: Clarendon, 1988), pp. 1–15.

182 This is the language of Alan E. Lewis, *Between Cross and Resurrection: A Theology of Holy Saturday* (Grand Rapids: Eerdmans, 2001). It is noteworthy that Torrance endorses the book, adding to the ambiguity of his thought at this point. For critiques of Lewis's approach see Thomas G. Weinandy, 'Easter Saturday and the Suffering of God: The Theology of Alan E. Lewis', *International Journal of Systematic Theology* 3 (2003): pp. 62–76; and Myk Habets, 'Putting the "Extra" Back into Calvinism', *Scottish Journal of Theology* (forthcoming).

183 Anthony Burgess, *The Ascension in Karl Barth* (London: Ashgate, 2004), p. 2. Burgess also notes that 'Thomas Torrance has provided one of the few significant twentieth century treatments of Jesus' ascension', p. 109.

184 See Douglas Farrow, *Ascension and Ecclesia: On the Significance of the Doctrine of the Ascension and for Ecclesiology and Christian Cosmology* (Edinburgh: T & T Clark, 1999), pp. 275–7.

185 Burgess reminds us, '...it is on matters related to Jesus' ascension and heavenly session that Torrance offers some of his strongest critique of Barth, suggesting that Barth's failures in this area of his thought leave him open to a charge of dualism and doceticism',

one of the great essential salvation events.'[186] The ascension is considered to be the requisite *anabasis* (ascent) of the Son of God corresponding to his *katabasis* (descent) in the incarnation.[187] Torrance specifically considers the resurrection and ascension to be two distinct but inseparable moments in one and the same event. The resurrection is the *terminus a quo*, its beginning, and the ascension is its *terminus ad quem*, its end.[188] Torrance has adopted Irenaeus's scheme of descent and ascent which involves a particular way of thinking about Jesus' history as the history of salvation.[189] The emphasis falls on the step-by-step recovery of the creation and creature through the obedience of Jesus, so that recapitulation is understood to mean that 'humanity is somewhat gradually redeemed and perfected through [Christ's] life-acts'.[190] Once again, our intent is not to present Torrance's doctrine of Christ's ascension as such but to investigate the relationship between Christ's ascension and Torrance's conception of *theosis*, which is unmistakably present throughout.[191]

In his ascension to the right hand of the Father the risen Jesus Christ is still a human; in fact he is the ultimate or true human.[192] In returning to heaven Christ must be thought of as ascending above space and time without ceasing to be human or without any diminution of his physical human existence. 'For Torrance the absence of Jesus via His ascension is therefore specifically the absence of His *risen humanity*',[193] writes Burgess, which in turn thrusts the church back to the previous earthly history as the place in which we are still to meet Christ. As Burgess explains, 'It is in the God-man Jesus of Nazareth that God and humanity are *hypostatically* united, and Jesus' ascension simply throws us back upon that truth – for the one who is ascended and "absent" is none other that [sic] this same

The Ascension in Karl Barth, p. 109. Burgess also notes how the work of William Milligan, cited by Torrance (*Space, Time and Resurrection*, 111, fn. 5), is influential on Torrance, see pp. 116–19.

186 Torrance, *Theology in Reconstruction*, p. 151.

187 Torrance, *Space, Time and Resurrection*, p. 123; cf. pp. 115, 132–5.

188 Torrance points the reader to Barth, *CD*, IV/2, p. 150.

189 According to Irenaeus the descent of the Son into human flesh and the ascent of the Son in human flesh joins the creation he has assumed to the eternity of God. Human being is now understood only in Jesus' humanity before the Father. See Gerrit S. Dawson, *Jesus Ascended: The Meaning of Christ's Continuing Incarnation* (Phillipsburg: P & R Publishing, 2004), pp. 164–5, who situates Torrance's concept of ascended humanity within the broader tradition from Irenaeus through to Andrew Murray.

190 Burgess, *The Ascension in Karl Barth*, p. 115.

191 On Torrance's doctrine of ascension in general see Burgess, *The Ascension in Karl Barth*, pp. 109–34; Farrow, *Ascension and Ecclesia*, who, while building on Torrance's work critiques his ascension theology; and Dawson, *Jesus Ascended*, a work which draws much of its inspiration from the theology of Torrance, see especially pp. 163–84.

192 Torrance, 'The Christ Who Loves Me', p. 18.

193 Burgess, *The Ascension in Karl Barth*, p. 111.

Jesus'.[194] 'In the incarnation,' writes Torrance, 'we have the meeting of man and God in man's place, but in the ascension we have the meeting of man and God in God's place.'[195] The ascension represents the exaltation of humanity into the life of God and on to the throne of God. In the ascension the Son of Man, New Man in Christ, is given to partake of the divine nature.[196]

> The union of God and man in Christ was assumed into the immediate presence of God the Father on his throne – there Christ wears our human life, and it is in our name that he is there at the right hand of God the Father Almighty, standing in for us.[197]

It is precisely here that Torrance considers we reach the goal of the incarnation – for we are beside Jesus, gathered up in him and included in his own self-presentation before the Father. Without using technical vocabulary, Torrance states that the goal of the incarnation is *theosis* and this is finally achieved by the ascension of Jesus Christ.

The importance of this for Torrance's doctrine of *theosis* is that Jesus Christ *as man* (human) now resides in intimate communion with the Trinity in heaven. As a man, Jesus Christ has perfect fellowship with God, and because of the eternity of the hypostatic union, the one person of the Son is the 'place' (*topos*) and 'space' (*chora*) of humanity in and with God. Because the ascended Lord fills this place and space:

> the ascension is the exaltation of new man, with his fully and truly human nature, and therefore of man with his 'place' as man, with the 'room' which he is given for his human life, *to participate in the divine 'place'*...It is ascension in which our humanity in Christ is taken up into the full Communion of Father, Son and Holy Spirit in life and love.[198]

This is why Dawson, in continuity with Torrance, can speak of deification as a kind of humanisation.

> The deification is actually a radical *humanization.* It is based on the life of Jesus lived as a man in the power of the Holy Spirit. We do not become the divine Son

[194] Ibid. Burgess suggests that Torrance's ascension theology is troubling at this point because it can tend to imply a bifurcation between Jesus' earthly-historical life and being, and the being he now has in heaven (p. 112). In my reading of Torrance there is no bifurcation and Torrance utilises the emphasis upon the ascended humanity of Christ to present a thoroughly Reformed doctrine of Christ's ascended work as High Priest.

[195] Torrance, *Space, Time and Resurrection*, p. 129.

[196] Ibid., 135. See Dawson, *Jesus Ascended*, p. 167.

[197] Torrance, *Scottish Theology from John Knox to John McLeod Campbell*, 21. Torrance goes on to link the Heavenly Session of Christ with the Eucharist in Knox and Scottish theology more generally (ibid., 22). See further in Chapter Four, pp. 170–85.

[198] Torrance, *Space, Time and Resurrection*, p. 133 (italics mine).

> – he is unique. Rather, we, too, are fitted by the Spirit for communion with the Father and empowered for service as the Spirit unites us continually to Jesus the new Adam. In Christ, we become men and women of the Spirit; our exaltation is the re-creation of humanity lived in joyful dependence on God, out of his very life, as we were meant to be.[199]

For Torrance and other recent thinkers, the ascension achieves *theosis*.[200] In the ascended Lord, believers are enabled to participate in the Divine nature and achieve immortality, becoming like God without ceasing to be human, and they do so precisely 'in Christ'.

In presenting the implications of the ascension of Jesus Christ in this way, Torrance again affirms that in *theosis* we never leave behind our creaturely status even in becoming 'gods'. This is made patently clear when he writes:

> The staggering thing about this is that the exaltation of human nature into the life of God does not mean the disappearance of man or the swallowing up of human and creaturely being in the infinite ocean of the divine Being, but rather that human nature, remaining creaturely and human, is yet exalted in Christ to share in God's life and glory.[201]

He is also affirming that we never leave behind Jesus Christ in his role as our Mediator and High Priest. Knowledge of God and communion with God in eternity adhere in the same way they do in the present – exclusively through Jesus Christ:

> Therefore we are sent back to Jesus, for there and there only may we hear God speaking in person, and there and there only at the foot of the Cross, where God, and man meet over the judgment and expiation of sin and guilt may we meet with God face to face and live, may we be judged and cleansed and have living communion with him in love through the propitiation of Jesus Christ.[202]

How is this communion and *theosis* made possible? Torrance answers, *only through the Spirit*. It is through the Spirit that Christ is made known to us and that intimate communion is maintained between Father and Son – between divinity and humanity. 'Through the Spirit Christ is nearer to us than we are to ourselves, and we who live and dwell in earth are yet made to sit with Christ "in heavenly

---

[199] Dawson, *Jesus Ascended*, p. 167.

[200] With reference to Torrance see Burgess, *The Ascension in Karl Barth*, p. 126, fn. 55, who levels several criticisms against Torrance's ascension theology which deserve thorough treatment, however, this falls outside the scope of the present work.

[201] Torrance, *Space, Time and Resurrection*, p. 135.

[202] Ibid., p. 134.

places", partaking of the divine nature in him.'[203] While the dynamics of the Holy Spirit will be highlighted in Chapter 4, what Torrance highlights through his discussion on the ascension is that as vicarious man, the Man for others, Jesus has deified humanity through the divinisation of his humanity. As believers participate in Jesus' ascended humanity, they participate in the fellowship of the Trinity. The ascension thus forms the capstone of Torrance's doctrine of vicarious humanity.

Conclusion

Chapter 2 has outlined Torrance's commitment to an incarnational redemption; Jesus Christ as Mediator has achieved salvation for humanity in his own person. By presenting a christology in which Christ is fully human and fully divine, Torrance asserts that in Christ human nature has been redeemed, reconciled, ascended, and 'divinised'. As Last Adam, Christ has made possible the full realisation of salvation, understood as something that transcends a legal and external transaction in favour of a relational and internal reality. The life and death of Christ, his so-called active and passive obedience, along with the retrospective and prospective aspects of atonement, all contribute to a Christian doctrine of *theosis*. Torrance thus understands the incarnation as inherently redemptive, yet not in a merely physical or mechanical sense.

Torrance's doctrine of the incarnation raises critical questions at several points, including: the accuracy of his reading of patristic sources, especially Athanasius; his adoption of a theology of 'vicarious humanity'; the coherence of his claim that the Word assumes a *fallen* human nature; along with his espousal of the reality of universal pardon but not universal salvation.

What remains is to see more clearly how *theosis* is communicated to the believer through the 'wondrous exchange' in Torrance's theology. How does a past event (incarnation) effect present salvation? This will occupy our attention in Chapter 3, as we examine how Torrance moves from an appropriation of Athanasian christology to a more explicit dependence on Calvin's soteriology of exchange, in which union with Christ and the blessings this bestows are communicated to the believer. Torrance contends in this discussion that justification is understood as both declaration *and* deification. It is Torrance's doctrine of *reconciliation* which now occupies our attention and further articulates how he understands the concept of *theosis*.

---

[203] Ibid., p. 135. While Torrance places some stress on the work of the Spirit he is highly critical of Barth's doctrine of ascension for emphasising 'the presence and work of the Spirit in such a way that the risen humanity of Christ becomes somewhat lost', Burgess, *The Ascension in Karl Barth*, p. 109.

Chapter 3
Partaking of the Divine Nature

Reconciliation and Redemption

In this chapter we examine in more detail the soteriological aspects of *theosis* as Torrance moves from a consideration of Christ's deification of human nature in the Incarnation to believers' partaking of the divine nature. Torrance's doctrine of reconciliation, his favoured term for soteriology, is heavily influenced by Calvin and Barth and thus critically draws upon the Reformed tradition while also contributing what he believes to be significant corrections and advancements to it. While not materially separate, incarnation and reconciliation are formally distinct as theological *loci*, and for the purposes of systematic study it has been necessary to deal with each under a separate chapter.

The consensus of Torrance scholarship to date is that his doctrine of reconciliation can be expressed in terms of a theology of union with Christ.[1] This study highlights the central role the concept of union with Christ plays in Torrance's theology, but proposes a further question: to what extent is Torrance's theology of union underpinned by his concept of *theosis*? Torrance believes *theosis* constitutes,

> the sustaining inner cohesion of our cognitive union with Christ through faith and the very substance of our personal and corporate union with Christ through the Word and Sacraments, for in Christ our human relations with God, far from being allowed to remain on a merely external basis, are embraced within the Trinitarian relations of God's own Being as Father, Son and Holy Spirit.[2]

Union with Christ is thus informed by the more determinative doctrine of *theosis* within Torrance's theology. Against the background of *theosis* one can discern how union with Christ has a pretemporal basis (in God's electing will), an historical application (in the incarnate life and death of Jesus Christ and the work of the Spirit), and an eschatological orientation (in both sanctification and glorification).

---

[1] See C. Baxter Kruger, 'The Doctrine of the Knowledge of God in the Theology of T.F. Torrance: Sharing in the Son's Communion with the Father in the Spirit', *Scottish Journal of Theology* 43 (1990). p. 373; Kye W. Lee, *Living in Union With Christ: The Practical Theology of Thomas F. Torrance* (New York: Peter Lang, 2003); and Jason H–K. Yeung, *Being and Knowing: An Examination of T.F. Torrance's Christological Science* (Hong Kong: China Alliance Press, 1996), p. 158.

[2] Thomas F. Torrance, *The Mediation of Christ*, 2nd edn (Edinburgh: T & T Clark, 1992), p. 64.

Theosis provides a controlling metaphor that gives coherence to the disparate themes of Torrance's soteriology.[3]

Torrance's articulation of *theosis* presents a theology of both reconciliation and redemption, adopts the language of personal and cognitive union with Christ, and outlines the progress the believer can make in partaking of the divine nature. Each of these features is compatible, Torrance believes, with the Reformed tradition and thus requires examination.

By 'redemption' Torrance means the emancipation of humanity from bondage, corruption, and nothingness; that which is often synonymous with 'atonement'.[4] Given the centrality and singularity of Jesus Christ for Torrance, he is obliged to view the entire history of redemption from a christocentric perspective when he looks at the Old Testament terms and images that speak of redemption and atonement, namely, *pdh, kpr,* and *ga'l*. These express 'something of the ineffable truth of atonement in its various but profoundly interrelated aspects'.[5] These three aspects of redemption must all be present in any biblically-based doctrine of redemption. If any one of these is missing or a single aspect made the sole basis of an atonement theory, then a serious distortion creeps into our soteriology.

The first aspect is the dramatic/dynamic aspect of atonement (*pdh*). This is the mighty act of God's saving deliverance out of the power and oppression of evil and the judgement of God upon it. The second is the cultic/priestly aspect of atonement (*kpr*). This has to do with redemption through atoning sacrifice for the expiation of sin and guilt whereby God incarnate in Christ draws near to us and draws us near to himself, cleansing us through his blood, sanctifying and healing us by the power of his Spirit, ransoming us from servitude to the world, delivering us from slavery into liberty, from darkness to light, thereby constituting us as a new priesthood and a special people belonging to himself for ever. The third aspect involves the ontological implications of atonement (*ga'l*). This has to do with redemption out of destitution or forfeited rights, perdition and death, for it depends on the divine-human nature of the Redeemer who stands in for us in our need and makes our desperate condition his own on the ground of his incarnate oneness with us. It is this third feature that is the most important of the three, as apart from it the other two tend to fall apart in our understanding.

---

[3] This is overlooked in many studies of his theology as for example in Lee, *Living in Union With Christ*. This is most evident in Lee's confusion over Torrance's use of *theosis*.

[4] Thomas F. Torrance, *Space, Time and Resurrection* (1976. Edinburgh: T & T Clark, 1998), p. 74.

[5] Thomas F. Torrance, 'The Atonement the Singularity of Christ and the Finality of the Cross: The Atonement and the Moral Order', in *Universalism and the Doctrine of Hell*, ed. Nigel M. de S. Cameron (Carlisle: Paternoster, Grand Rapids: Baker, 1992), p. 239. See a survey of these terms as used by Torrance in Gunther Pratz, 'The Relationship Between Incarnation and Atonement in the Theology of Thomas F. Torrance', *Journal for Christian Theological Research* 3 (1998): http://apu.edu/~CTRF/articles/1998_articles/pratz.html, pars. 24–9.

The above outline of redemption carries with it several implications, one of which is epistemological union with the incarnate Christ. According to Torrance, ontology and epistemology are essentially related: personal union also effects epistemological union. Both themes are subsumed under the concept of *theosis*. While Torrance's commitment to developing the epistemological foundations of Christian thinking has already been noted,[6] it is worth exploring in a little more detail the crucial role epistemology plays in his thinking on *theosis* when, for example, Torrance holds together revelation and reconciliation.[7]

Outside of Christ there is no real knowledge of God.[8] This is what lies behind Torrance's (and Barth's) rejection of a natural theology as traditionally conceived.[9] God cannot be known 'behind his back' as Torrance phrases it, nor can we know God without his willing himself to be known.[10] It is only in and through the eternal Word that God is known. This raises the question of the possibility of a genuine knowledge of God before the incarnation. Torrance deals with this at length when he speaks of the mediation of Christ within Israel.[11]

This is a crucial aspect of Torrance's doctrine of the knowledge of God. 'As the full and final self-revelation of God, however, Jesus Christ confronts us as One who is identical with the divine Self whom he reveals.'[12] In this one person we have revelation and reconciliation. Based on such verses as Jn 14.6, 'I am the Way the Truth and the Life, no one comes to the Father but by me', and Jn 14.9, 'Anyone who has seen me has seen the Father', Torrance concludes that:

---

6 See Chapter 2, pp. 60–65, and also Chapter 4, pp. 159–62. Especially important to this discussion is Torrance, *The Mediation of Christ*.

7 See Kruger, 'The Doctrine of the Knowledge of God in the Theology of T.F. Torrance', p. 366. Here Torrance is building upon Barth's method. See Barth, *CD* IV/3, p. 8; and Hunsinger, 'Karl Barth's Christology: Its Basic Chalcedonian Character', in *The Cambridge Companion to Karl Barth*, ed. John Webster (Cambridge: Cambridge University Press, 2000), p. 137.

8 See Chapter 2, pp. 61–5.

9 Torrance's doctrine of natural theology is highly nuanced and shows similarities and differences to that of Barth. See the discussion in Alister E. McGrath, *A Scientific Theology*, vol. 1, *Nature* (Grand Rapids: Eerdmans, 2001), pp. 279–86; and Paul D. Molnar, 'Natural Theology Revisited: A Comparison of T.F. Torrance and Karl Barth', *Zeitschrift für dialektische Theologie* 20 (2005): pp. 53–83.

10 This is most succinctly put in Thomas F. Torrance, 'The Christ Who Loves Me', in *A Passion for Christ: Vision that Ignites Ministry*, eds Gerrit S. Dawson and Jock Stein (Edinburgh: The Handsel Press, 1999), pp. 17–18.

11 Torrance, *The Mediation of Christ*, p. 9. In addition to 'matrix' Torrance speaks of Israel as the 'womb' for the incarnation of the Word, *God and Rationality* (Eugene, Or.: Wipf & Stock, 1997), p. 149. Cf. *Conflict and Agreement in the Church*, vol. 1, *Order and Disorder* (London: Lutterworth, 1959), pp. 285–303.

12 Ibid., p. 23.

> The Father and the Son are One, one in Being and one in Agency. Thus in Jesus Christ the Mediation of divine Revelation and the Person of the Mediator perfectly coincide. In Jesus Christ God has given us a Revelation which is identical with himself. Jesus Christ *is* the Revelation of God.[13]

Here again we see a consistent principle within Torrance's theology – the identity of Jesus Christ as both the Revealer and the Revelation of God. God is one in being and act.[14]

The significance of this christocentric epistemology is that in order to know God we must know Jesus Christ. 'In the Hebrew idiom revelation implies not only the uncovering of God but the uncovering of the ear and heart of man to receive revelation.'[15] Revelation is neither static nor passive; standing firmly within the Barthian tradition Torrance sees revelation as *event*. When we wish to come to know a personal being we must, by necessity, participate in the life of that personal being for true knowledge to be realised. This holds true for human relationships as well as divine. 'That is why', Torrance contends, 'we cannot know God without love, and if we are estranged without being reconciled to him.'[16] Torrance draws the following conclusion: 'Knowing God requires cognitive union with him in which our whole being is affected by his love and holiness. It is the pure in heart who see God.'[17]

This seeing or knowing is a personal participation in the triune relationship of the Father's love for the Son by the Holy Spirit and the Son's love for the Father by the Holy Spirit. Knowledge is fundamentally relational, not merely cognitive; it is a *personal* knowing that comes only by *personal* participation.[18] In accurately summarising Torrance's position Kruger writes, 'our knowledge of God arises through the sharing in the incarnate Son's communion with the Father in the Spirit. This can be stated in other words either as "sharing in the Son's knowledge of the Father in the Spirit" or as partaking of "God's own Self-knowledge"'.[19] This vocabulary takes us into the domain of *theosis* with its emphasis on knowing, participation, and communion through Christ in the Spirit within a trinitarian framework.[20]

---

13 Ibid.; and see Torrance, 'The Christ Who Loves Me', pp. 10–16.

14 See the perceptive treatment of these issues in Colin E. Gunton, *Act and Being: Towards a Theology of the Divine Attributes* (London: SCM, 2002).

15 Torrance, *The Mediation of Christ*, p. 11.

16 Ibid., pp. 25–6.

17 Ibid., p. 26.

18 See Thomas F. Torrance, *Belief in Science and in Christian Life: The Relevance of Michael Polanyi's Thought for Christian Faith and Life*, ed. Thomas F. Torrance (Edinburgh: Handsel, 1980), p. 141.

19 Kruger, 'The Doctrine of the Knowledge of God in the Theology of T.F. Torrance', p. 368, citing Torrance, *God and Rationality*, p. 174.

20 Kruger, ibid., structures his exploration of Torrance's knowledge of God around his emphasis upon communion, considering three aspects: the self–knowing or communion of

'Cognitive union' with God amounts to another cognate for *theosis* within Torrance's theology. As he makes clear, *theosis* 'does not mean "divinisation", as is so often supposed, but refers to the utterly staggering act of God in which he gives *himself* to us and *adopts* us into the communion of his divine life and love through Jesus Christ and in his one Spirit…'.[21] The relevance of this for our present discussion is made clear by the words immediately following this quotation: 'That is what constitutes the sustaining inner cohesion of our cognitive union with Christ… .'[22] For Torrance knowing God, the cognitive dimension of the faith, is a significant aspect of *theosis*.

From this epistemological basis Torrance articulates his doctrines of revelation, reconciliation, and redemption. Cognitive union is the first stage in a process of union with Christ in which the believer partakes of the divine nature. For this to happen there has to be a complete identification of Christ with humanity and in turn humanity with Christ, something Torrance calls the 'wonderful exchange', the central feature of his theology of union with Christ. Before considering the 'wonderful exchange' we shall first examine Torrance's doctrine of union with Christ as it relates to his understanding of *theosis*.

Union with Christ

Union with Christ is a central theme in Torrance's theology and provides a basis from which he is able to speak about *theosis*. In order to understand what Torrance means by union with Christ an understanding of how he has appropriated insights of Calvin and his Scottish theological tradition, especially that of H.R. Mackintosh, is required.

Torrance considers union with Christ as fundamental to Calvin's theology and in his own work it also occupies a central place.[23] He states: '…the doctrine of union with Christ in his vicarious human nature and priesthood remains central to the Reformed tradition and is surely one of its most helpful contributions to

---

the triune God; the actualisation of that communion in our humanity in Jesus Christ; and our sharing in that fulfilled communion through the Spirit. Yeung, *Being and Knowing*, largely follows this order.

[21] Torrance, *The Mediation of Christ*, p. 64.

[22] Ibid.

[23] See Charles Partee, 'Calvin's Central Dogma Again', *Sixteenth Century Journal* 18 (1987): pp. 191–9; I. John Hesselink, 'Calvin, The Holy Spirit, and Mystical Union', *Perspectives* 13 (1998): pp. 15–18; Dennis E. Tamburello, *Union With Christ: John Calvin and the Mysticism of St. Bernard* (Louisville: Westminster John Knox, 1994), p. 84; and Marcus Johnson, 'Union with Christ in Luther and Calvin', *Fides et Historia* 39 (2007): pp. 59–77.

the Ecumenical Church'.[24] Throughout Calvin's theology three distinct but interrelated 'unions' are presented. The first is the incarnational union, the second, the *unio mystica*, and the third, a spiritual union.[25] While Torrance adopts each sense of *unio cum Christo* into his own theology he does not follow Calvin's exact vocabulary. In the present study Torrance's more general vocabulary of union with Christ is followed rather than Calvin's precise delineation of the term.

Calvin specifically cuts out any 'extrinsecist' notions of justification or reconciliation by positing justification as a benefit of union with Christ.[26] Through participation in Christ we receive all the benefits of salvation, including Christ's righteousness; which equates to the filial life. Calvin insists on the forensic nature of justification but is equally adamant that we are justified as a result of our union with Christ.[27] This is affirmed when he writes, 'You see that our righteousness is not in us but in Christ, that we possess it only because we are partakers in Christ; indeed, with him we possess all its riches'.[28]

Christ is the *mediating* bond of union (Calvin's first sense of 'union'). The *unio mystica* is a personal union as men and women participate in a real way in Christ (Calvin's second sense of 'union'). This union is not without the Spirit who functions as the *unitive* bond of union with Christ (Calvin's third sense of 'union').[29] Tan summarises Calvin's position well:

---

24 Thomas F. Torrance, 'The Distinctive Character of the Reformed Tradition', in *Incarnational Ministry: The Presence of Christ in Church, Society, and Family. Essays in Honor of Ray S. Anderson*, eds Christian D. Kettler and Todd H. Speidell (Colorado Springs: Helmers and Howard, 1990), pp. 6–7.

25 See John Calvin, *Letter to Martyr, Geneva, August 8, 1555,* trans. George C. Gorham in *Gleanings of a Few Scattered Ears*, ed. George C. Gorham (London: Bell and Daldy, 1857).

26 See especially Calvin, *Institutes*, 3.1.1. There is a sustained polemic at the back of Calvin's thought in which he distinguishes his theology from that of Osiander who argued that the divine *Logos*, stripped of his humanity, is the indwelling and transforming Christ within. Cf. *Institutes,* 3.11.5–10. See Torrance, 'The Distinctive Character of the Reformed Tradition', pp. 5–9.

27 The forensic nature of justification is explicit in all editions of the *Institutes*, see Alister E. McGrath, *Iustitia Dei: A History of the Christian Doctrine of Justification*, 2nd edn (Cambridge: Cambridge University Press, 1998), pp. 223, 462, fn. 31, 32, 33. McGrath sees Calvin following Melanchthon in this respect but also preserving an important aspect of Luther's standing on justification as the personal union of Christ and the believer. As a result of his stress on union with Christ, Calvin was able to affirm both imputation and impartation of righteousness, understood christologically. The study of J. Todd Billings, *Calvin, Participation, and the Gift: The Activity of Beleivers in Union with Christ* (Oxford: Oxford University Press, 2007), examines these themes in detail.

28 Calvin, *Institutes*, 3.11.23.

29 See Seng-Kong Tan, 'Calvin's Doctrine of Our Union with Christ', *Quodlibet Journal* 5 (2003): http://www.quodlibet.net/tan-union.shtml, for these distinctions.

> Through the unitive operation of the Holy Spirit, Christ and the elect are brought into reciprocal relationship. The one is the humanward trajectory – Christ's participation in us – where 'he had to become ours and to dwell within us'; the other is the Christward movement – our participation in Christ – where we are said to be 'engrafted into him' [Rom 11.17], and 'to put on Christ' [*Institutes* 3.1.1].[30]

Finally, within Calvin's doctrine of *unio cum Christo* he presents the organic union created, not only between Christ and the believer, but also between believers in the body of Christ. Again Tan is helpful:

> [T]he inseparable corollary of communion with Christ is 'the communion of saints.' Although salvation has an intensely personal dimension, viz. an individual person's relation to God, nonetheless, it is not a private affair, since its context is ecclesiologically framed [*Institutes* 4.1.3]. Hence, a proper understanding of the reality of *unio mystica*, which recognizes the Spirit's function as its *vinculum*, demands that righteousness and holiness be interpreted communally.[31]

According to Torrance, 'This evangelical conception of union with Christ governed Calvin's teaching about justification and sanctification, Holy Communion, and the Church as the body of Christ'.[32] It also governs Torrance's own doctrine of union with Christ, as we shall see.

The fundamental basis of *unio mystica* for Calvin is to 'put on Christ' and to be 'engrafted into him'.[33] With this in mind Tamburello's study includes a detailed appendix of references to union with Christ in Calvin's writing and includes as cognates the following: engrafting, communion, fellowship, in the Spirit, mysterious/incomprehensible, one flesh/marriage, spiritual union, mystical union, growing together/becoming one, union with God, adoption, regeneration, and partakers of Christ.[34] This is important for our study because it shows that within Calvin's theology, one that exerted an immense influence over Torrance and Reformed theology generally, the ideas behind the classical formulations of *theosis* are already present. Torrance adopts many of these same cognates into his own soteriology in order to present his doctrine of salvation with a concept of *theosis* at its heart.[35]

---

30 Ibid.

31 Ibid.

32 Torrance, 'The Distinctive Character of the Reformed Tradition', p. 7.

33 Calvin, *Institutes*, 3.1.1.

34 Tamburello, *Union With Christ*, pp. 111–13.

35 Barth does the same although he is careful not to use the term *theosis* and he is as reticent as Torrance to use the actual term *unio mystica*. See Barth, *CD*, IV/3.2, pp. 538–49. Torrance shares Barth's reticence over the term 'mysticism', but in a manner significant for the present study, Torrance consciously adopts the concept of *theosis* in a way that Barth never could. See Bruce L. McCormack, 'Participation in God, Yes, Deification, No:

The most concise definition Calvin gives to the *unio mystica* is found in *Institutes* 3.11.10:

> Therefore, that joining together of Head and members, that indwelling of Christ in our hearts—in short, that mystical union—are accorded by us the highest degree of importance, so that Christ, having been made ours, makes us sharers with him in the gifts with which he has been endowed. We do not, therefore, contemplate him outside ourselves from afar in order that his righteousness may be imputed to us but because we put on Christ and are engrafted into his body—in short, because he deigns to make us one with him. For this reason, we glory that we have fellowship of righteousness with him.

The 'putting on Christ' metaphor, according to Tan, operates within Calvin's theology to represent the imputed righteousness received in justification. The 'engrafting' metaphor stands for the imparted holiness of Christ received in sanctification. While distinct concepts, they are not separate and they are both the benefits received in faith through the *unio mystica*.

> Thus, the distinction between the once-for-all 'alien' righteousness of Christ freely imputed on [*sic*] a sinner (justification) and the progressive holiness imparted through the indwelling Spirit in the regenerated person (sanctification) is obtained without separation, since they are simultaneous realities within *unio mystica*.[36]

One can clearly see how Calvin's theology informs Torrance's. An external transaction between Christ and the Father applied to the believer as imputed righteousness is not wrong *per se* but it is insufficient if it is made to represent the entire doctrine of salvation. When this happens, Torrance argues, exclusively juridical categories of atonement are accepted and salvation becomes something less than evangelical (the so-called 'Latin Heresy').[37] This is not a rejection of the Reformation doctrine of imputation but its relocation into the context of participation. Imputation is correctly understood when viewed, 'not just in terms of imputed righteousness but in terms of a participation in the righteousness of Christ which is transferred to us through union with him'.[38] When salvation is viewed through the lens of the *unio mystica* – a personal participation in Christ

---

Two Modern Protestant Responses to an Ancient Question', in *Denkwürdiges Geheimnis: Beiträge zur Gotteslehre. Festschrift für Eberhard Jüngel zum 70. Geburtstag,* eds Inglof U. Dalferth, Johannes Fischer, and Hans-Peter Großhans (Tübingen: Mohr-Siebeck, 2004), pp. 347–74.

[36] Tan, 'Calvin's Doctrine of Our Union with Christ', np.

[37] See Thomas F. Torrance, 'Karl Barth and the Latin Heresy', *Scottish Journal of Theology* 39 (1986): pp. 461–82.

[38] Torrance, 'The Distinctive Character of the Reformed Tradition', p. 6.

– we discern that *all* the benefits he won for us are actually imputed and imparted to us simply because we are *in Christ.*

The final goal of salvation is not only to be united to Christ by the Spirit but also to commune with the Father through the incarnate Son in or by the Holy Spirit. Union with Christ is thus understood as a participation in the divine life. In his commentary on 2 Pet 1.4, the key patristic text on *theosis*, Calvin rejects outright any Platonic idea of imitation, Manichean emanationism, or Neoplatonic mysticism by which human being and divine being are blurred or mixed. In its place he argues the biblical text asserts that the goal of justification and sanctification is that we may become 'partakers of divine immortality and the glory of blessedness, and thus we shall be in a way one with God so far as our capacity allows'.[39] In unequivocal terms Calvin affirms a doctrine of *theosis* when he concludes, 'We should notice that it is the purpose of the Gospel to make us sooner or later like God: indeed it is, so to speak, a kind of deification'.[40]

Does Calvin mean to imply that there is some ontological union with Christ achieved in *theosis*? Clearly he does. In arguing against the views of Servetus and Osiander,[41] Calvin contends that in our union with Christ the divine essence is not mixed with our own but an energetic or spiritual union is achieved through 'the secret power of his Spirit'.[42] To be a partaker of the divine nature means a participation not of 'essence but of quality', and so it is not, strictly speaking, a *substantial* union. It is, nevertheless, an ontic participation in the divine nature, for it involves a sharing in the *properties* of the essence or what Calvin preferred to term 'nature'.[43] Believers participate in divinity through *Christ*'s humanity and so

39 Calvin, *Calvin's New Testament Commentaries*, vol. 12, *Hebrews and 1 and 2 Peter* (2 Peter 1.4), p. 330.

40 Ibid.

41 Calvin accused Servetus of an emanationistic theological anthropology by which believers participate in the actual substance (essence) of God (*Institutes*, 1.15.5), while Osiander sought to equate the bond of union between the divine Persons with the bond of union between believers and Christ. For Calvin, the two are not symmetrical (*Institutes*, 3.11). Compare *Institutes*, 3.11.5 with John Calvin, *Commentary on John* (17.21) in vol. 5 of *Calvin's New Testament Commentaries*, trans. T.H.L. Parker, eds David W. and Thomas F. Torrance (Grand Rapids: Eerdmans, 1959), pp. 147–9. See Thomas F. Torrance, *Conflict and Agreement in the Church*, vol. 2, *The Ministry and the Sacraments of the Gospel* (London: Lutterworth, 1960), p. 143.

42 See John Calvin, *Sermons on the Epistle to the Ephesians*, Sermon 42 on Eph 5.31–33 (1562. Edinburgh: Banner of Truth Trust, 1973), p. 614.

43 Debate continues over the nature of human participation in the Divine within Calvin's thought. Partee, 'Calvin's Central Dogma Again', p. 198, suggests that Calvin does not posit an ontic participation in his use of 'union' for it is not 'mystical', nor 'substantial' but merely 'real' in a general but unspecifiable sense. According to Partee, Calvin does allow in his theology of the *unio mystica* an echo of the Platonic idea of imitation, but guards it from Platonic mysticism. See comments on Plato in Calvin, *Calvin's New Testament Commentaries*, vol. 12, *Hebrews and 1 and 2 Peter* (2 Peter 1.4), p. 330. Tan agrees with

the *unio mystica* is formulated within an asymmetrical relationship to Christ's *unio* with the Father. Like classical formations of *theosis*, this upholds Christ as God and Son by nature and believers as 'gods' and 'sons' by grace.

In Calvin's presentation of the believer's participation in the divine nature through union with Christ, understood within a strictly trinitarian context, the concept of *theosis* is clearly in view. More recent Reformed scholarship has identified Calvin's commitment to *theosis* and thus the possibility for a thoroughly Reformed construal of the doctrine.[44] It is this Calvinist construction of union with Christ that Torrance adopts almost point-for-point and builds upon in his own theology, allowing him to speak of the believer's real participation in the divine nature, and not just of *fellowship* with God.[45]

The second major influence behind Torrance's theology of union with Christ is his reading of Scottish Reformed theology, especially H.R. Mackintosh. Torrance believes Calvin's doctrine of union with Christ was given 'an essential place in the Reformation theology of the Church of Scotland beautifully expressed in the *Scots Confession*, and several sixteenth-century catechisms', however, it

---

Partee that Calvin does not speak of an essential participation, 'and yet it must be affirmed that *unio mystica* is not idealistic, but ontic', Tan, 'Calvin's Doctrine of Our Union with Christ', np. Tamburello, *Union With Christ*, pp. 88–9, provides evidence of this 'spiritual' union throughout Calvin's works. The recent work of Julie Canlis, 'Calvin, Osiander, and Participation in God', *International Journal of Systematic Theology* 6 (2004): pp. 169–84, also supports the notion that it is right to speak of 'participation in God' but for Calvin this participation is of a non-substantialist type. Cf. Billings, *Calvin, Participation, and the Gift*, pp. 53–65; Jonathan Slater, 'Salvation as Participation in the Humanity of the Mediator in Calvin's *Institutes of the Christian Religion*: A Reply to Carl Mosser', *Scottish Journal of Theology* 58 (2005), pp. 39–58; and McCormack, 'Participation in God, Yes, Deification, No', pp. 347–74.

44 See especially Carl Mosser, 'The Greatest Possible Blessing: Calvin and Deification', in *Scottish Journal of Theology* 55 (2002), pp. 36–57; Canlis, 'Calvin, Osiander, and Participation in God', pp. 169–84; Myk Habets, 'Reforming Theōsis', in *Theōsis: Deification in Christian Theology*, eds S. Finlan and V. Kharlamov (OR.: Pickwick Publications, 2006), pp. 146–67; Gannon Murphy, 'Reformed *Theosis*?' *Theology Today* 65 (2008): pp. 191–212; and Myk Habets, 'Reformed *Theosis*? A Response to Gannon Murphy', *Theology Today* 65 no. 4 (January, 2009), pp. 489–98.

45 As the title infers, McCormack, 'Participation in God, Yes, Deification, No', pp. 347–74, considers participation to be a thoroughly Reformed concept, as evident in the theology of Barth and Jüngel, but he is totally opposed to construing this as *theosis*, especially Torrance's approach, on the basis that Reformed theology occupies a different ontology than a doctrine of *theosis* requires. Torrance's trinitarian theology provides an answer to this objection when it presents what may be termed a relational ontology which makes it entirely compatible with a doctrine of *theosis*. This is evident throughout Thomas F. Torrance, *The Christian Doctrine of God: One Being Three Persons* (Edinburgh: T & T Clark, 1996), and *The Trinitarian Faith: The Evangelical Theology of the Ancient Catholic Church* (Edinburgh: T & T Clark, 1995). Cf. Stanley J. Grenz, *Rediscovering the Triune God: The Trinity in Contemporary Theology* (Minneapolis: Fortress, 2004), pp. 200–215.

was given 'scanty placc in subsequent Scottish theology due to the Westminster Confession of Faith, with its exiguous attention to the Trinity, and the Puritan form of Calvinism that characterized it'.[46] According to his reading of the tradition, the doctrine of union with Christ as Calvin explicated it survived only through the efforts of certain 'Christ-centered churchmen and theologians'.[47]

Without exploring the entire history of Scottish theology as read through the eyes of Torrance, we may note a few key influences on his thinking about union with Christ from this context. Torrance gives Robert Leighton (1611–84) praise for not considering union with Christ simply as a 'judicial union' but as a 'real union' which occupies the centre of the whole redemptive activity mediated through Christ as saving grace. Utilised in this way union with Christ is fundamentally related to both election in Christ and the concept of saving exchange whereby Christ gives to humanity what is his – his righteousness and filial status – and takes to himself what is not his own – our sin and alienation.[48] Thomas Boston (1676–1732) viewed union with Christ not merely as a legal union but a 'real and proper union with "the whole Christ" transformed through his death and resurrection, that is, a union of an ontological kind'.[49] Boston often spoke of this as a 'mystical union' in which all the benefits of the covenant of grace are given to the elect.

Of special interest to Torrance is H.R. Mackintosh (1870–1936) who made the concept of the *unio mystica* central to his soteriology.[50] For Mackintosh, the concept of the *unio mystica* was merely a dogmatic restatement of the biblically rich material on the believer's *participatio Christi* found throughout the New Testament. By participating in Christ there is an 'importation of another's personality into him; the life, the will of Christ has taken over what once was in sheer antagonism to it, and replaced the power of sin by the forces of a divine life'.[51] There is a twofold objectivity here: on the one hand, there is a 'Christ-in-you' relationship, and on the other hand there is a 'you-in-Christ' aspect. The former has to do with Christ being present within the believer as the source of new

---

46 Torrance, 'Thomas Torrance Responds', in *The Promise of Trinitarian Theology: Theologians in Dialogue with T.F. Torrance*, ed. Elmer M. Colyer (Lanham, Md.: Rowman & Littlefield, 2001), p. 310.

47 Ibid.

48 Leighton especially used the biblical concept of *Goel* or 'kinsman-redeemer' applied to Christ the incarnate Son. See Torrance, *Scottish Theology from John Knox to John McLeod Campbell* (Edinburgh: T & T Clark, 1996), p. 175.

49 Ibid., p. 207.

50 See Hugh R. Mackintosh, 'The Unio Mystica as a Theological Conception', *The Expositor* 7 (1909): pp. 138–55. Robert R. Redman, 'Participatio Christi: H.R. Mackintosh's Theology of the Unio Mystica', *Scottish Journal of Theology* 49 (1996): pp. 201–22, has observed how the theme serves as a *leitmotif*.

51 Hugh R. Mackintosh, 'The Unio Mystica as a Theological Conception', in *Some Aspects of Christian Belief* (Hodder & Stoughton, 1923), p. 103, cited in Redman, 'Participatio Christi: H.R. Mackintosh's Theology of the Unio Mystica', p. 202.

life, while the latter points to the foundation of this new life as lying *outside* of the believer in Christ. The Holy Spirit mediates the union. Torrance adopts these two aspects of participation in Christ into his own thinking.

Mackintosh was attempting to postulate a union with Christ Jesus that went beyond the merely moral or ethical. Like Torrance, Mackintosh had reservations over using the term 'mystical union' (despite teaching its substance), but chose to define what he meant by *unio mystica* more willingly than discard the term altogether. Redman considers this to be an ill-advised move as Mackintosh rarely used the words 'mystic' or 'mystical' except from his defence of them against their detractors, and he substantially reinterpreted the phrase so that in the end the continued use of it was a confusing distraction.[52] By 'mystical' Mackintosh means, according to Redman, 'that the believer's relationship to Christ transcends human relationships and human experiences of solidarity and union'.[53] In place of a mere moral union Mackintosh presents a spiritual union that, while rational, is beyond human comprehension. By 'union' Mackintosh does not mean a complete identification in which Christ and the believer become indistinguishable; this would be an *essential* union, something characteristic of certain medieval mystics. Mackintosh was aware of the risk of pantheism and avoided this in his christology. Through *participatio Christi*, Mackintosh argues, one has communion with God *as a human being* because it is through union with the *incarnate* Christ that we come to commune with God. By defining union with Christ in such a way Mackintosh is in basic agreement with Calvin's three senses of the term – incarnational, mystical and spiritual. One can clearly see why Torrance is so attracted to Mackintosh's theology.

Within this very specific trajectory of Reformed theology Torrance posits his own insights. Torrance articulates the dimensions of union with Christ in various ways but consistently he sees three realities involved. First, there is union with Christ made possible objectively through the *homoousion* of the incarnate Son (Calvin's 'incarnational union').[54] Second, there is the hypostatic union, and its significance for the reconciling exchange wrought by Christ in his life, death and resurrection (Calvin's *unio mystica*). Finally, these two aspects of union with Christ are fulfilled or brought to completion in the communion that exists between believers and the triune God (broadly corresponding to Calvin's 'spiritual union').

In a paraphrase of Torrance's theology, Hunsinger presents three aspects that correlate approximately to our outline. Firstly, *reception*, a past event that involves what Christ has done for us, received by grace through faith alone. Secondly,

---

[52] Redman, 'Participatio Christi: H.R. Mackintosh's Theology of the Unio Mystica', p. 218. Perhaps this explains Torrance's own refusal to use the term at all in his own work.

[53] Ibid., p. 203.

[54] Torrance also speaks of this incarnational or hypostatic union as a 'carnal union'. See Thomas F. Torrance, *The School of Faith: The Catechisms of the Reformed Church*, trans. and ed. with Introduction by Thomas F. Torrance (London: James Clarke and Co, 1959), pp. cvi–cvii; and W. Duncan Rankin, 'Carnal Union with Christ in the Theology of T.F. Torrance', Unpublished PhD Thesis (University of Edinburgh, 1997).

participation, a present event, in which believers are clothed with Christ's righteousness through partaking of Christ by virtue of his vicarious humanity. Thirdly, *communion*, the future or eschatological aspect that equates to eternal life itself in which believers enjoy communion in reciprocal love and knowledge of the triune God.[55]

Turning to Torrance himself, three words are used to elaborate what union with Christ means: *prothesis* – divine purpose, *mystērion* – mystery, and *koinonia* – fellowship/communion.[56] This triadic structure reflects the trinitarian action of the triune God: *prothesis* – the Father, *mystērion* – the Son, and *koinonia* – the Holy Spirit. A brief consideration of each will be instructive.

Prothesis refers to divine election whereby the Father purposed or 'set forth' the union of God and humanity in Jesus Christ. Divine election is a free, sovereign decision, a contingent act of God's love; as such it is neither arbitrary nor necessary.[57] Torrance thus holds to the Reformed doctrine of unconditional election, one which represents a strictly theonomous way of thinking, from a centre in God and not in ourselves.[58] Torrance draws on aspects of Barth's doctrine of election for he equates the incarnation as the counterpart to the doctrine of election so that 'the incarnation, therefore, may be regarded as the eternal decision or election of God in his Love…'.[59] Calling upon Calvin's analogy, Torrance insists that 'Christ himself is the "mirror of election", for it takes place *in him* in such a way that he is the Origin and the End, the Agent and the Substance of election…'.[60]

The second key expression Torrance uses is *mystērion*; the term is applied to Christ, and specifically to the mystery of his hypostatic union.[61] In relation to God this means that the consubstantial union of the Trinity upholds the hypostatic union so that God does not merely come *in* man but *as* man. In this union of God and man a complete *henosis* between the two is effected, and they are 'perfectly at one'.

> He had come, Son of God incarnate as son of man, in order to get to grips with the powers of darkness and defeat them, but he had been sent to do that not through the manipulation of social, political or economic power-structures, but by striking

---

55 George Hunsinger, 'The Dimension of Depth: Thomas F. Torrance on the Sacraments of Baptism and the Lord's Supper', *Scottish Journal of Theology* 54 (2001): pp. 164–5.

56 Torrance, *Conflict and Agreement in the Church*, vol. 2, pp. 82–92.

57 Thomas F. Torrance, *Christian Theology and Scientific Culture* (New York: Oxford University Press, 1981), p. 131.

58 See further in ibid., p. 132. Torrance does not, however, endorse either limited atonement or universal salvation (ibid., pp. 134–6).

59 Ibid., p. 133.

60 Ibid., p. 135. Cf. Calvin, *Institutes*, 3.24.1–5, and 3.22.7. See Myk Habets, 'The Doctrine of Election in Evangelical Calvinism: T.F. Torrance as a Case Study', *Irish Theological Quarterly* 73 (2008): pp. 334–54.

61 Torrance, *Conflict and Agreement in the Church*, vol. 2, pp. 84, 88–91, 141; and *Conflict and Agreement in the Church*, vol. 1, p. 266.

> beneath them all into the ontological depths of Israel's existence where man, and Israel representing all mankind, had become estranged from God, and there within those ontological depths of human being to forge a bond of union and communion between man and God in himself which can never be undone.[62]

Hence the hypostatic union is also a 'reconciling union' in which estrangement between God and humanity is bridged, conflict is eradicated, and human nature is 'brought into perfect sanctifying union with divine nature in Jesus Christ'.[63] Torrance refers to this as a 'dynamic atoning union'.

This reconciling union is not merely external or juridical but actual, and points to the higher reality of communion. Hence Torrance can assert that:

> [I]t is not atonement that constitutes the goal and end of that integrated movement of reconciliation but union with God in and through Jesus Christ in whom our human nature is not only saved, healed and renewed but lifted up to participate in the very light, life and love of the Holy Trinity.[64]

Reconciliation thus refers to the real participation of believers in the divine nature made possible by the dynamic atoning union of Christ. Torrance contends this is atonement in effect. As a result of the incarnation, humanity is united to divinity in the hypostatic union so that:

> In the Church of Christ all who are redeemed through the atoning union embodied in him are made to share in his resurrection and are incorporated into Christ by the power of his Holy Spirit as living members of his Body…Thus it may be said that the 'objective' union which we have with Christ through his incarnational assumption of our humanity into himself is 'subjectively' actualised in us through his indwelling Spirit, 'we in Christ' and 'Christ in us' thus complementing and interpenetrating each other.[65]

In addition to the hypostatic union Torrance applies the concept of *mystērion* to the mystery of the one-and-the-many, or Christ and his body the church. Torrance thus understands union with Christ to be largely corporate in nature but applicable to each individual member of his body who is ingrafted into Christ by baptism and continues to live in union with him as they feed upon his body and blood in Holy Communion.[66] Understanding the church as the body of Christ is thus another way of asserting an ontological union between the community of believers and Christ the Head.[67]

---

62 Torrance, *The Mediation of Christ*, p. 30.

63 Ibid., p. 65.

64 Ibid., p. 66.

65 Ibid., pp. 66–7.

66 Ibid., p. 67.

67 The corporate nature of *theosis* is explored in more detail throughout Chapter 4.

The third term Torrance uses is *koinonia*, and it too has a double reference. First, vertically, it represents our participation through the Spirit in the mystery of Christ's union with us. Second, horizontally, it is applied to our fellowship or communion with one another in the body of Christ.[68] At the intersection of the vertical and horizontal dimensions of *koinonia* is the church, the community of believers united to Christ, who is himself united to humanity through the incarnation. Torrance asserts that 'in and through *koinonia* the divine *prothesis* enshrining the eternal *mystērion* embodies itself horizontally in a community of those who are one with God through the reconciliation of Christ'.[69] It is this theology of union with Christ by means of fellowship or participation in God that links Torrance's doctrines of soteriology and ecclesiology.

In summarising Torrance's use of these three concepts Lee's study helpfully concludes that 'the cause (*causa*) of "union with Christ" is *prothesis*, the election of God. Its substance (*materia*) is *mystērion*, the hypostatic union in Jesus Christ, and its fulfilment (*effectus*) is *koinonia*, the communion of the Holy Spirit'.[70] This outline focuses on the trinitarian foundation inherent throughout Torrance's work that reminds readers not to see the work of reconciliation as exclusively that of the Son, or the Son and the Spirit, but as the work of the triune God.[71]

Lee's study of Torrance's theology of union and communion further outlines eleven characteristics of Torrance's conception of union with Christ, which emphasise the elements of *unio cum Christo*.[72] Two in particular are germane for our present purposes. Lee's fifth characteristic of union with Christ is Torrance's perceived rejection of deification: 'Torrance is strongly opposed to the notion of the deification of human nature through participation in the divine nature through sacramental grace, for this notion discloses a form of Monophysitism or docetism.'[73] According to Lee, Torrance concludes that this is the error in both mysticism and pantheism, where creaturely being is identified with the divine being. Lee acknowledges that Torrance posits a real union with Christ in his human nature as well as our exaltation to participate in the divine life and love, but this participation is that of a human in the Divine and as such constitutes *koinonia* and not *methexis* throughout.

Lee is right to distinguish between *theosis* and mystical forms of deification in Torrance's theology. He is also right to assert that *theosis* has a humanising

68 Torrance, *Conflict and Agreement in the Church*, vol. 2, pp. 88–90; and *Theology in Reconciliation: Essays Towards Evangelical and Catholic Unity in East and West* (London: Geoffrey Chapman, 1975), pp. 68–9.

69 Ibid., p. 91.

70 Lee, *Living in Union With Christ*, p. 200. Cf. Torrance, *Conflict and Agreement in the Church*, vol. 1, pp. 118–20.

71 Torrance is in basic agreement with a Reformed position on union with Christ. See Louis Berkhof, *Systematic Theology* (Edinburgh: Banner of Truth Trust, 1958), pp. 448–9.

72 Lee, *Living in Union With Christ*, pp. 201–11.

73 Ibid., p. 203.

function in contrast to certain depersonalising notions of mystical union, in which the human literally becomes divine. What Lee's study fails to highlight, however, is how robust Torrance's doctrine of *theosis* is and how union, communion and participation function as cognates of *theosis* in both Greek patristic theology and Torrance's work. Lee affirms Torrance accepts a doctrine of *theosis* over one of deification/divinisation.[74] However, in his conclusion we read:

> Torrance strongly rejects the notion of divinization through union with Christ, and instead argues for the Greek notion of *theosis*. Contrary to this, he sometimes states that union with Christ means 'the exaltation of man to be a partaker of the life and love that God is, and thereby to be a partaker of *divine nature*.' Having said this, one may wonder how one cannot be divinized or deified when one partakes of divine nature.[75]

By failing to see the comprehensive use Torrance makes of *theosis*, understood within the context of Greek patristic theology and the Reformed tradition, Lee is unable to appreciate how Torrance can reject a *form* of divinisation/deification and yet endorse a *doctrine* of *theosis*. By limiting his vision of Torrance's corpus to *union* and *communion* Lee finds himself unable to account for a central feature of Torrance's thought.

The other relevant feature of Lee's account of Torrance's doctrine of union with Christ is his sixth point, which focuses on the doctrine of *perichoresis* and involves the human participation in the divine life and love. Torrance explains that *perichoresis* is not a union of identity but 'a real sharing in the union of the incarnate Son with the Father, through a sharing not only in his human nature but in the life and love of God embodied in him'.[76] The end or goal of union with Christ is thus to participate in the Divine life by being lifted up into a *perichoretic* union. While Lee does not identify this with *theosis*, this is surely Torrance's point when he repeatedly speaks of ontological communion, real participation, *perichoresis*, and partaking of the divine life and love, all cognates for *theosis* within his theology.[77]

Lee's analysis of Torrance's doctrine of union with Christ is succinct and helpful at numerous points. It highlights the many dimensions union with Christ takes in Torrance's theology, especially the movement from Christ's prior union

---

74 See Lee, *Living in Union With Christ*, pp. 115, 150, 204, 212, 214, 235, 303, 316, 317.

75 Ibid., p. 317. Citations from Torrance, *Space, Time and Resurrection*, p. 70; and *Conflict and Agreement in the Church*, vol. 1, pp. 109–10.

76 Torrance, *Space, Time and Resurrection*, p. 70.

77 For examples see: Torrance, *Theology in Reconciliation*, pp. 17, 201; *Theology in Reconstruction* (Grand Rapids: Eerdmans, 1965), pp. 135, 184, 186, 247–8, 252; *Space, Time and Resurrection*, pp. 69–70; *The Ground and Grammar of Theology*, p. 159; *Reality and Scientific Theology* (Edinburgh: Scottish Academic Press, 1985), p. 187; and *Conflict and Agreement in the Church*, vol. 1, p. 26.

with us (incarnational union) and subsequently the believers' union with Christ (mystical and spiritual union). It brings to the fore the role of the Father, the Son and the Holy Spirit, and it shows how union with Christ unites the various *loci* of his dogmatics; all worked out within a trinitarian framework with a christological concentration. The weakness of Lee's analysis is his dismissal of the doctrine of *theosis* in Torrance's theology and his inability to see how pervasive and controlling this concept is for Torrance's doctrine of union and communion, which incorporates the various other cognates such as participation, engrafting, spiritual union, sacramental union and cognitive union, to name just a few. An otherwise fine study is hindered by a myopic concentration on union and communion and by a failure to see, in his own words, the 'meta-sacramental' dimensions involved.

According to Torrance, union with Christ is not simply evangelical detachment or a monistic merging with the divine. In accordance with his reading of Scripture, the tradition, and Reformation insights, Torrance sees union with Christ retaining the distinction between Christ and the Christian, along with a spiritual union, in which believers become partakers of the divine nature through participation in Christ (and fellowship with the Spirit). Reflecting Barth's comments on union with Christ, Torrance is adamant that this process does not involve any 'dissolution', 'disappearance', 'identification', 'conjunction' or 'reversibility' of the human with the Divine. However, it is for all that a 'true' but not 'ideal' union. It is a 'total' but not 'physical or intellectual' union, an 'indissoluble' not a 'transitory' union.[78] It is a union commensurate with *theosis*.

Mirifica Commutatio!

Torrance's concept of participation in Christ finds further expression in the notion of the 'wonderful exchange' (*mirifica commutatio*), according to which Christ takes upon himself the sinful nature of humanity and bestows his own righteousness upon that humanity. Reconciliation involves not only forgiveness of sins and freedom from bondage, but in particular, new life in union with God.[79] Hunsinger points out that Torrance presents five features of the atonement as faithful to the New Testament: (1) *self-giving*: the self-giving of the Son through the Father for the sake of the world; (2) *exchange*: the wondrous exchange that takes place between the innocent one for the guilty; (3) salvation *from* something: from the consequences of sin and the bondage to evil and death; (4) salvation *for* something: for participation in the eternal life of the Trinity; and finally (5) *initiative*: the whole process of reconciliation derives from the initiative of God's love.[80] According to Torrance,

---

[78] Barth uses all these designations throughout his discussion of union with Christ in *CD*, IV/3.2, pp. 538–49.

[79] Torrance, *The Trinitarian Faith*, p. 180.

[80] George Hunsinger, *Disruptive Grace: Studies in the Theology of Karl Barth* (Grand Rapids: Eerdmans, 2000), pp. 30–34. Hunsinger also notes the same sequence in

the prospective aspect of atonement fills out the retrospective aspect[81] so that this blessed or wonderful exchange involves the 'redemptive translation of man *from* one state *into* another brought about by Christ who in his self-abnegating love took our place that we might have his place, becoming what we are that we might become what he is'.[82] Atoning or reconciling exchange (*katallagē*) is thus central and forms a *leitmotif* running throughout Torrance's soteriology.[83]

According to Torrance:

> Theological expression was early given to this redemptive translation as the 'exchange' (ἀνταλλαγη) effected between God and sinful humanity described by the New Testament term for 'reconciliation' (καταλλαγη), thereby bringing out its profound import as 'atoning exchange'. Thus the unknown author of the Epistle to Diognetus spoke of 'the sweet exchange' (γλυκεια ἀνταλλαγη)...at the same time this concept of atoning exchange was linked to that of 'sacrificial exchange' (ἀνταλλαγμα) which brought out further its substitutionary significance.[84]

By means of a 'wonderful exchange', 'reconciling exchange', 'atoning exchange', 'sweet exchange', or 'atoning propitiation', all terms Torrance uses,[85] Christ takes what is his and gives it to fallen humanity and takes what is ours and heals, restores, forgives, and judges it within his own being and life.[86]

What is the relation between the *unio mystica* already considered and the doctrine of the *mirifica commutatio*? Taking his lead from Scripture and patristic thinkers, Torrance uses the concept of reconciling or wonderful exchange as a bridge idea between the *unio mystica* and a fully-fledged doctrine of *theosis*.[87] A failure to understand this aspect of Torrance's theology is a failure to understand any of it. Torrance reminds us that 'It is, then, upon this concept of atoning exchange as its inner hinge that the whole doctrine of incarnational redemption through the descent (καταβασις) and ascent (ἀναβασις), the death and resurrection, the humiliation and

---

the theology of Hans urs von Balthasar, cf. *Theo-Drama*, vol. 4 (San Francisco: Ignatius, 1994), pp. 240–44; 317–19.

81 See Chapter 2 , pp. 53–5.

82 Torrance, *The Trinitarian Faith*, p. 179 (italics in original).

83 Colyer, *How To Read T.F. Torrance*, p. 93, agrees that: 'Atoning exchange is at the center of Torrance's understanding of incarnational redemption.'

84 Torrance, *The Trinitarian Faith*, pp. 179–80.

85 Thomas F. Torrance, *Preaching Christ Today* (Grand Rapids: Eerdmans, 1994), pp. 32–4.

86 See Torrance, *Theology in Reconciliation*, p. 167.

87 Torrance derives the concept of 'exchange' from Scripture (especially such texts as Rom 5.15–21; 2 Cor 5.21, 8.9; Gal 3.27; Heb 4.14–15.10; 9.26–8), and from the early church where from the second century the theme of the 'wonderful exchange' (*admirabile commercium*) is found.

exaltation, of the Son of God rests'.[88] Yeung rightly concludes, 'in this way a set of intrinsic relations between God, Christ and humanity becomes the main pattern of the faith, with the dynamics of reconciling exchange at its heart'.[89]

Torrance identifies the 'wonderful exchange' with certain elements of Irenaeus's doctrine of recapitulation[90] and Calvin's *mirifica commutatio*.[91] Anticipating more recent interpretation Torrance sees Luther's soteriology as emphasising much the same elements of an atoning exchange.[92] According to Mannermaa, at the heart of Luther's soteriology lies the doctrine of participation understood as a 'happy exchange'. In Luther's theology what takes place between Christ and the believer is a communication of identifying properties where the righteousness of Christ is exchanged for the sin, death, and curse of the sinner: 'Because faith involves a real union with Christ and because Christ is the divine person, the believer does indeed participate in God.'[93] In a particularly clear passage in the *Church Postil*, Luther presents a doctrine of *theosis* as follows:

> This is one of those apposite, beautiful, and (as St. Peter says in 2 Pet 1) precious and very great promises given to us, poor miserable sinners: that we are to become participants of the divine nature and be exalted so high in nobility that we are not only to become loved by God through Christ, and have His favor and grace as the highest and most precious shrine, but also to have Him, the Lord Himself, dwelling in us in His fullness. Namely (he wants to say), His love is not to be limited only to the removal of His wrath from upon us, and to having the fatherly heart which is merciful to us, but we are also to enjoy this love…and gain great benefit and riches from it.[94]

---

88 Torrance, *The Trinitarian Faith*, p. 180.

89 Yeung, *Being and Knowing*, p. 205.

90 Irenaeus, *Adv. Haer.,* 5. *praef.*, 'Out of his measureless love our Lord Jesus Christ has become what we are in order to make us what he is himself', cited in Torrance, *The Trinitarian Faith*, pp. 156, 179. Also see Athanasius, *Con. Apol.*, 1.17; *De inc.*, 54. Cf. Torrance, *The Trinitarian Faith*, p. 188, fn. 147.

91 For a clear example see Calvin, *Institutes*, 4.17.2.

92 Torrance points out that this theme is common in Luther's works, citing *Tr. De lib. Christ*, *WA*, pp. 7, 25f, and that even the Roman Missal calls this the *mirabile commercium* (wonderful trade). Torrance, *Preaching Christ Today*, p. 32. See also *Karl Barth: Biblical and Evangelical Theologian* (Edinburgh: T & T Clark, 1990), p. 204. On Luther see Introduction, pp. 10.

93 Tuomo Mannermaa, 'Justification and *Theosis* in Lutheran-Orthodox Perspective', in *Union With Christ: The New Finnish Interpretation of Luther*, eds Carl E. Braaten, and Robert W. Jenson (Grand Rapids: Eerdmans, 1998), p. 32.

94 Cruciger's *Summer Postil* 1544, cited in Mannermaa, 'Justification and *Theosis* in Lutheran-Orthodox Perspective', pp. 33–4.

Torrance rejects the idea that propitiation relates to a just God placating his own wrath through the exaction of the death of his Son on the cross. Propitiation has to do with 'the two-way movement on the part of God who in his prevenient love freely draws near to us in order to draw us near to himself on the ground of the atoning self-sacrifice of Christ offered for us'.[95] And further, 'Any adequate account of the atoning life and work of Christ must consider it from two aspects, the life and faithfulness of the Incarnate Son toward man, and the life and faithfulness of the Incarnate Son toward the Father'.[96] Torrance's soteriology, like his christology, is centred on the Person of the incarnate Son.[97]

While it is true that on the cross God's inexorable opposition to sin is exhibited, it is evident as much in forgiveness as in judgement. God's judgement is based on his holiness and has a redemptive as well as a condemnatory aspect and so his judgement is finally a manifestation and instrument of his grace as much as his wrath.[98] From Mackintosh, Torrance learnt 'to think of the wrath of God as the obverse of the moral passion of his love when he stooped down to suffer in behalf of men and bring them forgiveness at unspeakable cost to himself; and it was always on this ground that he exposed the moral superficiality and soteriological deficiency of any attempt to eliminate the notion of wrath from the doctrine of God'.[99] Whether this is how propitiation is used within Scripture or the tradition is not of immediate concern, how Torrance interprets the term 'propitiation' for his own purposes is.

The expression 'atoning propitiation' is another way Torrance explains how the sinner is saved by grace.

> It is only on the ground of the reconciliation with God effected through the cross that the Holy Spirit is mediated to us, and it is only as Christ Himself is mediated to us through the presence of the Spirit that we may be united to Christ in his vicarious humanity and participate in the fruit of his saving and redeeming work.[100]

Here we find in more exact terms the theology that underlies *theosis*: the exchanging of sin for holiness; a saving knowledge of God as Father; and access to the inner relations of the triune Being.

---

[95] Torrance, 'The Atonement the Singularity of Christ', p. 242. The influence of Macleod Campbell is here unmistakably present.

[96] Torrance, 'The Atoning Obedience of Christ', p. 65.

[97] This is elaborated on in Thomas F. Torrance, 'Hugh Ross Mackintosh: Theologian of the Cross', *Scottish Bulletin of Evangelical Theology* 5 (1987), p. 168.

[98] Ibid., p. 169.

[99] Ibid.

[100] Torrance, 'The Atonement the Singularity of Christ', p. 243.

> It is not too much to say, then, that a proper understanding of God as Father, Son and Holy Spirit takes place only within the movement of atoning propitiation whereby God himself draws near to us and draws us near to himself and thereby enables us to have communion with him in his inner trinitarian relations, for it is only within that two-way movement of divine reconciliation that God's self-giving and self-revealing to mankind achieve their full end.[101]

What we find again is a constitutive doctrine of *theosis* at the centre of Torrance's soteriology. While the technical vocabulary is used sparingly, the theological foundations are clearly in place and the various aspects that contribute to such a doctrine are unmistakably articulated.

The life *and* death of Jesus Christ form the *locus* of redemption. Jesus Christ is the response of God to humanity and of humanity to God, so in him we have salvation and in him we have union and communion with God. For Torrance, union with God is 'in and through Jesus Christ in whom our human nature is not only saved, healed and renewed but lifted up to participate in the very light, life and love of the Holy Trinity'.[102] Here we see the vital link between the wonderful exchange and *theosis*. As Colyer succinctly puts it: 'The atoning exchange *is* incarnational redemption, and incarnational redemption *is* atoning exchange, all worked out in the one person of the incarnate Son of God within the twisted depths of our fallen humanity.'[103]

So profound is the doctrine of exchange for Torrance that it comes to embrace the whole relationship between Christ and the believer, as illustrated by his employment of Gregory Nazianzen's statement:

> Let us become like Christ, since Christ became like us. Let us become divine for his sake, since he for ours became man. He assumed the worst that he might give us the better; he became poor that we through his poverty might be rich; he took upon himself the form of a servant that we might receive back our liberty; he came down that we might be exalted; he was tempted that we might conquer; he was dishonoured that he might glorify us; he ascended that he might draw us to himself, who were lying low in the fall of sin. Let us give all, offer all, to him who gave himself a ransom and reconciliation for us.[104]

---

101 Ibid., p. 243.

102 Torrance, *The Mediation of Christ*, p. 66.

103 Colyer, *How To Read T.F. Torrance*, p. 94 (italics in original).

104 Torrance, *The Trinitarian Faith*, pp. 180–81, citing Gregory of Nazianzus, *Or.*, 1.5. Torrance also points the reader to Athanasius, *Con. Ar.*, 1.41; 4.6–7; *De decr.*, 14; *Ad. Epict., 6; Ad Adel.*, 4.

The doctrine of *theosis* thus provides a window into Torrance's soteriology, articulated here by means of the concept of 'exchange', opening up other aspects of his theology.[105]

From the concept of exchange Torrance draws a direct link to a doctrine of *theosis* when, in reference to Rom 8.32, he suggests that this speaks of the infinite worth of Christ's sacrifice, which, by the blessed exchange, has the effect of finalising and sealing the ontological relations between every person and Jesus Christ.[106] Why? Precisely because the soteriological exchange takes place within the incarnate Person of the Mediator. Torrance contends, 'That is the staggering truth of the Gospel that so overwhelmed the early church which they sought to express in their doctrine of *theopoiesis*…'.[107]

The Holy Spirit also plays a vital role in Torrance's account of the reconciling exchange and *theosis*: 'for to have the Spirit dwelling in us is to be made partakers of God beyond ourselves. This is made possible through the atoning exchange that took place in the incarnation'.[108] Through the presence of the Holy Spirit we are 'deified', our humanity is lifted up beyond itself into Christ and enjoys a new fullness of human life in blessed communion with the divine.[109] This is a result of what the Spirit accomplished in the life of the incarnate Son. Through Jesus Christ the Spirit descended upon a man and effected the union between human and divine nature. The Holy Spirit is now mediated to believers by and through the humanity of Christ who sanctified himself in the Spirit so that we might be sanctified in him. Torrance explains how the Pentecost event is integrally related to the atonement and united by the concept of *theosis*:

> This twofold movement of the giving and receiving of the Spirit actualised within the life of the incarnate Son of God *for our sakes* is atonement operating within the ontological depths of human being. It constitutes the 'deifying' content of the atoning exchange in which through the pouring out of the same Spirit upon us we are given to participate. The indwelling of the Spirit mediated to us through Christ is the effective counterpart in us of his self-offering to the Father through the eternal Spirit. In other words, Pentecost must be regarded, not as something added on to atonement, but as the actualisation within the life of the Church of the atoning life, death and resurrection of the Saviour.[110]

The hypostatic union is eternally grounded in the communion between the Father, the Son, and the Holy Spirit. It is, in a secondary sense, the 'projection…of that communion in and through Christ into mankind, creating κοινωνια as its

105 Torrance *The Trinitarian Faith*, p. 181, acknowledges this.

106 Ibid., pp. 182–3.

107 Ibid., p. 184, see pp. 188–90.

108 Ibid., p. 189.

109 Ibid.

110 Ibid., p. 190.

counterpart'.[111] It is a trinitarian reality of ontological import.[112] Once again we have an explicit movement from union with Christ to communion with God. The former, union with Christ, is represented by the first stage of *theopoiesis* – *henosis*, Christ's hypostatic union; the latter, communion with God, is the higher theological level in which believers, through the Spirit and in Christ, are in a sort-of-perichoretic communion with the triune God – *theosis*. It is *theosis* that represents the ultimate state of communion with God, which will one day reach perfect expression in the *eschaton*.

The Blessings of Union

Central to all of Torrance's theology is a strong emphasis on grace.[113] According to Torrance a drastic change, if not a revolution, took place during the Reformation in the Western understanding of the doctrine of grace.[114] Going back to Nicene theology the Reformers identified in the incarnate Son and in the Holy Spirit the realisation that the gift and giver are one and the same. The Nicene Creed explicitly states that the Holy Spirit is the 'Lord and Giver of Life who proceeds from the Father and who with the Father and the Son together is glorified and worshipped'. At the Reformation that Nicene principle was applied not only to the Word and Spirit of God but also to the grace of God.[115] Accordingly, Torrance concludes that 'the grace of God given to us in Christ is not some kind of gift that can be detached from Christ, for in his grace it is Christ himself who is given to us. *Properly understood grace is Christ*, so that to be saved by grace alone is to be saved by Christ alone'.[116] This is how Torrance understands the Reformers' use of *sola gratia* – grace alone implies Christ alone.

To illustrate further the revolutionary advance in the Reformation concept of grace Torrance discusses the differences between a Roman Catholic and a Reformed doctrine of grace, utilising the idea of *theosis* as a case study.[117] Roman Catholic theology posits a created grace between God and humanity which Torrance views as deeply Pelagian in its outworking, even if not in its intention. It is Pelagian insofar as there are attendant notions of co-operation and co-redemption implicit in its doctrine of deification. Accordingly, grace becomes a commodity of the church, the church is considered an extension of the incarnation, and the priest becomes a second Christ who mediates grace. In response, Reformed theology associates

---

111 Torrance, *Conflict and Agreement in the Church*, vol. 2, p. 91.

112 The pneumatological aspects of Torrance's theology will be examined in Chapter 4.

113 This has been evident since his doctoral work published as Thomas F. Torrance, *The Doctrine of Grace in the Apostolic Fathers* (Edinburgh: Oliver and Boyd, 1948).

114 Torrance, *Preaching Christ Today*, p. 21.

115 Ibid., p. 20.

116 Ibid. (italics mine).

117 Torrance, *Theology in Reconstruction*, pp. 167–91.

grace specifically with the incarnate Jesus Christ. When the *homoousion* is applied to the grace of the Lord Jesus Christ all distinctions between 'this' and 'that' type of grace with which Roman Catholic theology operates are abolished. Along with the *homoousion* of Nicaea is added the doctrine of the hypostatic union of Chalcedon, for if grace is God's self-giving to us in Christ, then grace must be understood in terms of his human and divine natures as well. 'It is from this point of view that the notion of deification through grace must be tested',[118] writes Torrance. This *test* proves insightful for our study.

In order to examine this christologically, Torrance asks how it is that if, according to Roman doctrine, deification is achieved through grace in union with the divine, the human nature of Jesus is deified? What is the relation of his human nature to his divine nature in deification? In the Roman construction of deification Torrance believes an attempt is being made to go further than the doctrine of the hypostatic union, which pictures the union as taking place *inconfuse*, *immutatabiliter*, *indivise* and *inseparabiliter*. Torrance understands the use of grace in this way to betray a 'Monophysite' error of sinning against the *inconfuse* specifically. Torrance finds a similar 'error' inherent in Lutheran christology of the sixteenth century. Clearly, Torrance is accusing Roman doctrines of deification as advocating a form of mixture between human and divine natures rather than patristic and Reformed doctrines of *theosis* that posit a participation, union, or communion between divinity and humanity.

At the heart of the disparity between Catholic and Protestant conceptions of salvation lay these differing conceptions of grace. The Protestant (specifically Reformed) view emphasises the objective nature of redemption whereby God imputes Christ's righteousness (*dikaiosune*) to others, but does not constitute them as *dikaioi* in themselves. The Catholic view places the stress on the subjective nature of redemption, emphasising the reality of grace at work in the life of the believer so that such believers can be spoken of as *iusti*, recipients of an imparted righteousness. Each side has repeatedly accused the other of some form of heresy: from the Protestant side come claims of Pelagianism, from the Catholic the charge that the Protestant view is a 'legal fiction' which deals merely in external categories.[119] In his discussion of the doctrine of grace Torrance raises *both* objections about *both* groups! This leads us to ask what his view on the matter is. We find in Torrance's theology a familiar appeal to Calvin's soteriology and to Barth.

Due to a one-sided application of certain arguments utilised by Calvin against the erroneous views of Osiander,[120] many scholars in the Reformed tradition are

[118] Ibid., p. 183.

[119] According to Torrance, because of Rome's failure to appreciate the place union with Christ played in Calvin's soteriology they misunderstood his doctrine of justification to be a 'legal fiction'. See Torrance, *Conflict and Agreement in the Church*, vol. 1, pp. 66–7.

[120] This is chronicled in Canlis, 'Calvin, Osiander, and Participation in God', pp. 169–84.

reticent towards any notion of participation in their soteriology. Participation is a central feature in doctrines of *theosis* and so Torrance asks, what is the cause of this reticence? He finds the answer in divergent conceptions of grace. Trevor Hart presents the issue in its wider context:

> The problem with both Catholic and Protestant formulations of the doctrine of grace would seem to be not so much that which each seeks to affirm (for which both can provide considerable biblical warrant) but rather the framework within which they both operate, a framework which tends in practice to separate the person of Christ from his work, and to define salvation as humanity's direct and immediate participation in certain 'benefits' procured by the latter.[121]

From this deficient framework, both sides, in Hart's estimation, are unable to affirm adequately the truth that the human person reconciled to God in Jesus Christ is *simul iustus et peccator*. Hart provocatively writes, 'Do we really possess *iustitia* as Christians, or is the grace which we proclaim to be understood in terms of a cloak which covers a corpse? Is the church a Society of Saints or a School for sinners?'[122] Hart concludes that 'both points of view may be described as "extrinsecist": one makes grace something external to our being, and the other tears it away from its ontological moorings in the humanity of the Saviour; they both ultimately rob his humanness of its true *mediatorial* significance'.[123] We find within Torrance's theology exactly the same critique, something he typically terms the 'Latin Heresy'.[124] For Hart and Torrance alike, the solution is found within Calvin's soteriology:[125] we need to consider the questions of grace and justification again from a strictly *christological* perspective, asking ourselves, 'Who am I in Christ?' The basis for this lies in the already examined doctrine of the *unio cum Christo*. From this foundation Torrance constructs a theology that affirms at the same time a legal declaration *and* the 'deification' of the believer. This deserves our attention.

Declaration and Deification

In his doctrine of reconciliation Torrance offers a discussion of justification that upholds the Reformation insight of imputed righteousness but at the same time

---

121 Trevor Hart, 'Humankind in Christ and Christ in Humankind: Salvation as Participation in Our Substitute in the Theology of John Calvin', *Scottish Journal of Theology* 42 (1989): p. 69.

122 Ibid., p. 69.

123 Ibid.

124 See Torrance, 'Karl Barth and the Latin Heresy', pp. 461–82.

125 Hart, 'Humankind in Christ and Christ in Humankind', p. 70. Hart is influenced by James B. Torrance in this area and this accounts in part for his affinity with Thomas F. Torrance.

incorporates a more dynamic and relational application of the term so that it can be related to sanctification in a meaningful way. To do this the concept of *theosis* is appealed to which, controversially, results in viewing justification as declaration *and* deification. This, Torrance argues, adequately relates justification to sanctification. It is also a way to incorporate glorification as well as other blessings of union with Christ.

Because of his emphasis on incarnational redemption through the saving humanity of Christ, Torrance's doctrine of justification is profoundly shaped by this christology. In addition, given Torrance's emphasis on the prospective aspects of the atonement, it is not surprising that in dealing with justification he considers it from the 'positive side of salvation' and links it to the resurrection.[126] In many ways the resurrection is the starting point for soteriology, and the incarnation can be interpreted in its light.[127] According to Torrance, forgiveness is not just a word of pardon but a word translated into our existence by crucifixion *and* resurrection, by judgement *and* re-creation; it means the sinner is now given a right standing before God and is holy – justified.[128] The believer is even now holy *in Christ.* In stressing the *in Christ* dimension Torrance is exemplifying the sort of 'paradigm shift' called for by Hart:

> What would seem to be required…is for Western theology to undergo a 'paradigm shift', to leave behind the outlook which has been predominant ever since the writings of Tertullian, and to seek to recapture the missing dimension in our soteriology, namely the person of the Saviour himself.[129]

Torrance is insistent in opposing certain dogmas of scholastic Protestantism, seeing justification as not simply a declaratory act, but an actualisation of what is declared. Justification has to do with forgiveness and when forgiven, sinners *are* forgiven.[130] By implication, when 'the Protestant doctrine of justification is formulated only in terms of forensic imputation of righteousness or the non-imputation of sins in such a way as to avoid saying that to justify is to make righteous, it is the resurrection that is being by-passed'.[131] Why is this so? Because the resurrection means that the Word God sent on his mission does not return void but accomplishes that for which he was sent. The resurrection tells us that when God declares someone just, he or she is just on the ground of being in a real union with Christ. It is this

[126] See Torrance, *Theology in Reconstruction*, p. 151.

[127] See his dependence upon Barth in Torrance, *Karl Barth: Biblical and Evangelical Theologian*, pp. 105–10. Lee, *Living in Union With Christ*, p. 123, comes to the same conclusion.

[128] Torrance, *Space, Time and Resurrection*, p. 61.

[129] Hart, 'Humankind in Christ and Christ in Humankind', p. 70.

[130] Torrance, *Space, Time and Resurrection*, p. 62, uses the healing of the paralytic in Mark 2.1–12 to bear this out.

[131] Torrance, *Space, Time and Resurrection*, p. 63.

that leads us to affirm that Torrance articulates what we might term an account of justification as declaration *and* deification.

Forgiveness, intimately associated with justification, is experienced by believers united to Christ in a perichoretic bond in which we partake of all Christ's saving benefits precisely because we partake of Christ. This perichoretic union goes well beyond anything humans can experience with one another, 'for it involves a relation of mutual indwelling and spiritual coalescence between Christ and his people'.[132] On the basis of the resurrection union with Christ is not merely moral: it is a sharing in the inner life of Jesus, being united to him in the wholeness of his incarnate reality as the crucified and risen Son of God. Thus it is a personal-ontological union.[133] Echoing classical formulations on *theosis* Torrance contends, 'This must include, in some real measure, an intimate assimilation into that inner life through sharing in the power of Christ's resurrection…'.[134]

In Torrance's estimation: 'We require an active relation to Christ as our righteousness, an active and an actual sharing in his righteousness…when we approach justification in this light we see that it is a creative event in which our regeneration or renewal is already included within it.'[135] Torrance then cites Calvin, *Institutes*, 3.1.1–4; 3.3.9; 3.11.6ff. In the *Institutes* several arguments are obviously significant to Torrance. In 3.1.1–4 Calvin speaks of the work of the Holy Spirit in bringing about repentance and union; in 3.3.9 union with Christ is linked not only to Christ's death but also to his resurrection in which we are raised to new life in conformity with the righteousness of God. Calvin properly identifies this work with regeneration – hence he links it with the gift of the Holy Spirit – while Torrance prefers to treat it under the more general topic of justification. In 3.11 justification by faith is treated specifically, and in 3.11.6 righteousness and justification are directly linked so that 'as Christ cannot be divided into parts, so the two things, justification and sanctification, which we perceive to be united together in him, are inseparable'. In 3.11.5ff Calvin is countering a false claim which Osiander terms 'essential righteousness'. Osiander was advocating a 'Latin' doctrine of justification by faith and works, which Calvin equates with semi-Pelagianism. In Torrance's view of justification not simply as a declaratory act but as actually making righteous, one could be forgiven for thinking he was leaning towards a 'Latin' or even semi-Pelagian view of justification himself. However, the use of this passage from Calvin makes clear that this is precisely what he is *not* doing. Rather than confuse Christ's justification and righteousness with our own, Torrance wishes, like Calvin, to discern the inherent link between justification and

---

132 Torrance, 'Hugh Ross Mackintosh: Theologian of the Cross', p. 167.

133 Cf. Torrance, *Conflict and Agreement in the Church*, vol. 2, pp. 63–4; *Conflict and Agreement in the Church*, vol. 2, p. 143; and *Theology in Reconstruction*, pp. 141, 170.

134 Torrance, 'Hugh Ross Mackintosh: Theologian of the Cross', p. 167. Torrance traces this idea back to H.R. Mackintosh and John McLeod Campbell, styling their idea a soteriological restatement of the *unio mystica*.

135 Torrance, *Space, Time and Resurrection*, p. 63.

sanctification so that in being just before God we are actually united to Christ and his work. Thus what is Christ's truly becomes ours. This is yet another instance where the mediation of Christ is thoroughly worked out by Torrance, inspired at this point by Calvin.

Justification is a continuing act in Christ, in whom we are continuously being cleansed, forgiven, sanctified, renewed, and made righteous. This is not to imply that the process is fully completed in the present. This would be to deny the reality of the *eschaton* and of bodily resurrection at the *parousia*. There is a time-lag, in the context of space-time reality, between the resurrection of Christ, the Head of the body, and the resurrection of those who are members of his body. And yet in the power of the Spirit we have union and communion with God through the risen Christ in the present, a taste of the age to come.[136] *Theosis* is the culmination of Torrance's soteriology as he claims it as the effective or prospective aspect of justification.

In his 1960 Presidential address to the Scottish Church Theology Society, Torrance argues that a truly Reformed understanding of justification must go beyond a merely forensic or legal transaction to include the imputation of Christ's righteousness.[137] Torrance is highly critical of the way the *Westminster Catechisms* have separated justification from sanctification and dislocated the concept of union with Christ from justification.[138] Torrance suggests that Latin theology and its understanding of forensic justification has failed to comprehend the re-creation of the sinner effected by Christ's resurrection from the dead and for this reason it deserves the label the 'Latin Heresy'. Justification is not just a cancellation of guilt and the bestowal of a new status. New status is achieved through union with Christ; it is the resurrection of the sinful flesh into the new life of Christ, and thus the believer's holiness is found in Christ's.

> It is an outstanding characteristic of all the documents of the Scottish Reformation that a place of centrality is given to the union of God and Man in Christ, and therefore our 'blessed conjunction' or 'society' or 'fraternity' with Christ. That union with Christ lies at the heart of our righteousness in him, for it is through that union that we actually participate in his holy life.[139]

---

[136] Torrance sees this vividly portrayed in the sacraments. See Chapter 4, pp. 170–85.

[137] Torrance, *Theology in Reconstruction*, pp. 150–68.

[138] Recent Finnish interpretations of Luther criticise the Lutheran *Formula of Concord* on the same grounds. See Peura, 'Christ as Favor and Gift (*donum*): the Challenges of Luther's Understanding of Justification', in *Union With Christ: The New Finnish Interpretation of Luther*, eds Carl E. Braaten and Robert W. Jenson (Grand Rapids: Eerdmans, 1998), pp. 45–8.

[139] Torrance, *Theology in Reconstruction*, p. 151.

Participation or union with God makes us truly holy, not just legally so. 'Justification is not only the forgiveness of sins, but the bestowal of a positive righteousness that derives from beyond us, and which we have through union with Christ.'[140]

When Protestant theologians, especially Reformed ones, speak of justification in this way, the suspicion of Pelagianism, or at least semi-Pelagianism is aroused. Is this what Torrance advocates? Clearly it is not. Of crucial importance here is the idiosyncratic distinction Torrance draws between 'objective' and 'subjective' justification.[141] Objective justification is what has taken place in Christ before the Father and is equated with what the Reformed tradition terms the active obedience of Christ. Subjective justification has also already taken place in Jesus Christ, as he acts as our Substitute and Representative, thus assuming two roles simultaneously – the Justifier and the justified, the Sanctifier and the sanctified, what the Reformed tradition terms the passive obedience of Christ. In this way the active and passive obedience of Christ are held together as are justification and sanctification.[142] Torrance brings these themes into succinct summary in the following:

> Justification has been fulfilled subjectively as well as objectively in Jesus Christ, but that objective and subjective justification is objective to us. It is freely imputed to us by grace objectively and we through the Spirit share in it subjectively as we are united to Christ. His subjective justification becomes ours, and it is subjective in us as well as in him, but only subjective in us because it has been made subjectively real in our own human nature, in our human flesh in Jesus, our Brother, and our Mediator.[143]

Torrance continually stresses what Christ does and who Christ is – and applies the vicarious humanity of Christ to the theme of justification. Thus:

> Justification is not the beginning of a new self-righteousness, but the perpetual end of it, for it is a perpetual living in Christ, from a centre and source beyond us. To be justified is to be lifted up above and beyond ourselves to live out of the risen and ascended Christ, not out of ourselves.[144]

Torrance goes further and regards the term 'justifying faith' as inappropriate because it gives the question of assurance undue prominence. When speaking of 'subjective justification' Torrance is insistent that *our* faith is actually *Christ*'s faith made vicariously for us and so the quest for assurance by means of *our*

---

140 Ibid., pp. 151–2.

141 Ibid., pp. 152–61.

142 Torrance appeals to Calvin, Knox, and the Scottish Presbyterian tradition for upholding these truths against that of Reformed 'scholasticism', epitomized by the *Westminster Catechisms*, ibid., pp. 157–62.

143 Ibid., p. 160.

144 Ibid., p. 152.

faith, as in covenant or federal Calvinism, became an anthropologically-centred abstraction. It is not *our* faith that is determinative for salvation but *Christ*'s.[145] Torrance is critical of Roman Catholics, evangelicals and liberals alike, who, in direct antithesis to a Reformed doctrine of election, rest salvation upon our own personal or existential decision.[146] When Torrance states that in justification we actually *become* righteous his statement has an eschatological orientation. The only full realisation of righteousness is in the man Jesus Christ. Our union with him is what makes us righteous and is the basis upon which justification and sanctification rests.

According to Torrance, incarnation and atonement are intrinsically 'locked into one': 'It is surely in this way that we are to understand the teaching of the New Testament that the Lord Jesus Christ *is himself* our *justification, redemption, mediation and propitiation; he is himself the resurrection and the life*.'[147] We are united to Christ not only in his death but also in his perfect life of filial obedience and love to the Father. This is also what holds justification and sanctification together, and this explains Torrance's unusual appeal to objective and subjective justification.

The logic employed by Torrance, especially in his discussion of how justification is more than simply a declaratory act, is to be found in the theandric nature of Jesus Christ and his role as Mediator. Justification, sanctification, mediation, and propitiation took place principally in the person of the Mediator, not as a third party between God and humanity, for Christ was of one and the same being as God and of one and the same humanity as we are. 'His mediation took place, therefore, both within his ontological relations with God and within his ontological relations with mankind.'[148] Pratz brings out the force of this in relation to justification:

> [T]his essential element in the obedience of the Son is of supreme importance because solely through the hypostatic union Christ gives us not only his negative righteousness, which is the remission of our sins, but also his positive righteousness, which is his life in perfect love, obedience, and filial relationship to the Father…[149]

---

145 See ibid., pp. 159–61.

146 Ibid., p. 162. By a 'Reformed doctrine of election' Torrance implies the priority of God's action in salvation over and against that of human free will. On election see Thomas F. Torrance, 'Predestination in Christ', *Evangelical Quarterly* 13 (1941): pp. 108–41; *The School of Faith*, xi–cxxvi; *Conflict and Agreement in the Church*, vol. 2, pp. 83–8; *Christian Theology and Scientific Culture*, pp. 127–37; and *Scottish Theology from John Knox to John McLeod Campbell*. Torrance's doctrine of election is examined in detail in Habets, 'The Doctrine of Election in Evangelical Calvinism'.

147 Torrance, 'The Atonement the Singularity of Christ', p. 233 (italics in original).

148 Ibid., p. 235.

149 Pratz, 'The Relationship Between Incarnation and Atonement in the Theology of Thomas F. Torrance', par. 20.

This keeps Torrance's doctrine of justification from being simply a forensic non-imputation of sin, the flaw he sees in Western (Latin) doctrines of atonement. It also explains the relationship between justification and sanctification in his theology.

On the basis of the unity between the active and passive obedience of Christ, Torrance contends that in our justification:

> we have imputed to us not only the passive righteousness of Christ in which he satisfied for our sins in suffering the judgment of God in his death on the Cross, but the active righteousness of Christ in which he positively fulfilled the Father's holy will in an obedient life.[150]

The only possible conclusion for Torrance therefore is that justification means more than the non-imputation of our sins through the pardon of Christ, but in its place a positive sharing in his divine-human righteousness. Sanctification is correlative with justification so that to receive the one is to receive the other.

By viewing justification and sanctification as the result of our intimate union with Christ, Torrance shows his commitment to a deeper integrative motif at work behind his soteriology, ordering it, controlling it, and directing it to its ultimate object – Jesus Christ himself. That integrative motif has to do with the participation of believers in the True Man, Jesus Christ, and through Christ with God the Father (in the Holy Spirit). In short, it has to do with *theosis*.

Paul Achtemeier reminds us of a critical feature of Torrance's work: 'Union with Christ involves not simply a participation in the life of Christ, but also a sharing in the *mind* of Christ.'[151] Sharing in the mind of Christ takes on a heuristic force in Torrance's work, pointing the reader back to Jesus Christ himself whose life, thoughts, prayers, and particularly worship become ours in a trinitarian event of transposition. Drawing heavily on John McLeod Campbell's theology, Torrance contends that the believer is brought 'within the circle of the life of Christ', to know, love, and worship God.[152] According to Torrance, to reject the view that the believer is granted, in justification, access to the mind of the incarnate Christ is to fall foul to Apollinarianism, with its rejection of a real human soul and rational mind in Christ.[153]

By means of the Holy Spirit we have access through Christ to the Father, who creates a oneness of mind and will between believers and the triune God. 'Coming to us from the incarnate, crucified, risen and ascended Christ the Holy Spirit enables us to enter through the veil of the flesh of Christ into the holiest,

---

150 Torrance, *Theology in Reconstruction*, p. 155.

151 P. Mark Achtemeier, 'The *Union with Christ* Doctrine in Renewal: Movements of the Presbyterian Church (USA)', in *Reformed Theology: Identity and Ecumenicity*, eds Wallace M. Alston and Michael Welker (Grand Rapids: Eerdmans, 2003), p. 340.

152 Torrance, *Theology in Reconciliation*, p. 139. Torrance notes he could have taken the same idea from H.R. Mackintosh.

153 Torrance, *Theology in Reconciliation*, p. 140.

and connects us with Christ as he dwells in the immediate presence of God in unbroken communion with him.'

It is because justification and sanctification are commensurate within Torrance's theology that he can articulate a theology of declaration *and* deification. How successfully he does this, however, requires some examination of the coherence of justification and *theosis* in his work.

The coherence of justification and theosis Before closing this discussion of justification we must further enquire whether holding together the doctrines of justification and theosis can meaningfully be called Reformed theology. The recent comment by Kärkkäinen is significant:

> [A]ny expert on Reformation theology would have a hard time trying to reconcile the idea of *theosis* with the doctrine of justification. Historically, these two traditions have been considered to be diametrically opposed to each other.[154]

Kärkkäinen then attempts a synthesis within his own Lutheran-Pentecostal context. Lutheranism has been open to seeing justification and *theosis* as compatible for two reasons, first, the result of ecumenical dialogue and second, the 'Manermaa school's' reinterpretation of Luther.[155] According to Torrance, doctrines of justification and *theosis* can be reconciled for they are, in fact, not mutually exclusive. However, a 'Reforming' of *theosis* is required if the two traditions are to come together coherently. While Torrance has indicated the direction in which this theology might proceed, his is certainty not the final word on the issue.[156]

Torrance downplays the juridical or forensic elements in his soteriology, especially where one might most expect to see these features, in a doctrine of justification. While he is surely right to argue against an over-emphasis on juridical elements in contemporary Reformed soteriology, he does tend to obscure the fact that the New Testament language of justification (*dikaiosune* and its cognates) carries a forensic character that cannot be removed without doing violence to the

---

[154] Veli-Matti Kärkkäinen, 'Grace and the Ecumenical Potential of Theosis', in *Toward a Pneumatological Theology: Pentecostal and Ecumenical Perspectives on Ecclesiology, Soteriology, and Theology of Mission*, ed. Amos Yong (Lanham: University Press of America, 2002), p. 149.

[155] See *Dialogue between Neighbours: The Theological Conversations between the Evangelical-Lutheran Church of Finland and the Russian Orthodox Church 1970-1986*, ed. Hannu Kamppuri (Helsinki: Luther-Agricola Society, 1986); *Salvation in Christ: A Lutheran-Orthodox Dialogue*, eds John Meyendorff and Robert Tobias (Minneapolis: Augsburg, 1992), and Risto Saarinen, 'Salvation in the Lutheran-Orthodox Dialogue: A Comparative Perspective', in *Union With Christ: The New Finnish Interpretation of Luther*, eds Carl E. Braaten and Robert W. Jenson (Grand Rapids: Eerdmans, 1998), pp. 167–81.

[156] See the exploratory essays by Habets, 'Reforming *Theōsis*'; Murphy, 'Reformed *Theosis*?'; and Habets, 'Reformed *Theosis*? A Critical Reply to Murphy'.

biblical text. While his position is not as radical as Orthodox theologians Lossky and Ware,[157] Torrance does tend to diminish the nature of justification, something that provokes significant critique amongst Western theologians. However, Torrance's appeal to *theosis* is a welcome reminder to Protestant thinkers that even Reformation theologians such as Calvin did not separate justification from sanctification in a way that made the former external and forensic and the latter internal and progressive. Torrance has shown through his employment of both the doctrines of justification and *theosis* that one may coherently hold together a doctrine of salvation in its various tenses (perfect, present and future), *and* anchor them in the incarnate person of the Son.

Justification and *theosis* are complementary, as each plays its part in the process of salvation in Christ.[158] However, unlike a number of thinkers who have sought to account for both justification and *theosis*, Torrance does not see these as two stages in the process of salvation, with justification as the negative side and *theosis* the positive.[159] Neither does he consider justification to be prior to *theosis* within an *ordo salutis*. Torrance's use of *theosis* portrays it as an overarching concept that contains within it the entire dynamic of salvation. As such, justification is an aspect of the metanarrative of *theosis* and so it no longer has a static form as it arguably does in much Protestant orthodoxy. Alternatively, the explicitly dynamic character of justification can be maintained, alongside the other aspects of the *ordo* such as adoption and sanctification when *theosis* functions in the way Torrance employs it.

The introduction of *theosis* to a Western soteriology such as Torrance's removes the doctrine of the *articulus iustificationis* from a central position[160] and affords this place instead to union with Christ, from which flow all the blessings of salvation,

---

157 See, Vladimir Lossky, *Orthodox Theology: An Introduction*, trans. I. and I. Kasarcodi-Watson (1978. Crestwood, NY.: St Vladimir's Press, 2001); ibid., *The Mystical Theology of the Eastern Church* (1944, Crestwood, NY.: St Vladimir's Seminary Press, 1998); and Kallistos Ware, *How Are We Saved? The Understanding of Salvation in the Orthodox Tradition* (Minneapolis: Light and Life Publishing Company, 1996).

158 The compatibility of Eastern and Western soteriologies is argued by Bradley Nassif, 'Are Eastern Orthodoxy and Evangelicalism Compatible? Yes. [With Responses]', in *Three Views on Eastern Orthodoxy and Evangelicalism*, eds Stanley N. Gundry and James Stamoolis (Grand Rapids: Zondervan, 2004), pp. 25–114.

159 Paul R. *Hinlicky,* 'Theological Anthropology: Toward Integrating Theosis and Justification by Faith', *Journal of Ecumenical Studies* 34 (1997): pp. 38–74; and Lucian Turcescu, 'Soteriological Issues in the 1999 Lutheran-Catholic Joint Declaration on Justification: An Orthodox Perspective', *Journal of Ecumenical Studies* 38 (2001): pp. 64–72, attempt to combine justification and *theosis* as a two-stage process of salvation. See the critique of Turcescu's thesis by Reformed theologian George Vandervelde, 'Justification and Deification – Problematic Synthesis: A Response to Lucian Turcescu', *Journal of Ecumenical Studies* 38 (2001): pp. 73–8.

160 McGrath, *Iustitia Dei*, pp. 219–40, convincingly shows that in Reformation theologians justification never functioned as the *articulus iustificationis* at all. It was, rather, a post-Reformation development.

including justification and sanctification. Torrance grasps a central feature of Calvin's theology, that the question of justification is essentially an aspect of the larger question of humanity's relation to God in Christ, and these need not be discussed exclusively in terms of the category of justification. McGrath credits Calvin for overcoming this weakness inherent in Lutheranism and notes that this is how Scottish theology from Knox to Torrance has generally understood it.[161] The result of including *theosis* in a Reformed soteriology like Torrance's is that salvation is viewed in quite different terms. No longer is salvation thought of as exclusively salvation from sin, alienation, and hostility, although those themes are clearly part of any biblical soteriology. Instead, union, communion and participation are more meaningfully incorporated. A retrospective focus is replaced with a prospective one without losing the strengths of the former. The ultimate goal of salvation is no longer to appease the wrath of an angry God but to attain to participation in the divine life through the Son by the Holy Spirit. This still necessitates judgement on sin and justification of the sinner, but it does not end there. Salvation in a *theosis*-centred soteriology is accomplished by the incarnation in the hypostatic union. It is this perspective which focuses Torrance's theology.

Progress in Theosis

Having established the fundamental nature of salvation as declaration and deification, Torrance's work also articulates how progress in *theosis* may be achieved. He does this by appropriating the concept of *prokope*. The term *prokope* was appropriated by the fathers to refer to the Lukan account of the obedience and development of the child Jesus, who literally 'cut his way' (*proekopten*) as he 'grew in wisdom and favour with God and with men' (Luke 2.52).[162] This reveals, according to Torrance, what amounts to a model of the way of *theosis*. Knowledge is the basis of this aspect of *theosis*: knowledge of God the Father as revealed through God the Son.[163] Jesus Christ is the Truth who has accommodated himself to humanity in an economic condescension. He is also a man who hears and obeys the Divine Word in his incarnate life. As such he provides for us in his own obedient Sonship, within our human nature, the way whereby we are carried up to knowledge of God the Father – the attainment of true life.[164] This is where the use of *prokope* is taken up by Torrance as he cites his favourite work on the Holy Spirit, Basil's *De Spiritu Sancto*:

---

161 Ibid., p. 225, cf. p. 463, fn. 46.

162 The word 'grew' (*prokopto*) is literally a nautical expression meaning 'to beat one's way forward blow by blow', Gustav Stählin', 'προκοπη, προκοπτω', in *TDNT*, eds Gerhard Kittel, Geoffrey W. Bromiley and Gerhard Friedrich (Grand Rapids: Eerdmans, 1964–76), vol. 6, p. 704 (pp. 703–19). The word is also used in middle and later Stoicism to refer to moral progress (p. 706).

163 Torrance, *Theology in Reconstruction*, p. 38.

164 Ibid.

> We understand by Way that advance [*prokope*] to perfection which is made stage by stage, and in regular order, through the works of righteousness and the illumination of knowledge; ever longing after what is before, and reaching forth unto those things which remain, until we shall have reached the blessed end, the knowledge of God, which the Lord through Himself bestows on them that have trusted in Him. For our Lord is an essentially good Way, where erring and straying are unknown, to that which is essentially good, to the Father. For no one, He says, cometh to the Father but through me. Such is our way up to God through the Son.[165]

This is the christological side of *theosis* to which Torrance, by means of Basil, then adds the pneumatological aspect. Christ became incarnate through the operation of the Spirit and it was through the power of the Spirit that he advanced (*proekopte*) through life. This is the 'economy of the Spirit' that complements the 'economy of the Son'. Thus *theosis* moves from christology to pneumatology. The Holy Spirit is considered the 'perfecting cause' who brings Christ and all other creatures to their fulfilment in God and so consummates their creation.[166] This perfecting cause takes place perfectly in the *prokope* of Christ, for since he came to share our human nature and we are united to him through the Spirit whom he gives, it is through the power of the Spirit that we participate in his *prokope*. As a result, those in Christ rise through the Son to true knowledge of and communion with God the Father. This process continues throughout life, for according to Basil and Torrance, it is only in the *eschaton* that God's works of creation and redemption will be brought to their ultimate completion.[167]

Torrance is not alone in appropriating this biblical and patristic concept. His brother James also utilises the idea in order to present a model of incarnational redemption. In an essay in honour of James Torrance, Newell presents two competing models of atonement, the 'subject-centred appropriation model' and the 'object-centred participation model'. The latter is associated with Thomas and James Torrance and the Scottish tradition generally.[168] In endorsing this model Newell argues that it offers us a 'response to Christ's victory which is not cast in terms of our appropriating the benefits of Christ's victory through moral effort or our cessation of effort'. What we have in its place is 'an interior portrait of our participation through the *koinonia* of the Spirit in the one true man who has experienced the agonising conflict between sin and love'.[169] In real terms,

---

165 Basil, *De Spiritu Santo*, 8.18 (not 18.18 as Torrance records it), ibid., pp. 38–9.

166 Here Torrance points us to Basil, *De Spiritu Santo*, 16.38–9.

167 Torrance, *Theology in Reconstruction*, p. 39, see Basil, *De Spiritu Sancto*, 16.39.

168 Roger Newell, 'Participation and Atonement', in *Christ in Our Place: The Humanity of God in Christ for the Reconciliation of the World: Essays Presented to Professor James Torrance*, eds Trevor A. Hart and Daniel P. Thimell (Exeter: Paternoster, 1981), pp. 92–101.

169 Ibid., p. 98.

> When our life's conflicts, failures and triumphs are intersected by the atoning journey of the Son into the far country, our life becomes a pilgrimage of relational union with the One who was made perfect through what he suffered (Heb 5.8). We participate by the Spirit in the Son who bent back our twisted humanity as 'he grew in wisdom, stature and favour with God and man' (Luke 2.52).[170]

Participation in the *prokope* of Christ is used by both Torrance brothers to shed light on certain Pauline emphases found in Phil 1.12; 3.10–11; Acts 14.22; Eph 4.12–16; and 2 Cor 4.8–10, 16.

From his brief study of this term and its application to the atonement theology of Thomas and James Torrance, Newell concludes, 'It is never adequate to merely analyse the atonement intellectually…the twin movements of Christ's participation in our fallen creatureliness and our "blow by blow" participation in his life, death and resurrection cast us loose upon the gracious sea of the Trinity'.[171] Newell is surely right to see in Thomas Torrance's theology a vision of communion with God that goes well beyond the mundane confines of contemporary creaturely being.

The other aspects of the *beneficia Christi* that Torrance argues are parts of the *prokope* of the life in Christ now deserve brief examination. We shall limit our study to what Torrance means by appropriating the biblical language of believers as resurrected 'sons' of God and his exposition of the eschatological *visio Dei* as the *telos* of *theosis*, as these two features summarise much of his thought in this area.

Resurrected 'sons' of God In articulating the way of progress in theosis for the believer united to Christ, Torrance identifies reconciling aspects of the resurrection as yet another witness to communion with the triune God. The resurrection is to adoption, even though adoption is a proleptic reality this side of our resurrection. What makes this possible is the resurrection of Jesus Christ for us: when united to Christ the believer is also, proleptically, adopted.

Torrance asserts in unequivocal terms that human beings remain human beings, even in *theosis*, and it is in the resurrection of the man Jesus Christ, the man in whom our nature is assumed and healed, that redemption is achieved and set forth. 'It is thus the resurrection of our human nature in Christ into communion with the life of God that is the end and goal of atonement.'[172] In Torrance's words, 'resurrection as redemption means the restoration of man in all the fullness of his *humanity*, for it is redemption out of corruption and the lapse toward annihilation into the new being and new life of the new creation'.[173] The resurrection is the

---

[170] Ibid.

[171] Ibid., p. 100.

[172] Torrance, *Space, Time and Resurrection*, p. 67.

[173] Ibid., p. 74. He goes on to add, 'the resurrecting of Jesus is to be thought of as the recreating and restoring of man into the same sphere of real being as that to which we human creatures belong…', ibid., p. 87.

actualising of human reality, the humanising in Jesus of dehumanised humanity. Torrance summarises this ontological aspect:

> Now on the ground of the resurrection, and its final rejection of all contradiction between God and man, and therefore in its rejection of all negation of being in judgment, we can really believe that *man is*, that man is man. He is the creature God made him to be and may not now cease to be what he is. He is man in living communion with the creative Source of life. The resurrection of Jesus Christ and of human nature in him is therefore the foundation and source of a profound and radically new Christian humanism.[174]

In this way what God initiated at creation is finalised in the resurrection of Jesus Christ.

Reconciliation is nothing other than the everlasting union of God and humanity *in* Christ Jesus and God and humanity *with* Christ Jesus. The resurrection is the capstone to the work of Christ, the completion of all that was done for us in his life and death, so that he is our peace and our reconciliation. Christ is the living reconciliation in the form of personal being and reality in God.[175]

Reformed theology typically includes the glorification as the final aspect of the *ordo salutis* and Torrance, as a Reformed theologian, is no different. However, he speaks more of *resurrection* than of *glorification*, though it is clear that he means the same thing by this expression. This is not to imply that he collapses the resurrection into glorification, but he sees the one as integrally bound up with the other as one movement of glorification in two stages. Resurrection is to glory – thus the glorification of humanity through the exaltation of Jesus Christ forms the climax of Torrance's *ordo salutis*.[176]

---

174 Ibid., p. 79.

175 Ibid., p. 69.

176 Whether or not Torrance has a formal *ordo salutis* is debated. Lee, *Living in Union With Christ*, p. 214, argues that Torrance does not have one, while Colyer, *The Nature of Doctrine in T.F. Torrance's Theology*, p. 150, asserts that he does. It is evident that Torrance does offer at least a rudimentary *ordo salutis*, in the sense that he distinguishes between various aspects of reconciliation and an implicit logical and chronological articulation of them. From the foundational event of union with Christ several corollaries follow, and it is these corollaries which we may view as an *ordo salutis* in Torrance's work. Each aspect of the *ordo* is in effect an aspect of *theosis*, culminating in ultimate communion with God in glory. Cf. Torrance, *Conflict and Agreement in the Church*, vol. 2, p. 65; and *Theology in Reconstruction*, pp. 157–61; Torrance, *Scottish Theology from John Knox to John McLeod Campbell*, pp. 128–9; and James B. Torrance, 'Strengths and Weaknesses of the Westminster Theology', in *The Westminster Confession in the Church Today: Papers Presented for the Church of Scotland Panel on Doctrine*, ed. Alasdair I.C. Heron (Edinburgh: St Andrew Press, 1982), pp. 40–53.

When Christ comes again, we shall see him in his glory and in that seeing we shall know as we are known and so we shall become like him.[177] The resurrection of believers at the last day is not to an incorporeal spirit-state, but a physical resurrection like Christ's. To be spiritual is not to be *less* human but *more fully* and *truly* human, as it was for Christ before us.[178] As our Head, Christ's life experience will one day be that of those united to him by the Holy Spirit: as he was raised to newness of life and into a glorified state so we too will be. Torrance reminds us that as surely as in Holy Communion we eat the bread and drink the wine which become assimilated into our own physical existence, so surely we who partake of the body and blood of Christ given for us will rise with him out of the grave into newness of life, attaining at last the redemption of the body in the new creation.[179] Here Torrance echoes what the early Christians thought to be an indispensable aspect of *theosis*: that finite human beings can, in Christ and through the Holy Spirit, attain immortality.

The resurrection has the effect of initiating and achieving the adoption of women and men, a central theme in any doctrine of *theosis*. Torrance notes that adoption is more biblically termed *sonship* through Christ (Rom 8.15, 23; Gal 3.26, 4.5–7; Eph 1.5).[180] Accordingly, our human nature is now set within the Father-Son relationship. Through faith in Christ and union with him we share brotherhood with him and experience in him the Fatherhood of God, and in and through him we share in the Spirit of the living God. Unlike much post-Reformation theology, Torrance (along with Calvin and Jonathan Edwards) identifies adoption and justification as parallel benefits and not simply of adoption as the *result* of justification.[181] In making such a move Torrance replaces the overly juridical union evident in some Reformed soteriology with personal union as the centre of his soteriology.[182]

Here we see classical formulations of *theosis* again coming to the fore: participation in the divine Being while remaining human beings; communion with

---

177 Torrance, *Space, Time and Resurrection*, p. 140.

178 Myk Habets, 'Naked but Not Disembodied: A Case for Anthropological Duality', *Pacific Journal of Baptist Research* 4 no. 1 (2008), pp. 33–50.

179 Torrance, *Space, Time and Resurrection*, p. 142. Torrance cites Ignatius, *Epistle to the Ephesians*, 20.2; Serapion, *Euchologion*, 17.2; and Clement of Alexandria, *Protrepticos*, 10, who speak of the Eucharist as 'the medicine of immortality'.

180 On 'sonship' and 'adoption' see Eduard Schweizer, 'υἱος, υἱοθεσια', in *TDNT*, 8, pp. 382–4, 389–91; and 397–9; Brendan Byrne, *'Sons of God'– 'Seed of Abraham': A Study of the Idea of the Sonship of God of all Christians against the Jewish Background* (Rome: Biblical Institute, 1979); and James M. Scott, *Adoption as Sons of God: An Exegetical Investigation into the Background of* ΥΙΟΘΕΣΙΑ *in the Corpus Paulinum* (Tübingen: J.C.B. Mohr, 1992).

181 See for example, Francis Turretin, *Institutes of Elenctic Theology*, 3 vols trans. George M. Giger, ed. James T. Dennison (Phillipsberg: Presbyterian and Reformed, 1992–7), pp. XVI.4–6.

182 See the discussion on adoption in Chapter 4, pp. 162–5.

the Father of the Son by means of the Spirit; and adoption as 'sons' to participate in the Triune communion of love. Torrance himself makes this link when he relates the work of adoption to the Triune communion prayed for by Christ in the high-priestly prayer of John 17 and again in the Epistle to the Hebrews (4.14; 9.24). In these texts it is suggested that through the consecrated bonds of our union with Christ we are made to share in the union of the Son with the Father.[183] 'It is not surprising', concludes Torrance, 'that this could be spoken of as the exaltation of man to be a partaker of the life and love that God is, and thereby to be a partaker of divine nature.'[184]

The resurrection of Christ secures the adoption/sonship of believers and is the 'first fruits' (1 Cor 15.20) of our resurrection. It also has other effects. One in particular stands out for Torrance, the ultimate goal of *theosis* – a nuanced version of the *visio Dei.*

The visio Dei The theme of light occupies an exalted place in the Christian tradition, with notable roots in the New Testament's Johannine literature which defines God as Light which is foreign to all darkness (1 Jn 1.5), to Christ as the Light of the world who sends out his disciples to be as lights to the world (Jn 8.12; cf. Mt 5.14–16). The New Testament is also unanimous in its teaching that the saints and angels see God's face directly (Mt 18.10; 1 Cor 13.12; 1 Jn 3.2). The Nicene Creed represents the Son as Light proceeding out of Light. These themes have played an important part in the Christian tradition, especially within Byzantine Christianity, and have been intimately linked with doctrines of theosis.

Two examples of this may suffice. First, if God reveals himself to humanity as Light, and is able to be anticipated by them, can he also be inaccessible and transcendent, as Scripture affirms? This was the question put to the Hesychasts by Barlaam the Calabrian in the form of a bitter accusation. The Hesychast monk Gregory Palamas (1296–1359) answered Barlaam in his *Apodictic Treatises* (1336); *Triads in Defense of the Holy Hesychasts* (1338–41); and *Hagioretic Tome* (1340). Essential to his reply was the distinction between the *essence* and *energies* of God. Torrance rejects this distinction in favour of a more personalistic account, though he never ventured a full-scale critique of the distinction, perhaps on account of his close relations with the Eastern Orthodox Churches.[185] Second, within Reformed theology this is also evident, for instance, when Jonathan Edwards spoke analogously of *theosis* as the shining forth of light. Edwards once described believers as 'little suns, partaking of the nature of the fountain of their light'.[186]

---

183 Torrance, *Space, Time and Resurrection*, pp. 69–70.

184 Ibid., p. 70 (corrected).

185 See Vladimir Lossky, *The Vision of God*, 2nd edn, trans. Asheleigh Moorhouse, (Crestwood: St Vladimir's Seminary, 1973), pp. 25–44; and *The Mystical Theology of the Eastern Church*, pp. 217–35; and Torrance, *The Christian Doctrine of God*, pp. 187–8.

186 Paul Ramsey, in Jonathan Edwards, *Ethical Writings: The Works of Jonathan Edwards*, vol. 8, ed. P. Ramsey (New Haven, Yale University Press, 1989), pp. 343 and

According to Torrance, for Christ to be Light necessitates his being Word also, the two being hypostatically related. 'The very Light of God could not be consistently Light', he writes, 'and certainly could not be known as such, if Jesus Christ were not also Word of Word as well as Light of Light, and thus immutably, eternally God of God as both Light and Word.'[187] This conclusion is drawn from the deduction that if Jesus Christ is of one and the same being with God (*homoousios*) as incarnate Son, this must apply to him also as incarnate *Word* of God.[188] This is consistent with the tenor of Torrance's method and theology: what God is toward us in his self-revelation in Jesus Christ as the Word made flesh, he is in his own divine being.

Torrance forcefully reasons that 'God is himself the supreme Light, unapproachable and invisible', and yet, 'he is illuminatingly present in the world of thought'.[189] How? God is visible through the things he has made but is only knowable through the incarnate Word of God, Jesus Christ. True knowledge of God, even of his uncreated and invisible Light, is 'seen' and 'known' only in Christ. 'Through the mystery of the invisibility of light God guards and reflects the mystery of his own invisible Light before which our creaturely finite minds falter and fail, but nevertheless he allows us, as St Paul expressed it, to "see" him darkly or indirectly as in a mirror.'[190]

Drawing heavily on the insights of John Philoponos of Alexandria and John of the Cross, Torrance develops a theology of light – both scientifically and theologically. God is unapproachable in the radiance of his pure light. As one cannot look at the sun and see, one cannot see God and live. According to John of the Cross, this is so for two reasons: first, God is unapproachable because of the sheer invisibility of his uncreated Light. God is infinite and transcendent and our finite capacities have no means by which we may see or comprehend this Light. Second, 'God is unapproachable for us because of the inability of our impure minds to bear the sheer purity of his divine Light'.[191] The utter holiness of God that consumes all evil and impurity overwhelms the sight of the sinner.

Torrance draws from this the following significant conclusions concerning knowledge of God: first, God must establish a degree of reciprocity between himself and humankind in which his uncreated Light adapts itself to the lowly understanding of fallen minds so that men and women may be elevated to communion with God in such a way that they may have access to him beyond

---

347. See Michael J. McClymont, 'Salvation as Divinization: Jonathan Edwards, Gregory Palamas and the Theological Uses of Neoplatonism', in *Jonathan Edwards: Philosophical Theologian*, eds Paul Helm and Oliver D. Crisp (Aldershot: Ashgate, 2003), pp. 136–60.

[187] Torrance, *Christian Theology and Scientific Culture*, p. 107.

[188] Torrance cites John Reuchlin (1455–1522), the German humanist and great-uncle of Philip Melanchthon, as first articulating this connection. Ibid., p. 106.

[189] Ibid., p. 87.

[190] Ibid., p. 91.

[191] Ibid., p. 93.

their creaturely capacities.[192] This is a clear statement of *theosis* defined as the 'elevation' of the person to communion with God.[193]

Second, the reconciliation accomplished between God and humanity must ensure that guilt is expiated, sin is forgiven, and defilement is removed so that our minds may be equipped to 'see' the divine Light. This is accomplished through the 'two-fold [*sic*] relationship between God and humanity mediated through the incarnation and passion of God's beloved Son in Jesus Christ'.[194] In Christ the invisible Light of God is made visible and the 'indissoluble oneness' with the eternal Word and Love of God is made accessible to humankind. Jesus Christ is the 'Light of the world', and it is only in and through him that we are enlightened and may see and know the invisible God. Jesus Christ is thus 'Light of Light' and 'God of God'; the two terms being synonymous, 'thus he constitutes in the reality of his divine-human person both the invisible radiation and the creaturely reflection of the eternal Light which God is'.[195] By becoming one with us in our human nature and condition the incarnate Son is both the eternal Word of God and a human word, both the uncreated Light of God and created light, in the indivisible unity of his life and person.

Using the analogy of light Torrance extends his doctrine of *theosis* to include the idea that Jesus Christ is both 'luminous Word' and 'audible Light'.[196] In sermonic tone, Torrance writes:

> Jesus was completely and absolutely *transparent* with the Light of God. There was no darkness in him, nothing unreal, no deceit, no insincerity. He was utterly true and genuine, *translucent* with the sheer Truth of God himself, the one point in human existence where the divine Light shines through to the world purely and truly, unimpeded and unclouded by any distortion or refraction. Far from being less human because of that, he was more human than any other, indeed perfectly human, for with him the divine Light which is the source of all human life and light had its perfect way. He was so perfectly the man that he ought to have been that there was no gap in his nature resulting from a lapse from true humanity, as a result of which he was obliged to be what he was not but ought to be. The union between his human life and the humanising Light of the Creator was unbroken, so that it is through him that the eternal uncreated Light of God shines through to us.[197]

---

192 Ibid.

193 Torrance directly connects a theology of light to the concept of *theosis* in *The Trinitarian Faith*, p. 139, fn. 102.

194 Torrance, *Christian Theology and Scientific Culture*, p. 94. Torrance then draws on and updates Irenaeus's commentary on the prologue of St John's Gospel (ibid., p. 95).

195 Ibid., p. 95.

196 Ibid., p. 101.

197 Ibid., p. 96 (italics added).

To avoid misunderstanding Torrance adds, 'Jesus was not just the most perfect man, the most human being that ever lived, shot through and through with divine Light, but God himself in his divine Light living among us as man'.[198]

'Transparency' in this discussion functions as an analogy for *theosis*.[199] The experience of *theosis* is similar to a sense of *transparency*. The goal of *theosis* is to *reflect* God's uncreated Light fully and completely, without spot or blemish; to *mirror* God absolutely. This is not possible for the darkened sinful vessels that we are and consequently only in the incarnate Light of the Son is *theosis* realised.

> It is the living Light of God himself actively lived out among us as a human life, which continues to bear directly, personally, intimately upon the ontological depths of our human existence, searching, judging, cleansing, healing and renewing, and remains for ever the one light-bearing and life-giving Life for all mankind.[200]

The incarnate Son of God is the light of God and the light of the world and it is only as one is united to this light that one can apprehend it, reflect it, and *be* light oneself.[201] Torrance concludes, 'Since it is in this enlightening and saving Life of the crucified and risen Jesus that the eternal Light and Life of God himself are mediated to us in a form in which we can share in death as well as life, it is through union and communion with Jesus that we are enabled to see the invisible God and live'.[202]

All the familiar themes of *theosis* are represented here, this time 'illuminated' by a theology of light (pun intended). This is a remarkable description on Torrance's part, one that cuts through much of the confusion and debate between Eastern and Western views of mystical knowing and the role of light, and brings to the fore the christological aspects of *theosis*.[203] Christ alone is the true human and he alone is able to participate fully in the divine nature, for he shares that nature in his hypostatic union. Through participating in the humanity of Jesus Christ the

---

198 Ibid., p. 97.

199 There is an interesting parallel in the doctrine of *theosis* articulated by Jonathan Edwards recorded in Edwards, *Ethical Writings; The Works of Jonathan Edwards*, vol. 8, p. 640.

200 Torrance, *Christian Theology and Scientific Culture*, p. 97.

201 Clive S. Lewis, 'The Weight of Glory', in *Screwtape Proposes a Toast and Other Pieces* (London: Fontana, 1965), pp. 106–7, presents the same thought in his discussion of glorification. See Myk Habets, 'Walking *In Mirabilibus Supra Me*: How C.S. Lewis Transposes *Theosis*' (unpublished paper).

202 Torrance, *Christian Theology and Scientific Culture*, p. 99. On the biblical paradox of being able to 'see and not see' God consult Andrew S. Moore, 'The Invisibllity of God: A Survey of a Misunderstood Phenomenon', *Evangelical Quarterly* 79 (2007): pp. 311–29.

203 For more on Torrance's position on 'mystery' and 'mysticism' see Yeung, *Being and Knowing*, p. 191; Richardson, 'Revelation, Scripture, and Mystical Apprehension of Divine Knowledge', pp. 185–203; and Habets, 'Thomas Forsyth Torrance: Mystical Theologian *Sui Generis*'.

believer is also drawn into the Light and life of God, 'deified' without losing his or her created humanity in the process. To see God is to know God, and to know God is to know the incarnate Son who has made him known. 'But we all, with unveiled face, beholding as in a mirror the glory of the Lord, are being transformed into the same image from glory to glory, just as from the Lord, the Spirit' (2 Cor 3.18).

Conclusion: Reforming *Theosis*?

Before concluding this chapter the question of the compatibility of *theosis* and the Reformed tradition needs to be addressed.[204] In a provocative essay entitled 'The End of Reformed Theology?' Bruce McCormack suggests that for a theology to be 'Reformed' it must be able to be illustrated through the Reformed Confessions, and not simply by appeal to the early church or Calvin.[205] In his sights he has several of his 'friends' including Torrance, for he recognises that Torrance has sought to make union with Christ central to his dogmatics and has adopted categories of *theosis* in doing so. McCormack asks, 'Where is there in the soteriologies of T.F. Torrance, Colin Gunton or Mark Achtemeier…any element that might be responsibly called "Reformed"? He adds, 'the odd appeal to a few passages from Calvin will hardly suffice for making this case…'.[206] He then concludes:

> It could be that Torrance et al. are right to lift up the theme of 'union with Christ' (construed along lines that stand in very close proximity to the Eastern theosis doctrine) and to make it central to their soteriologies. But my question is: How can the doctrine that emerges from this procedure be justifiably called 'Reformed'?[207]

In response we may note several things. First, while there is certainly considerable logic to McCormack's argument, other essays of the same volume in which his comments appear point out that the Reformed tradition has no single confession which is binding on all the churches, nor is it a static tradition, but one which takes seriously *reformata sed semper reformanda* ('Reformed but always needing to reform'), the principle that the church should always be striving to conform to Scripture. While the *Westminster Confession* in particular is clearly prominent even it does not hold an exclusive place in Reformed theology. Second, Reformed theology holds up the Word of God as its supreme authority and thus appeal to Scripture always carries more weight than appeal to tradition. Third, Reformed

---

204 What follows is a partial defence. See further in Habets, 'Reforming *Theōsis*'; Murphy, 'Reformed *Theosis*?'; and Habets, 'Reformed *Theosis*? A Critical Reply to Murphy'

205 Bruce L. McCormack, 'The End of Reformed Theology? The Voice of Karl Barth in the Doctrinal Chaos of the Present', in *Reformed Theology: Identity and Ecumenicity*, eds Wallace M. Alston and Michael Welker (Grand Rapids: Eerdmans, 2003), pp. 46–64.

206 Ibid., p. 51, fn. 10.

207 Ibid.

theology is more than the sum total of its confessions as it includes the thinking of its church doctors, ministers, churchmen and women. Finally, Torrance, as has been shown, does not simply call upon the early church or Calvin, but appeals to diverse sources, not least Scripture, and repeatedly draws upon the theology evident in his own Scottish Reformed tradition to make his case.[208] While questions remain over the accuracy of Torrance's reading of the tradition, in drawing on such a range of Reformed doctors and confessions Torrance certainly appears to meet McCormack's requirements for a truly 'Reformed' theology.

McCormack's criticism appears unfounded. At best his treatment of Torrance is selective. It could be that McCormack lacked the space to work through Torrance's use of Reformed Confessions to prove his point. If he had perhaps he would have pointed to the *French (Gallican) Confession*, penned largely by Calvin and appearing in 1559, the same year as his definitive edition of the *Institutes*. In that *Confession* justification is placed before regeneration and sanctification and omits any mention of union with Christ. McCormack might then have concluded that union with Christ is not central in Calvin's thought or the Reformed confessions. In reply, clearly, no one confession can convey the entire scope of orthodoxy and it is clear that the *French Confession* was meant to supplement the *Institutes*. We also note that art. 36 of the *French Confession* does make mention of union with Christ in relation to the Eucharist, and in so doing shows that this *Confession* is not at odds with the *ordo docendi* of the 1559 *Institutes*. It is also evident that the *Westminster Shorter Catechism*, although quite long, contains no section on the church and has little to say about the Holy Spirit, yet it would be amiss to suppose that meant Reformed theology has little to say of importance on ecclesiology or pneumatology!

Torrance has examined his tradition in depth, highlighted certain tendencies within it which he believes need to be reemphasised, and has reflected that in his theology. His soteriology thus provides a model of what a Reformed doctrine of *theosis* might look like. Torrance is convinced that a doctrine of reconciliation worked out around the theme of exchange and the broader concept of *theosis* is utterly compatible with Reformation thought. Other contemporary Reformed thinkers clearly disagree.[209]

Drawing on the Great Tradition Torrance firmly believes that '[Reformed theology] interprets "deification" precisely in the same way as Athanasius in the *Contra Arianos*'.[210] Deriving impetus from Calvin, Torrance argues that it is only

---

[208] See for instance Torrance, *The School of Faith*, pp. xi–cxxvi, especially cx–cxi; *Scottish Theology from John Knox to John McLeod Campbell*, which can be viewed as an extended discussion on the theology of union with Christ throughout the history of Scottish Reformed theology.

[209] McCormack, 'Participation in God, Yes, Deification, No', pp. 347–74. Another example includes Lewis B. Smedes, *My God and I: A Spiritual Memoir* (Grand Rapids: Eerdmans, 2003), pp. 71–2; and *Union With Christ: A Biblical View of New Life in Jesus Christ*, 2nd edn (Grand Rapids: Eerdmans, 1983).

[210] Torrance, *Theology in Reconstruction*, p. 184.

through 'real and substantial union' with Christ in his human nature that we partake of all his benefits, and it is only in him that we are really made to partake of the eternal Life of God himself. He writes, 'He had come deliberately to share with us our life and death in order to make us share with him his eternal life in God'.[211] The movement from union to communion, *henosis* to *theosis*, is not one in which the distinctions between the believer and God are dissolved. In communion believers relate to the Father in his distinct role as our heavenly Father, to the Son in his distinct role as our Saviour and Lord, and to the Spirit in his distinct role as the Holy One who unites believers to Christ, empowers them, and continually applies the benefits of salvation. At this point Torrance goes no further when he states:

> We are unable to describe this participation in positive language any more than we can describe the hypostatic union in positive language – refusal to do so does not by itself import that a real and creative and therefore an ontological relation is not envisaged in this participation.[212]

Despite the radical distinction between divine and human being in the Reformed tradition, we have seen that room is still left for a real communion between the two. According to Torrance, this is effected through *theosis*, the participation of human being in the divine being through the Son.

> As both God of God and Man of man Jesus Christ is the actual Mediator between God and man and man and God in all things, even in regard to space-time relations. He constitutes in Himself the rational and personal Medium in whom God meets man in his creaturely reality *and brings man without, having to leave his creaturely reality*, into communion with Himself.[213]

The language of leaving behind creaturely reality when a person is in communion with God is largely foreign to the Western tradition. However, it is certainly the language of the East, from which Torrance has drunk deeply, and as we have seen, it is also compatible with the Reformed tradition within which Torrance stands.

For Torrance *theosis* is not so much the 'divinisation' or 'deification' of humanity, as popularly (mis)understood, but the re-creation of our lost humanity in the dynamic, atoning interaction between the divine and human natures within the one person of Jesus Christ, through whom we enter into the triune communion of God's intra-trinitarian life.[214] Torrance states that 'our "deification" in Christ is

---

211 Torrance, *Space, Time and Resurrection*, p. 57.

212 Torrance, *Theology in Reconstruction*, p. 186. As should be clear by now, Torrance posits an ontological, not a metaphysical union. A metaphysical union is the underlying idea of a pantheistic concept of communion in which the believer becomes dissolved into the essence of the divine nature so that they cease to exist as a distinct entity.

213 Torrance, *Space, Time and Incarnation*, p. 52 (italics added).

214 Torrance, *The Trinitarian Faith*, p. 189.

the obverse of his "inhominization"'.[215] As far as Torrance is concerned this is what distinguishes *theosis* in Reformed thought from other expressions of deification or divinisation.

Torrance is able to affirm the eternal distinction between God and creation both in the incarnate Christ (hypostatic union), and in our participation in Christ through the reconciling exchange. This leads him to incorporate *theosis* into his Reformed theology. *Theosis* is the work of the triune God in graciously allowing human persons to participate or partake of the divine nature. Through being united to Jesus Christ, the God-man, we are united to his divinised humanity and through that relationship we enjoy fellowship with God. Torrance has written that the goal of the incarnation is that we may be gathered up in Christ Jesus and included in his own self-presentation before the Father and in that relationship, to partake of the divine nature.[216] But significantly, Torrance acknowledges the truth inherent in the doctrine of *theosis*:

> [T]he staggering thing about this is that the exaltation of human nature into the life of God does not mean the disappearance of man or the swallowing up of human and creaturely being in the infinite ocean of the divine Being, but rather that human nature, remaining creaturely and human, is yet exalted in Christ to share in God's life and glory.[217]

The present chapter has highlighted the unique role the eternal Son plays in the process of *theosis* along with the participation of believers into Christ's humanity and through him to communion with the Father by the Spirit. Torrance often speaks of this as the 'wonderful exchange'. While the present chapter has tended to focus on individual believers, Torrance's vision of *theosis* is inherently corporate, involving the work of the Holy Spirit at each step, the details of which are the concern of the next chapter.

---

215 Ibid.

216 Torrance, *Space, Time and Resurrection*, p. 135.

217 Ibid.

Chapter 4
Community and Communion

The Eternal Spirit

Throughout this examination of Torrance's theology the role of the Holy Spirit has been mentioned frequently but not specifically analysed. The present chapter examines the role of the Holy Spirit as it relates to Torrance's use of *theosis*, a role that is constitutive of *theosis* in epistemological and ontological terms. Torrance's pneumatology deals with the human person as an individual and, significantly, human persons in *relation* both to God and to those in the body of Christ. Consequently Torrance develops a pneumato-ecclesiology in which both community and communion are emphasised, as the church is understood as the communion of *theosis*.

Pneumatology is fundamental to the discussion of *theosis* as it is here that the reality of the believer's participation in the divine nature emerges. Torrance's pneumatology provides a basis for this, yet due to his focused attention on other issues, it never received the detailed treatment one may have hoped for.[1] Central to the present study is the relationship between the Spirit and Christ, which Torrance develops around the theme of their mutual mediation; the relationship between the Spirit and the believer, developed primarily in the motif of communion; and the relationship between the Spirit and the church, most fully expressed within a theology of the sacraments. The Holy Spirit equips and enables the incarnate Son to make the wonderful exchange for us; the Holy Spirit is the bond of love who unites believers to the incarnate Son and enables them to be drawn into the life of God; and the Holy Spirit is the bond of communion who constitutes the church as the *locus* of *theosis*. Through this pneumatologically-oriented ecclesiology Torrance's doctrine of *theosis* justifies trinitarian prayer and worship: true worship, as understood by Torrance, is the gift of participating in the incarnate Son's communion with the Father by the Spirit – a most fitting goal of *theosis*.

---

[1] One of these other issues includes Torrance's proposed resolution to the *Filioque* debate, see Torrance, 'The Agreed Statement on the Trinity', in *Theological Dialogue Between Orthodox and Reformed Churches*, ed. Thomas F. Torrance, 2 vols (Edinburgh: Scottish Academic Press, 1985, 1993), vol. 2. pp. 219–26; *The Trinitarian Faith: The Evangelical Theology of the Ancient Catholic Church* (Edinburgh: T & T Clark, 1995), pp. 231–47; and his final position on the issue in *The Christian Doctrine of God: One Being Three Persons* (Edinburgh: T & T Clark, 1996), pp. 168–92.

Pneumatology is perhaps the least examined aspect of Torrance's theology,[2] and yet it constitutes one of the more significant features of his work, leading one scholar to remark: 'The Spirit is the hero behind the curtain of Torrance's theological stage.'[3] For others the curtain is still very much drawn, when, for instance, Yeung concludes, 'It seems that Torrance does not yet have a full doctrine of the Holy Spirit', and then, 'Torrance definitely rejects the charge of binitarianism but that is without doubt the way towards which his theology leans'.[4] Yeung's charge is all the more surprising given that he is allegedly following closely Chapter 6 of *The Trinitarian Faith*, a chapter in which Torrance shows why and how the Spirit is *homoousios* with the Father and the Son![5] Torrance's major monographs, *The Trinitarian Faith* and *The Christian Doctrine of God*, provide no evidence of binitarianism. Yeung errs in thinking that because Torrance presents a *christologically-conditioned* pneumatology, his theology of the Holy Spirit is somehow radically deficient. Torrance's purpose is to give the Holy Spirit a place of significance along with the incarnation of the Son in Christian theology.[6] The Holy Spirit is constitutive for it is by the Spirit that we participate in the Son and through him in God. The question is not, 'Does Torrance have a robust pneumatology?' but rather, 'How should a robust pneumatology be expressed in a scientific dogmatics?' While Yeung's critical comments are mistaken, he is right to suggest that Torrance's pneumatology is not as thoroughly developed as it could be, and that at key points where an extended exposition on the role of the Spirit is called for, in *theosis* for example, little exists. However, lack of a developed pneumatology is a different claim from the allegation that Torrance's theology is binitarian!

Torrance's theology is rigorously trinitarian, however, the intrinsic relations between the Holy Spirit, the Son, and the Father need not occupy our attention, or many other aspects of pneumatology that he deals with.[7] The preceding analysis

---

2 Only two articles deal specifically with Torrance's pneumatology: Elmer Colyer, 'Thomas F. Torrance on the Holy Spirit', *Word and World* 23 (2003): pp. 160–67; and Deddo, 'The Holy Spirit in T.F. Torrance's Theology', in *The Promise of Trinitarian Theology: Theologians in Dialogue with T.F. Torrance*, ed. Elmer M. Colyer (Lanham, Md.: Rowman & Littlefield, 2001), pp. 81–114. Elmer M. Colyer also includes a chapter on pneumatology in *How To Read T.F. Torrance: Understanding his Trinitarian and Scientific Theology* (Downers Grove: IVP, 2001), pp. 211–41.

3 Kye W. Lee, *Living in Union With Christ: The Practical Theology of Thomas F. Torrance* (New York: Peter Lang, 2003), p. 316.

4 Jason H-K. Yeung, *Being and Knowing: An Examination of T.F. Torrance's Christological Science* (Hong Kong: China Alliance Press, 1996), p. 208.

5 Ibid., p. 169, fn. 65.

6 Torrance, *The Trinitarian Faith*, pp. 63–4.

7 For Torrance's pneumatology see Thomas F. Torrance, *The School of Faith: The Catechisms of the Reformed Church*, trans. and ed. with Introduction by Thomas F. Torrance (London: James Clarke and Co, 1959), pp. xcv–cxxvi; *Theology in Reconstruction* (Grand Rapids: Eerdmans, 1965), pp. 192–258; '*Spiritus Creator*', in *Le Traité sur le Saint-Espirit de Saint Basile*, ed. L. Visher (Taizé: Presses de Taizé, 1969); *God and Rationality* (Eugene,

of Torrance's doctrines of creation, anthropology, incarnation, and reconciliation holds equally for his pneumatology, as I have pointed to the constituent role of the Holy Spirit already at many points throughout the previous discussion.

In order to further clarify how Torrance presents a doctrine of *theosis* it must be repeated that the work of the Spirit is never independent of the Son. Torrance draws upon the work of Athanasius to affirm that the only correct way to gain knowledge of the Holy Spirit is through knowledge of the Son.

> [U]nless we know the Holy Spirit through the objectivity of the *homoousion* of the Son in whom and by whom our minds are directed away from ourselves to the one Fountain and Principle of Godhead, then we inevitably become engrossed with ourselves, confusing the Holy Spirit with our own spirits, and confounding the one Truth of God with notions of our own devising.[8]

To go back to Basil's distinctions, the Spirit perfects what the Son has moulded and so the two work together.[9] Through the inner linking of the work of the Spirit (perfecting), and the work of the Son (moulding), the specifically personal nature of humanity's subject-being and personal mode of rationality arises.

> Through Jesus Christ, the Incarnate Son or Word of God, and in the Holy Spirit, it is possible for man to have direct access to God, to meet and know him personally, to hear him and speak to him face to face or person to person, and thus to experience in himself the transforming impact of God's personal Reality and Being.[10]

By linking the Spirit's work with the Son in this trinitarian fashion, Torrance thrusts us back to christology as the proper place to examine the nature of human being and person. Through the incarnation Christ perfects human nature and heals it in soul and body as the Holy Spirit decisively and perfectly sanctifies him.

Here we come full circle to theological anthropology to see that salvation understood from the standpoint of the Spirit must be expressed in inherently relational terms in which Christ is central.[11] Once again we are reminded that the

---

Or.: Wipf & Stock, 1997), pp. 165–94; *Karl Barth: Biblical and Evangelical Theologian* (Edinburgh: T & T Clark, 1990), pp. 208–12; *The Trinitarian Faith*, pp. 191–251; and *The Christian Doctrine of God*, pp. 59–67, 147–55, and 180–94.

[8] Torrance, *Theology in Reconstruction*, p. 227. Torrance was particularly influenced by Athanasus's Letters to Serapion on the Holy Spirit, referring back to them repeatedly. See further in *The Trinitarian Faith*, pp. 140–41; 191–251.

[9] Basil, *De Spiritu Sancto*, 16.37–40; 18.46; 19.48; and 24.55. See Torrance, *Theology in Reconstruction*, pp. 220–25.

[10] Thomas F. Torrance, 'The Soul and Person in Theological Perspective', in *Religion, Reason, and the Self: Essays in Honour of Hywel D. Lewis*, eds Stewart R. Sutherland and T.A. Roberts (Cardiff: University of Wales Press, 1989), pp. 113–14.

[11] Ibid., p. 115.

incarnation proleptically conditions creation.[12] Through the vicarious life, death, and resurrection of Jesus Christ, humanity is made to participate in the divine life in the Spirit through the Son. Through the incarnation divinity and humanity were united thus enabling the fullness of the Spirit's presence to sanctify human nature. 'This is the new spiritual and ontological condition of people which the New Testament refers to by the expressions "in Christ" and "in the Spirit".'[13] It is this new ontological level of human existence made possible by the incarnation and the pouring out of the Spirit that led the Greek fathers to assert a doctrine of *theosis* in relation to John 10.34: 'the Scripture calls "gods" those to whom the Word of God came': 'Such was the exalted status', writes Torrance, 'they felt obliged to accord to man "in Christ" and "in the Spirit".'[14]

The Spirit thus comes 'as the Spirit of a Manhood wholly offered to God in perpetual glorification and worship and praise'.[15] Worship is *epiclesis* and *paraclesis*, the invocation of the *Paraclete* Spirit and the coming of the other *Paraclete* to help us. In our worship the Holy Spirit comes from God, uniting us to the response, obedience, faith, and worship of Jesus Christ (also our *Paraclete*), and returns to God, raising us up in Jesus to participate in the worship of heaven and in the eternal communion of the Holy Trinity.[16]

Aware of the dangers inherent in identifying the Holy Spirit with the human spirit, Torrance insists on the radical objectivity of the Spirit.[17] Torrance defines pneumatology as 'the objective reality and personal Being of the Spirit…'.[18] How then can the Spirit be present in creation without confusing God's Spirit for the human spirit? Only through the mediation of Son and Spirit can these be distinguished. God became human without ceasing to be divine in order to enable believers to participate in the divine nature without ceasing to be human. In the incarnation God drew so near to humanity that he entered within our creaturely life, and the completion of the atoning work of Christ led to an outpouring of the Spirit of God upon human flesh that created the church. The church is thus the sphere within which reconciliation is actualised and God makes himself present. Torrance's doctrine of *theosis* would be incomplete, and incoherent, even anti-Christian, if the objectivity of the Spirit was not maintained by it.

According to Torrance, the persistent error of both Protestantism and Roman Catholicism lies in confounding the Holy Spirit with the human spirit on the one

---

12 See Chapter 1, pp. 25–8.

13 Thomas F. Torrance, 'The Goodness and Dignity of Man in the Christian Tradition', *Modern Theology* 4 (1988): p. 321.

14 Ibid.

15 Torrance, *Theology in Reconstruction*, p. 248.

16 Ibid., p. 250.

17 This is echoed many times in Torrance's theology but is concisely stated in ibid., pp. 233–5.

18 Ibid., p. 235.

hand (*homineque*), or with the spirit of the church on the other (*ecclesiaque*).[19] Both views must be rejected. Based on his understanding of the objectivity of the Spirit, Torrance maintains that by the Holy Spirit '*God is closer to us than we are to ourselves*'.[20] Colyer remarks, 'In Torrance's theology, the Holy Spirit is as profoundly, personally, and intimately present to us and all of creation as in any form of panentheism, but in a way that acknowledges the majesty, objectivity, and freedom of the Spirit…'.[21] God became incarnate without ceasing to be God and now, after Pentecost, God is present to us in a real way by his Spirit without reducing his majesty or being to the creaturely realm.[22]

Consistent with Nicene theology Torrance understands *theosis* as an affirmation of the 'immediate personal and ineffable presence of the Holy Spirit, in and through whom we are united to Jesus Christ, and through Christ with the Father…'.[23] Explaining the central role of the Holy Spirit to the process of *theosis* Torrance observes:

> By coming *into* man the Holy Spirit opens him *out* for God. But at the very heart of this movement is the act of God in which he became man in order to take man's place, and give man a place within the communion of the divine life… Hence when we speak of the Spirit as pouring out the love of God in our hearts, we are to think of his activity in strict correlativity to the atoning substitution in the life, death and resurrection of Jesus Christ – that is to say, we are to think of the work of the Spirit not simply as the actualizing within us of what God has already wrought for us in Jesus Christ once and for all, but as opening us up within our subjectivities for Christ in such a radical way that we find our life *not in ourselves but out of ourselves, objectively in him*.[24]

Torrance outlines the goal and purpose of creation as it relates to the vital role of the Holy Spirit. In a lengthy citation he argues:

> It is from the free ground of that transcendent otherness in himself in his Triune Being, that God freely and spontaneously creates others outwith [*sic*] himself for fellowship with himself and brings them into actual communion with himself. This free-flowing unconditioned outgoing movement of his Being means that God refuses to be shut off from us in his unapproachable Majesty, infinite otherness and incomprehensibility. He makes himself really accessible to us, and does so not only in communicating himself to us in the incarnation of his

---

19 Ibid., p. 231.

20 See Colyer, *How To Read T.F. Torrance*, pp. 219–20.

21 Colyer, 'Thomas F. Torrance on the Holy Spirit', p. 167. Colyer works this out in more detail in, *How To Read T.F. Torrance*, pp. 211–21.

22 Colyer, 'Thomas F. Torrance on the Holy Spirit', p. 167.

23 Ibid.

24 Torrance, *Theology in Reconstruction*, p. 238 (italics in original).

> Son, but in imparting to us his Holy Spirit in such an utterly astonishing way as to actualise among us his self-giving to us as the Lord and at the same time to effect our receiving of him in his self-giving.[25]

Modern charges against a doctrine of *theosis* claim that it is a Platonic accretion that ultimately confuses humanity and divinity. Torrance's theology, in direct contrast to such claims, declares that because of the utter objectivity of the Holy Spirit, *theosis* can in no way be construed as confusing, mixing, or melding divinity with humanity in either Christ or the Christian.

As in his doctrines of incarnation and reconciliation, Torrance does not start his pneumato-ecclesiology afresh but proceeds from within the Reformed tradition, especially as influenced by Calvin. Following the lead of Calvin, 'the theologian of the Holy Spirit', Torrance seeks to build bridges between Eastern and Western theologies in order to achieve a more ecumenical, and more biblical, expression of the body of Christ:[26] his use of *theosis* is a key to this.

There is in Calvin's thought a strong emphasis on the work of the Spirit in the renewal and sanctification of believers summarised in the assertion: 'the Holy Spirit is the bond by which Christ effectually unites us to himself'.[27] Thus Calvin set the agenda for the theological discussion to follow. In the third book of his 1559 *Institutes* he prefaces his treatment of the 'Mode of attaining the Grace of God' with a remark about the Holy Spirit as the active agent of God who applies the benefits of Christ to individual believers and to the church. One of Calvin's great legacies to Protestantism was his emphasis that the work of the Spirit is inseparable from the work of the Son and the Father. Torrance rigorously adopts this in his theology.

According to Torrance the Holy Spirit incorporates believers into Christ in a profound way. Everything that is Christ's as the 'man' for us becomes ours through our spiritual union with him. This christological focus and the Pauline language of 'in/with Christ' help our understanding of the two aspects of the work of the Spirit. First, in relation to Christ, the Spirit is the one who empowers, enables, bonds and mediates the presence and power of God. Second, in relation to the believer the Spirit places us 'in' or 'with' Christ, so that his justification, adoption, sanctification, and glorification become ours. According to Torrance and Reformed theology more generally, union with Christ thus provides the framework within which the work of the Spirit may be considered.[28]

The Holy Spirit is central to Torrance's doctrine of *theosis* but only when understood within a truly trinitarian framework. It is not, as Yeung suggests, that

---

25 Torrance, *The Christian Doctrine of God*, p. 150.

26 'Gregory the Theologian and Calvin the Theologian together build a bridge in Christian doctrine between East and West', writes Torrance, *Trinitarian Perspectives: Toward Doctrinal Agreement* (Edinburgh: T & T Clark, 1994), p. 21.

27 Calvin, *Institutes*, 3.1.1.

28 See Chapter 3, pp. 97–109.

the Holy Spirit is less significant than the Son or the Father but that the 'deifying' activity of the Spirit has a christological focus: to incorporate the believer into Christ and through Christ to bring the believer to participate in the divine nature. Having said this, it is evident that Torrance only spoke of the work of the Holy Spirit in the process of *theosis* in the ongoing lives of believers in specific and thus limited ways.

Treating pneumatology and ecclesiology together in this chapter highlights the way in which the Holy Spirit and the church function in close reciprocity in Torrance's use of *theosis*. This chapter expressly limits itself to an investigation of the specific work of the Spirit in relation to *theosis* and its outworking on several levels: the Holy Spirit in relation to Jesus Christ, to believers, and within the church.

The Mutual Mediation of Son and Spirit

In Scripture and in the early church the Holy Spirit emerges most fully in relation to Christ, and thus for Torrance, a proper christocentrism allows for and sponsors a robust pneumatology.[29] Basing his pneumatology largely on Greek patristic insights, Torrance contends that the creative and redemptive work of the Spirit is to be thought of in terms of his inseparable relation to Christ. 'Not only does the Spirit have *koinonia kata physin* with the Father and the Son, but he is peculiarly closely related to the nature of the Son, and it is in this connection that his operations are to be discerned and understood.'[30] Torrance finds confirmation of this throughout the Gospels, where the Spirit is intimately involved with every stage of Jesus' earthly career: virgin conception (Mat 1.18 par.), baptism (Mat 3.16, par.), temptation (Mk 1.12 par.), ministry (Lk 4.14; Mat 12.31 par.), cross (Mk 14.36; Heb 9.14), resurrection (Rom 8.11), and Pentecost (Acts 2.4). The Spirit is not an addendum to theology. Instead, he is active before and after the cross, empowering and defining Jesus the Son and empowering and actualising the words and works of Christ in the church. This emphasis in Torrance leads one of his commentators to declare:

> In and through the incarnation of the Son of God the being and action of the Holy Spirit is revealed in two dimensions. Thus the church in its own worship and doctrine traced out the two dimensions in terms of two relations: the relation of the Holy Spirit with the Triune life and also in relation to creation.[31]

---

[29] See for instance Thomas F. Torrance, *Theology in Reconciliation: Essays Towards Evangelical and Catholic Unity in East and West* (London: Geoffrey Chapman, 1975), p. 253; and *Divine Meaning: Studies in Patristic Hermeneutics* (Edinburgh: T & T Clark, 1995), pp. 60–62, 216.

[30] Torrance, *Theology in Reconstruction*, p. 221. Torrance is drawing specifically upon St Basil's *De Spiritu Sancto*.

[31] Deddo, 'The Holy Spirit in T.F. Torrance's Theology', p. 84.

Torrance uses this twofold relation to great effect to highlight the identity and mission of the Holy Spirit, explaining that the Spirit makes *theosis* a reality in the life of the believer.

Torrance goes back to Basil the Great for his definition of the distinction between the three persons of the Godhead. The Spirit is distinguished as 'the perfecting cause' (*he teleiotike aitia*), the work of the Father as 'the originating cause' (*he prokatarktike aitia*), and the work of the Son as 'the moulding cause' (*he demiourgike aitia*).[32] The Spirit as the 'perfecting cause' brings to completion the creative purpose of God for human persons in the Son, thereby linking 'the creature in an enduring ontological relation to God'.[33] The perfecting work of the Spirit is applied to believers who are at once 'in Christ' and 'in the Spirit', and thus granted a 'personalising communion' which is what Torrance believes Greek patristic theology terms θεοποιησις.[34] The Spirit is thus the quickening Spirit, the Lord who is *autozoe*, the Author of Life.[35] Created being, while having no inherent qualities that would place it in ontological union with God, nevertheless, by the work of the Spirit, acquires ontological communion with the triune God. Thus, it is in the role of the Holy Spirit that Torrance identifies the point of contact in Christ Jesus with God and between God and humanity. Pneumatology must be our focus if we are to know how *theosis* is incorporated throughout his theology.

Approaches to the theology of the Spirit have tended to bifurcate, as Rowan Williams has pointed out.[36] On the one hand, the Spirit may be regarded as an epistemological bridge between Creator and creature or; on the other, the Spirit may be seen as an ontological link between the triune God and the believer. Torrance's theology develops both themes, epistemological and ontological, and sees both as essential to a doctrine of *theosis*.[37] Having already considered Torrance's reading of Calvin's theology we need not rehearse those themes again.[38] Our immediate concern is with the salvation of men and women understood as *theosis*, which Torrance derives from the 'mutual mediation of the Son and the Spirit'.

To understand Torrance's theology we must appreciate that while the missions of the second and third Persons of the Trinity are distinct, they are never separated. Accordingly, 'the doctrine of the Spirit must be allowed to interpenetrate the doctrine of Christ and his revealing and reconciling work, for it is the Spirit who

---

32 Torrance, 'The Soul and Person in Theological Perspective', p. 111. Cf. Basil, *De Spiritu Sancto*, 16.38.

33 Ibid., p. 111.

34 Torrance, *The Trinitarian Faith*, p. 231.

35 Torrance, *Theology in Reconstruction*, p. 216.

36 Rowan Williams, *On Christian Theology* (Oxford: Blackwell, 2000), pp. 107–27.

37 See Eugene F. Rogers, 'The Mystery of the Spirit in Three Traditions: Calvin, Rahner, Florensky or, You Keep Wondering Where the Spirit Went', *Modern Theology* 19 (2003): p. 245.

38 See Introduction, pp. 10–12, Chapter 1, pp. 29–37, and Chapter 3, pp. 97–109.

mediates the Son as it is the Son who mediates the Spirit'.[39] As Colyer has warned, 'failure to take note of this can lead to serious misunderstandings of Torrance's position'.[40] This doctrine of mutual mediation applies to the extent that the work of the Spirit may be understood as correlative to the traditional Reformed view of Christ's threefold Office as Prophet, Priest and King.[41] In regard to the Prophetic office, both Christ *and the Spirit* are referred to in the New Testament as the 'quickening Spirit' and as 'Advocate' (Rom 8.2, 1 Cor 15.45, Jn 14.16, 1 Jn 2.1). In this twofold advocacy and intercession the work of Christ is not only fulfilled in a single act of redemption at the cross but is also applied in time to those who believe in him. In regard to the Priestly office, the Spirit applies the blood of Christ to believers through baptism, but this cannot be separated from Pentecost, the occasion on which the risen Christ baptises his church. In regard to the Kingly office, the Spirit works as the power and operation of God, effectively applying Christ's victory over the powers to believers, and so delivering them from bondage into the freedom of the 'sons' of God.

According to Torrance, the Holy Spirit is not given to us as an empty sign, 'naked' or 'isolated', but, comes to us as the Spirit *of Jesus Christ*, and is thus 'charged with all the experiences of Jesus'.[42] This explains the sending of the Holy Spirit after Christ's ascension. 'Then he came down freely upon the Body that had been prepared, the church purchased by the blood of Christ, and lifted it up, unhindered by guilt and sin or the divine judgment, to participate freely in the very life of God.'[43] The Holy Spirit is thus the Spirit of holiness, the Spirit of redemption, the Spirit of glory *because* he is the Spirit of Christ.

Torrance makes explicit the inseparability of the Spirit from the Son when, in a direct discussion of *theosis* he argues:

> [The Holy Spirit] is not divine because he participates in God, for he is himself fully and wholly God, of one and the same being with the Father. In virtue of his divine reality and presence incarnate within mankind he acts upon people in an utterly divine and creative way, making them partake of himself through grace and thus partake of God. Θεοποιησις or θεωσις, then, was used to describe the unique act of God incarnate in Jesus Christ…in the nature of the case we are not saved or renewed by the activity of Christ without being united to him and partaking of him.[44]

---

[39] Torrance, *Karl Barth: Biblical and Evangelical Theologian*, pp. 209–10.

[40] Elmer M. Colyer, *The Nature of Doctrine in T.F. Torrance's Theology* (Eugene, Ore.: Wipf and Stock, 2001), p. 148.

[41] Torrance, *The School of Faith*, p. ciii.

[42] Torrance, *Theology in Reconstruction*, p. 247.

[43] Ibid., p. 248.

[44] Torrance, *The Trinitarian Faith*, p. 139.

Partaking of Christ is made possible because of Christ's union with humanity in the incarnation, and by the believer's union with Christ, all of which is enabled by the Spirit.

> Christ alone is *Theos* (Θεος), true God of true God, he alone is properly (κυριως) Son of the Father, but through his divine activity (θεοποιησις) we are adopted and made sons of God in him, and in that respect, as those who through union with Christ receive the grace and light of his Spirit, are said to be *theoi* (θεοι).[45]

Thus *theosis* is able, within Torrance's theology, to stand for salvation in all its tenses, applications, stages, and contours. Torrance, following his Greek patristic mentors and before them, Jesus (Jn 10.34, cf. Ps 82.6), is able to assert that believers are *gods*. This bold assertion is only comprehensible within a trinitarian context.

It is precisely because the Holy Spirit is the Spirit of Christ that he can be identified as the Spirit of 'Manhood' by Torrance – 'the Spirit comes as the Spirit of Manhood wholly offered to God in perpetual glorification and worship and praise'.[46] The mutual mediation of Son and Spirit is applied to believers so that they have the Spirit of Sonship/Manhood applied to them in order to enable them to live an obedient, humble life of faithful service to God. To sever the Spirit from the Son is to strip the Spirit of his identity and of his unique work. It is only in and by the Spirit of Christ that a believer can participate in the divine nature, for that is precisely what the Spirit does, both with Christ *the* Son by nature, and with believers, sons and daughters, by grace. As Torrance clarifies, 'The Holy Spirit is God in his freedom not only to give being to the creation but through his presence in it to bring its relations with himself to their end and perfection'.[47] That end and perfection is union with the humanity of Christ and through that union a communion with the Father through the Son in the Holy Spirit.

Seen in this light 'the creative work of the Spirit is, so to speak, proleptically conditioned by that of redemption'.[48] Once again we find the familiar themes of Torrance's doctrines of creation, anthropology and christology reworked and restated, this time from the perspective of the Holy Spirit. The Holy Spirit is not operating on some independent plane from the Son or the Father; neither is the Spirit merely applying the results of an already accomplished work of the Son. The Spirit is crucial to Jesus' incarnate existence – his life, death, and resurrection – and is now at work in the world to further the mission of the Son.

We may observe the parallel between Torrance's doctrine of the Spirit and certain Eastern Orthodox understandings.

---

45 Ibid.

46 Torrance, *Theology in Reconstruction*, p. 248.

47 Ibid.

48 Ibid., p. 217, cf. p. 221.

> According to the Eastern view, the descent (*katabasis*) of the divine person of Christ makes human persons capable of an ascent (*anabasis*) in the Holy Spirit. It was necessary that the voluntary humiliation, the redemptive *kenosis* of the Son of God should take place, so that fallen humans might accomplish their vocation of theosis, the deification of created beings by uncreated grace.[49]

According to many Eastern Orthodox theologians, doctrines of *theosis* cannot be expressed on a christological basis alone, but demand a pneumatological development as well. The goal of *theosis* is not the cancellation of sin, although this is a necessary outcome; it is, more profoundly, creatures' worship of God, defined in trinitarian terms as the gift of participating through the Spirit in the incarnate Son's communion with the Father.[50] It is the Holy Spirit who affects *theosis* with all its constituent parts and cognates: justification, sanctification, adoption, glorification, communion, participation and perfection. Eastern Orthodoxy 'teaches that that which is common to the Father and the Son is the divinity which the Holy Spirit communicates to humans within the church, in making them partakers of the divine nature. Deification is the highest gift and blessing of the Holy Spirit'.[51] Torrance's pneumatology is in general agreement with this.[52]

So central is the theme of pneumatology throughout Eastern Orthodox thought that, echoing the words of St Seraphim of Sarov, Lossky affirms 'the true end of the Christian life is the acquiring of the Holy Spirit'.[53] Lossky explains that through praxis and contemplation (*theōria*), the power of divine love is communicated to the human by the Holy Spirit, 'creating a gift, a divine and deifying energy in which we really participate in the nature of the Holy Trinity, by becoming partakers of the divine nature'.[54]

This fundamental vision of the mutual mediation between Christ and the Spirit, operative within the church, is employed by Torrance, but with important qualifications. Orthodoxy often appears to imbibe an element of Pelagianism in its doctrine of synergistic salvation, something Torrance vehemently rejects throughout his work. According to Torrance the point of the Reformation is that

---

49 Veli-Matti Kärkkäinen, 'Grace and the Ecumenical Potential of Theosis', in *Toward a Pneumatological Theology: Pentecostal and Ecumenical Perspectives on Ecclesiology, Soteriology, and Theology of Mission*, ed. Amos Yong (Lanham: University Press of America, 2002), p. 152. Cf. Torrance, *Theology in Reconstruction*, pp. 248–9.

50 While this is the specific terminology of James B. Torrance, it is consciously constructed along Cappadocian lines and is faithful to an understanding of worship which Thomas F. Torrance ascribes to as well. See James B. Torrance, *Worship, Community and the Triune God of Grace* (Downers Grove: IVP, 1996), pp. 9, 15, 20–21, 30 and 41.

51 Kärkkäinen, 'Grace and the Ecumenical Potential of Theosis', p. 154.

52 Torrance, *Theology in Reconstruction*, pp. 248–9.

53 Vladimir Lossky, *The Mystical Theology of the Eastern Church* (1944. Crestwood, NY.: St Vladimir's Seminary Press, 1998), p. 196.

54 Ibid., pp. 213–14.

humans lost their freedom in the Fall and the Holy Spirit is required to create this anew. What Torrance does have in common with Orthodoxy, however, is the stress on the communal or corporate nature of salvation along with the context within which the Holy Spirit operates – the Church.

The culmination of the Spirit-empowered mission of Christ is Pentecost. This means, as Badcock has made clear, that 'there can be no adequate pneumatology where the centrality of Jesus is lost from sight, and therefore no theology of the Spirit or of the spiritual life in which the historical context and content of the central Christian story as presented in the New Testament is relinquished'. Badcock then asserts: '"The spirit was not", in the *Christian* sense, until Jesus had been "glorified" (John 7.39) – a glorification that in the New Testament is inseparable from the passion.'[55] Pentecost plays a considerable role in Torrance's discussion for it is the historical climax of the incarnation and the occasion on which the risen and ascended Lord bestows upon his church his new life.[56] 'In other words', as Pinnock phrases it, 'something happened through the total journey of Jesus that literally changed the world and opened the door wide to union with God.'[57] He adds, 'With the glorification of Jesus a process began which will end in the divinization of the world'.[58] Torrance's theology echoes these same themes, albeit without the implication of universalism.

Thus something decisive happened on the Day of Pentecost, a new coming of the Holy Spirit in power in order to do for humanity what humanity could not do for itself. Pentecost is as new, distinct, and unique, as the incarnation itself. Pentecost commenced a new mode of the Spirit's entry into the lives of men and women. This was made possible by the incarnation by which human and divine natures were inseparably united in the eternal Person of God the Son. In him, therefore, Torrance would say that the closed circle of the inner life of God was made to overlap with human life, and human nature was taken up to share in the eternal communion of the Father, the Son and the Spirit.

While much theology has concentrated on the descent of the Spirit, fewer theologians (in modernity at least) have developed the theme of the ascent of the Spirit back to God. Torrance provides the following presentation:

> By his very nature the Holy Spirit not only proceeds from the Father but lifts up to the Father; he is not only the Spirit sent by Christ but the Spirit of response to Christ, the Spirit in whom and by whom and with whom we worship and glorify the Father and the Son. Not only is God the Holy Spirit descending to us, the Spirit by whom God bears witness to himself, but God the Holy Spirit lifting

---

[55] Gary D. Badcock, *Light of Truth and Fire of Love: A Theology of the Holy Spirit* (Grand Rapids: Eerdmans, 1997), p. 267.

[56] Torrance, *Theology in Reconstruction*, pp. 240–49.

[57] Clark H. Pinnock, *Flame of Love: A Theology of the Holy Spirit* (Downers Grove: IVP, 1996), p. 93.

[58] Ibid., p. 94.

> up all creation in praise and rejoicing in God, himself the Spirit of worship and witness by whom the Church lives and fulfils its mission to the glory of God.[59]

This movement back to God is clearly an aspect of *theosis* in Torrance's theology.[60]

In the introduction to a work on the Reformed Catechisms, *The School of Faith*, Torrance emphasises that the Spirit actualises within the believer subjectively what Christ has accomplished objectively.[61] This is a natural and logical extension of the mutual mediation of Son and Spirit into the creaturely realm. The work of the Spirit must be understood as correlative to the union of God and humanity wrought in the incarnate life of Jesus Christ. As the Spirit unites the divinity and humanity of Christ, so the Spirit unites believers to God. Thus Torrance asserts:

> The Reformed doctrine of the Communion of the Spirit is not a doctrine of communion in spirit or even simply a doctrine of communion in the Spirit, but a doctrine of Communion in Christ through the Spirit or, to put it otherwise, of *union with Christ through the Communion of the Spirit*.[62]

Communion thus stands for a corporate dynamic of mutual participation through the Spirit in Christ and a personal communion which each may have with Christ within the corporate communion. 'That is the doctrine of the Church as the Communion of Saints, in which each shares with the other and all share together in the life and love of God in Jesus Christ.'[63] This is a fundamental insight that Torrance builds upon when articulating the role of the Spirit as the agent of participation of the believer in Christ and through Christ with the Father.

The Spirit as Agent of Participation

Central to the process of Christian transformation, according to all traditions, is the work of the Holy Spirit precisely because it is *spiritual* growth. Torrance's own position on the spiritual growth of the believer attempts to bring together

---

59 Torrance, *Theology in Reconstruction*, p. 242.

60 See ibid., p. 243, and Roland Spjuth, *Creation, Contingency and Divine Presence: In the Theologies of Thomas F. Torrance and Eberhard Jüngel* (Lund: Lund University Press, 1995), p. 129. Torrance's explanation of the redemptive significance of Pentecost has certain parallels with the theology of recapitulation developed by Irenaeus (*Adversus Haereses*, *ANF*, 1, pp. 612–1156; see Trevor A. Hart, 'Irenaeus, Recapitulation and Physical Redemption', in *Christ in Our Place: The Humanity of God in Christ for the Reconciliation of the World: Essays Presented to Professor James Torrance*, eds Trevor A. Hart and Daniel P. Thimell (Exeter: Paternoster, 1981), pp. 152–81.

61 Torrance, *The School of Faith*, p. cvi.

62 Ibid.

63 Ibid., p. cxxiv.

Eastern and Western conceptions of spirituality and growth in holiness. By adapting doctrines of *theosis* from Eastern Orthodoxy and combining it with a Western, Reformed spirituality, Torrance's theology holds out significant promise for explaining how the believer actually becomes deified or progresses in *theosis*. However, as we shall see, because Torrance emphasises the objective elements of salvation his articulation of the subjective elements remain largely undeveloped. Thus his theology promises more than it delivers as it contains little by way of clearly articulated practical application. This is not to imply that his theology is impractical, as the rest of this chapter will show, but rather, that he has not elaborated on many of these points in detail.[64]

That said, a work of the Spirit is certainly decisive for Torrance's account of *theosis*. 'The counterpart to the doctrine of the Incarnation and saving work of Christ', Torrance asserts, 'is the doctrine of union with Christ and of participation in Him and all His benefits – that takes place through the Communion of the Holy Spirit...'.[65] After all, the Spirit is not an intermediary force that unites the believer to the Son but is the *Holy* Spirit, the Spirit of God and the Spirit of Christ, who alone can effect the union between God and humanity. This union is understood by Torrance as *theosis*, as Colyer affirms:

> Torrance is also similarly concerned to reject any notion of a created medium between God and humanity by affirming the direct creative activity of the Holy Spirit as God and Lord, and to restore what the Greek fathers called *theosis* (deification), though understood in terms of humanity being made free for God by God (including knowledge of God that cannot be separated from soteriology) and not in terms of the divinization of humanity.[66]

Based upon the mutual mediation of Son and Spirit, there is both a God-humanward movement and a human-Godward movement and Jesus through the Spirit mediates both. This means, as Deddo explains, 'the Spirit not only brings to us the objective effects worked out in the vicarious life of Christ, but also the subjective effects worked out in his humanity. That is, the Spirit enables us to share in Jesus' own faithful response to the Father'.[67] Torrance's doctrine of human response as previously analysed[68] provides a foundation for what is developed here by way of the Holy Spirit.

Through the Spirit we share in Christ's response to the Father. The Spirit empowers the believer to cry 'Abba, Father', in the same way that comes naturally

---

64 Compare this with, for instance, the 'stages of justification' in Stăniloae outlined by Emil Bartos, *Deification in Eastern Orthodoxy: An Evaluation and Critique of the Theology of Dumitru Staniloae* (Carlisle: Paternoster, 1999), pp. 290–96.

65 Torrance, *The School of Faith*, p. xcv.

66 Colyer, *The Nature of Doctrine in T.F. Torrance's Theology*, p. 147.

67 Deddo, 'The Holy Spirit in T.F. Torrance's Theology', p. 97.

68 See Chapter 2, pp. 72–81.

to the Son of God; for to be 'in the Spirit' is to be 'in Christ'. Deddo notes that according to Torrance, 'our whole lives in every part are constituted a participation: a dynamic life of union and communion with God'.[69] Torrance insists that our holiness or sanctification is realised in Christ by the *Holy* Spirit: our repentance, faith, and obedience are actualised in Christ by the Holy Spirit; every part of our relationship with and response to God is thus achieved in, through, and by the Son and the Spirit.[70] Not only is the Holy Spirit instrumental in justification, but now, also, to sanctification. Critically, however, both are located *in* Christ. Here we have, in effect, the other side of redemption: 'the side of the subjectification of revelation and reconciliation in the life and faith of the church. That means the Spirit is creating and calling forth the response of man in faith and understanding, in thanksgiving and worship and prayer'.[71] As we shall see, worship and prayer are the climax of Torrance's vision of *theosis* in the present in-between time of the church.[72]

Torrance's doctrine of *theosis* is again thoroughly patristic, particularly Athanasian, in its pneumatological orientation, especially in three areas. First, *theosis* is the special work of the Holy Spirit in the triunity of God, understood as the *Spiritus Creator*.[73] Like Athanasius, Torrance follows the traditional teaching of the church in ascribing 'the creative work of the Spirit in *renewing* or *sanctifying* the creature, and consummating (or bringing to its *telos*) the relation of the creature to the Godhead'.[74] Second, Torrance contends that the Spirit is ineffable and couched in mystery, a mystery that cannot be fully illuminated without overstepping the bounds of godly reverence.[75] Third, the work of the Spirit is always associated with the work of the Son.[76] Because the work of the Spirit is not to be conceived independently of the Son, the work of the Spirit in creation can only be understood within the context of his sanctifying, renewing or perfecting operation. This leads Torrance to affirm, 'the creative work of the Spirit is, so to speak, proleptically conditioned by that of redemption'.[77] It is within the context of the *Spiritus Creator* that Athanasius and Torrance deal directly with a doctrine of *theosis* and in turn the theme of the *Spiritus Redemptor*. As Torrance states: 'To be concerned with the Spirit, to know him, to be acted on by him, is immediately

69 Deddo, 'The Holy Spirit in T.F. Torrance's Theology', p. 97.

70 See Torrance, *Theology in Reconstruction*, pp. 250–51; *Theology in Reconciliation*, p. 118; and *The Christian Doctrine of God*, p. 65.

71 Yeung, *Being and Knowing*, p. 175. See Torrance, *The School of Faith*, p. cv.

72 See the discussion further in this chapter, pp. 185–91. On the relation of time to the church see Torrance, *Royal Priesthood*, Scottish Journal of Theology Occasional Papers No. 3 (Edinburgh: Oliver and Boyd, 1955), pp. 43–62.

73 Torrance, *Theology in Reconstruction*, pp. 209–28. Cf. Athanasius, *Ad Ser.* 1.28, 30; 3.4f; *C. Arianos* 3.5.

74 Ibid., p. 216. Cf. Athanasius, *Ad Ser.* 1.20, 30f.

75 Ibid., p. 217, where he refers to Athanasius, *Ad Ser.* 4.1ff., 6.

76 See Athanasius, *Ad Ser.* 1.18; 1.22ff; 3.1.

77 Torrance, *Theology in Reconstruction*, p. 217.

to be concerned with the Being or *ousia* of God the Creator. That, as I understand it, is the import of the patristic notion of *theosis* or "deification".'[78]

As examined in Chapter 3, Torrance mentions the role of the Holy Spirit in his relation to Light, a key patristic image or cognate of *theosis*.[79] In a discussion on the hiddenness and self-effacing character of the 'invisible Spirit of Truth', Torrance argues that the Spirit is not directly known in his own person (*hypostasis*): 'He is the invisible Light in whose shining we see the uncreated Light of God manifest in Jesus Christ, but he is known himself only in that he lights up for us the Face of God in the Face of Jesus Christ.'[80] As such the Holy Spirit has a 'distinctive, transparent and translucent *hypostasis*'.[81] This leads Torrance to contend that the goal of *theosis* consists in our being 'enabled to apprehend [God], yet only in such a way that what he is as God…is completely veiled from us'.[82] This is strikingly parallel to certain features of Eastern Orthodox apophaticism. Here again Torrance stands in continuity with the Greek fathers, though not uncritically so.[83]

Controlling Torrance's discussion of *theosis* and the work of the Holy Spirit is the consistent assumption that the being and act of God belong inseparably together. In the giving of the Holy Spirit, God's being and act are made visible and knowable as God gives *himself*, his self-revelation and self-communication in the Holy Spirit.[84] This is the other side of the unknowability of God. While God is ultimately unknowable, in his outgoing movement in the sending of the Son and the Holy Spirit 'he takes us into communion with himself, making himself open to our knowing of him and making us open to him and receptive of his self-revealing to us'.[85] While Torrance accepts an apophatic reticence in his theology he is not prepared to adopt the Orthodox distinction between the *essence* and *energies* of God. He is explicit: 'To know God *kata physin*, in accordance with his own nature, is to know him under the impact of his distinctively divine *energeia*, that is, to know him through a living empirical relation determined by *theosis*.'[86] Thus, the divine *energeia* are not impersonal for Torrance as in Eastern Orthodoxy. Such an Orthodox understanding actually undermines a doctrine of *theosis*.[87] It also reduces the act of God to something other than a revelation of his being, thus demoting Christ and the Holy Spirit to intermediaries of God, not God himself.

78 Ibid., p. 214.

79 See Chapter 3, pp. 131–5.

80 Torrance, *The Christian Doctrine of God*, p. 151.

81 Ibid.

82 Ibid.

83 Ibid. Cf. Athanasius, *Ep. Ad Serap* 1.17: 'thus far human knowledge goes. Here the cherubim spread the covering of their wings'.

84 Ibid., p. 152.

85 Ibid.

86 Torrance, *Theology in Reconciliation*, p. 248.

87 For a defence of this position see Habets, 'Reformed *Theosis*? A Critical Reply to Murphy'.

The Holy Spirit, Torrance contends, is the direct *parousia* of the divine *ousia* of God Almighty.[88] Torrance marvels at God's freedom to remain transcendent and at the same time to become incarnate for our sake in Jesus Christ and to impart God's self to us in sending the Holy Spirit. The Holy Spirit is free to be present and actualise God's relation to us, but also free to be with and in us and actualise our relation to God and thereby bring our lives as God's creatures to their goal of participation in God.[89] It is this *analogia relationis* that makes possible real knowledge of and communion with God and it is this that Torrance uses to define *theosis*. In *The Christian Doctrine of God* he writes:

> Through the presence of the Holy Spirit we are certainly put in sanctifying and enlightening touch with the dynamic Being and Act of the All-Holy and Almighty God resulting in a transcendental determination of our own being *for God* – the experience which the Greek Fathers spoke of as *theosis* (θεωσις) – and are thereby enabled to apprehend him.[90]

Earlier in the same work Torrance states that, 'emphasis was laid also upon the redemptive mission and the saving efficacy of the Holy Spirit as the Lord and Giver of Life, whose renewing and sanctifying operation in the faithful was identical with the direct act of God himself, that is as θεωσις'.[91] Torrance then qualifies these statements and adopts an apophatic reticence in regard to how much of God we can truly know, in his remark that we can comprehend God,

> Yet only in such a way that what he is as God (τι ἐστι Θεος) is completely veiled from us. Even in his self-revelation to us God reserves the hiddenness of his Being and does not come under the control of our knowing of him – before him all our human forms of thought and speech break off in wonder and adoration.[92]

Torrance is asserting that human persons can participate in the divine nature; a relational knowing and experiencing of the Trinity. So the distinction between the economic and ontological aspects of the Trinity is employed with a different nuance than in the Eastern Orthodox use of the *theologia* and *oikonomia*. Torrance affirms that in the Son and Holy Spirit one comes to 'see', 'hear' and 'know' God as he is in himself, but they do so in a creaturely way that is at once a revelation of the 'hiddenness' of God. This means that God is always greater (*Deus semper maior*). Given Torrance's theological method of cognitive stratification,[93] he

---

88 Torrance, *The Christian Doctrine of God*, p. 149.

89 Ibid., p. 152.

90 Torrance, *The Christian Doctrine of God*, p. 151.

91 Ibid., p. 97.

92 Ibid., p. 151.

93 See Thomas F. Torrance, 'The Stratification of Truth', in *Reality and Scientific Theology* (Edinburgh: Scottish Academic Press, 1985), pp. 131–59; and *The Christian*

contends that this allows us to affirm simultaneously the knowability of God in the incarnate Son through the Holy Spirit and at the same time to stand with our hands over our mouths and fall on our knees to worship and adore that which will forever be beyond our comprehension.[94]

Due to the heuristic force of the *homoousion*, both in terms of the Son *and* the Holy Spirit, Torrance identifies the economic Trinity with the ontological Trinity (but only in a certain respect).[95]

> In this way the *homoousion* is found to have a critical significance in regard to what may and what may not be read back from God's revealing and saving activity in history to what he is antecedently, eternally and inherently in himself. It does tell us that what God is antecedently, eternally and inherently in himself he is indeed toward us in the incarnate economy of his saving action in Jesus Christ on our behalf, but it relates that economy ontologically to God in the ineffable Mystery of his Being who remains transcendent over all space and time, so that a significant distinction and delimitation between the economic Trinity and the ontological Trinity must be recognised as well as their essential oneness.[96]

As a result of the *homoousion*, we meet with the immanent Trinity (*theologia*) when we encounter Jesus Christ and the Spirit in space-time (*oikonomia*). Neither God nor human nature is changed by this fellowship (*koinonia*): however, as the Person of Christ remains the same in the incarnation despite the union of the two natures (*henosis hypostatikē*), so in the union (*henosis*) of humanity and God in salvation neither is changed ontologically but each relates to the other in a 'real' way.[97] This enables human beings to become more fully personed through participation in the divine nature.

Doctrine of God, pp. 88–111. See a discussion of these levels in Colyer, *The Nature of Doctrine in T.F. Torrance's Theology*, pp. 181–7; and an overview in Alan G. Marley, *T.F. Torrance: The Rejection of Dualism* (Edinburgh: Handsel Press, 1992), pp. 15–16; and Benjamin Myers, 'The Stratification of Knowledge in the Thought of T.F. Torrance', *Scottish Journal of Theology* 61 (2008): pp. 1–15. For a wider perspective which draws particularly upon Nicolai Hartman and Roy Bhaskar see Alister E. McGrath, 'Stratification: Levels of Reality and the Limits of Reductionism', in *The Order of Things: Explorations in Scientific Theology* (Oxford: Blackwell, 2006), Chapter 5.

94 Torrance, *The Christian Doctrine of God*, pp. 110–11.

95 For an analysis of the economic and ontological Trinity in recent thought, specifically Torrance's work, see Paul D. Molnar, *Divine Freedom and the Doctrine of the Immanent Trinity: In Dialogue with Karl Barth and Contemporary Theology* (London: T & T Clark, 2002), especially pp. 167–96; 317–30 and Stanley J. Grenz, *Rediscovering the Triune God: The Trinity in Contemporary Theology* (Minneapolis: Fortress, 2004), pp. 200–215.

96 Torrance, *The Christian Doctrine of God*, p. 97.

97 Thomas F. Torrance, 'Incarnation and Atonement: Theosis and Henosis in the Light of Modern Scientific Rejection of Dualism', *Society of Ordained Scientists*, Bulletin No. 7 (Edgeware, Middlesex, Spring 1992): pp. 8–20.

Anything short of a real participation in the divine nature is not *theosis,* and yet the Spirit's total objectivity safeguards Torrance from presenting what he calls a doctrine of 'divinisation'. *Theosis* is a reality in the life of the believer but not one that threatens the Creator-creature distinction from either direction. 'Divinisation', as Torrance employs the word here, posits a *direct* participation of the believer in the *essence* of God, and this is what Torrance rejects. *Theosis* however, in line with its biblical and patristic roots, posits participation by the believer in the divine nature, a relational union mediated by the Son and the Holy Spirit.

In one of Torrance's most crucial passages on the topic a variety of concepts are used to describe *theosis* and explain how it is that the Spirit at once opens up God to the world and the world to God. (Aspects of *theosis* are indicated parenthetically):

> The presence of the Holy Spirit to the creation imports an openness on the part of God's creation toward himself, for through the Spirit God is able to take possession of his creatures, to sustain them from below, and to be present within them in such a way as to lift them up to the level of (1)participation in God where they are opened out for (2)union and (3)communion with God far beyond the limits of their creaturely existence. To *be* (4)'in the Spirit' is to *be* in God, for the Spirit is not external but internal to the Godhead. But since it is only the Spirit of God who knows what is in God and it is he who unites us to the Son of God in his oneness with the Father, through the (3)Communion of the Spirit we are exalted to (5)know God in his inner trinitarian relations as Father, Son and Holy Spirit. When this actually takes place, however, we are restrained by the sheer Holiness and Majesty of the divine Being from transgressing the bounds of our creaturely being by inquiring beyond what is given through the Son and received in the Spirit, and therefore from intruding upon the mystery of God or thinking presumptuously and illegitimately of him. When God is present to us in his Holy Spirit we are on holy ground like Moses at the Burning Bush where he was bidden to take the shoes off his feet. Before the Face of God we are constrained by the Holy Spirit to (5)think of him only in a reverent and godly way worthy of him, in which (6)worship, wonder and silence inform the movement of our creaturely spirits to the Father, through the Son and in the Spirit, answering to the movement on God's part from the Father, through the Son and in the Spirit.[98]

Through the activity of the Spirit, who is, as Torrance points out, internal to the Godhead, we are united to the Son of God in his oneness with the Father, and through the communion of the Spirit we are exalted to know God in his inner trinitarian relations as Father, Son and Holy Spirit, an experience which transcends our comprehension.[99] The relational transcendence that the Spirit mediates even

98 Torrance, *The Christian Doctrine of God*, p. 153.

99 Torrance is fond of repeating the phrase of Basil's, 'We confess that we know what is knowable of God and yet what we know reaches beyond our comprehension'

now, as evidenced in such texts as Rom 8.26–7 is the source of Torrance's apophatic reticence regarding the consummation of *theosis*.

According to Torrance the double movement of the Spirit parallels that of the Son but in a reciprocal fashion, not as a separate process:

> When we consider this two-way activity of the Spirit in its coordination with the two-way activity of Christ, as we are bound to do in view of their oneness in Being and Act, we must think of the Spirit as participating in the vicarious and intercessory activity of Christ. Thus we must think of the presence of the Spirit as actualising within us the intervening and reconciling work of Christ when as the Son of God he assumed our wayward and disobedient humanity and through his own obedient life and atoning sacrifice offered himself to the Father in our place and in our stead, and thereby restored it in obedient sonship to the Father as our Father as well as his Father.[100]

Torrance places himself squarely within the patristic matrix of theology by asserting a thoroughgoing doctrine of *theosis*. He argues that *theosis* is centred in the incarnation of the eternal Son and with him, the vivifying, recreating, sanctifying and glorifying work of the Holy Spirit. In Christ and by his Spirit the believer is able to cry to God, not as a stranger but now, through the Spirit and in Christ, to their 'Abba, Father', as they have become children of God, joint-heirs of Christ, participants by grace in the divine nature.

Canlis notes that 'Calvin's genius was to perceive that without a genuine role for the Holy Spirit, you cannot help but have a fusion, or divine overwhelming of some sort'.[101] Calvin's doctrine of participation or union with God was made in response to the view of Osiander that the believer is united with or participates in the Divine Logos, not the incarnate Word. Canlis concludes, 'If in Melanchthon's causal scheme we are too far away from God, in Osiander's we are too close… Calvin approaches a very similar doctrine of indwelling and of union as Osiander, but strictly adheres to a trinitarian structure. He knew that the secret to our union was neither mechanistic imputation nor fusion, but rather participation in the Trinity'.[102]

Torrance, too, wishes to find a balance between positing a mixture or absorption of divine and human natures in salvation and the opposite tendency which regards the being of God as unknowable (*simpliciter*); hence only God's (impersonal) *energies* are able to be encountered. The first is too close, the second too distant. Torrance adopts the language of the 'blessed exchange' to indicate the principle that in Christ God has given us access to the divine life. However, as Colyer adds,

(*Epistulae*, 235.2).

100 Torrance, *The Christian Doctrine of God*, pp. 153–4.

101 Julie Canlis, 'Calvin, Osiander, and Participation in God', *International Journal of Systematic Theology* 6 (2004): p. 172.

102 Ibid., p. 172.

'A significant part of this "blessed exchange" throughout Christ's life, ministry, death, and resurrection, Torrance contends, is that "the eternal Spirit of the living God has composed himself, as it were, to dwell with human nature, and human nature has been adapted and become accustomed to receive and bear the same Holy Spirit"'.[103] In short, through the Son and in the Spirit the believer is enabled to participate in the divine nature. This, for Torrance, is what the doctrine of *theosis* means in the Christian church.

Deddo correctly summarises Torrance's soteriology when he asserts: 'The Spirit is the communion of the Father and the Son, so for us to have the Spirit is for us to share in the Son's union and communion with the Father. Thus salvation consists in being drawn up in the Son into the very Triune life by the power of the Spirit.'[104] A shorter but no less precise statement would be that salvation, as Torrance understands it, might be explicated as *theosis*.[105]

The Spirit of Truth

In Chapter 3 Torrance's doctrine of cognitive (epistemological) union was examined and linked to his doctrine of *theosis*.[106] Cognitive union is dealt with quite comprehensively in Torrance's treatment of the 'Spirit of truth', and it is worth rehearsing his basic moves in this context.

The epistemological importance of the Holy Spirit in Torrance's theology cannot be underestimated.[107] The Holy Spirit does not bring witness to himself but to Christ, and this, according to Torrance, is the force of Pentecost. The Holy Spirit is the Spirit of truth (*aletheia*), because:

> ...there is *aletheia*, for truth is the unveiling of what was hidden, the manifestation of the divine Reality – that is why He is called the Spirit of truth: it is through his agency that Jesus Christ is revealed as the Son of the Father...he does not show us Himself, but shows us the Face of the Father in the Face of the Son...yet because it is through Him that the Word of God was made flesh and through Him that the Word continues to be heard and believed, because it is in his Light that we see Light and by his creative operation that we know the unknowable and eternal God...he is Himself God of God, the Holy Spirit of one substance

---

103 Colyer, 'Thomas F. Torrance on the Holy Spirit', p. 162, citing Torrance, *Theology in Reconstruction*, p. 246.

104 Deddo, 'The Holy Spirit in T.F. Torrance's Theology', p. 93.

105 Ibid., pp. 94 and 95, notes this same fact slightly later in his exposition. See Torrance, *Theology in Reconciliation*, pp. 134, 238–40; *Divine Meaning: Studies in Patristic Hermeneutics* (Edinburgh: T & T Clark, 1995), pp. 198, 202; and *The Trinitarian Faith*, pp. 198–228.

106 See Chapter 3, pp. 92–7.

107 For an overview see Torrance, *The Trinitarian Faith*, pp. 213–15; and *God and Rationality*, pp. 165–92.

> with the Father and of one substance with the Son, who confronts us in His own person with the ultimate Godness of God...He utters the Word but does not utter Himself, and therefore He directs us through Himself to the one *Logos* and *Eidos* of Godhead in Jesus Christ in accordance with whom all our knowledge of God is formed in our minds...[108]

The Spirit's presence is that of the being of God within human experience and human knowledge, and creates a relation to God in Christ that is required for true knowledge to exist.[109] In an insightful statement Torrance summarises the role of the Holy Spirit in *theosis* as follows:

> The Spirit of God the Father and the Son is God in his freedom personally to meet and be with man, to address him in his Word, making himself known to him and creating in him capacity to respond as a rational subject and agent to himself. It is through this inter-personal mode of his presence to man that the Spirit makes man's being open for fellowship with God, and thereby brings his creaturely relations to their true end and fulfilment in God. He is essentially the living Spirit who, coming from the inner communion of the Holy Trinity, creates communion between man and God.[110]

Torrance argues that until the Spirit interprets the historical actions of God in Christ, revelation has not yet occurred. Torrance draws one corollary from this axiom:

> The Christ who is the whole fact of faith is thus the Christ of the Gospel period extended into a further period through the Holy Spirit. The whole Christ is thus not the bodily Christ but the Christ of actual event carried out into the actual experience and faith of the Church by the indwelling mind of Christ, the Holy Spirit, who indwells the believer.[111]

This leads Torrance to the concise statement: 'The significant thing about the Lordship of Christ, the Deity of Christ, is that it may be confessed by people only in the power of the Holy Spirit.'[112] Word and Spirit are kept in the closest proximity as they mutually condition one another, both in revelation and reconciliation.

Torrance forcefully presents the idea that God can only be known by encountering him and his saving work in space and time. The ascension connects us to the incarnation, and to the historical Jesus, and so to a word and act of God inseparably implicated in our space and time. Thus all true knowledge of God is

---

108 Torrance, *God and Rationality*, p. 167. Cf. *The Trinitarian Faith*, pp. 191–250; and *The Ground and Grammar of Theology*, pp. 164–7.

109 Torrance, *The Mediation of Christ*, pp. 115–19.

110 Torrance, 'The Soul and Person in Theological Perspective', pp. 111–12.

111 Torrance, *The Doctrine of Jesus Christ*, p. 49.

112 Ibid., p. 55.

mediated through the historical Jesus. But the obverse is also true: that through the historical and crucified Jesus we truly meet with the risen and ascended Lord; we meet with God in his transcendent glory of majesty, and we really are gathered into the communion of the Son with the Father, and of the Father with the Son, and are raised up through the Spirit to share in the divine life and love that have overflowed to us in Christ Jesus.[113] Thus, within the heart of his theological construction of the atoning and reconciling work of Christ, Torrance returns to the theme of *theosis* to clarify his point.

It is Torrance's contention that we can only think of these two aspects of the ascension through the Spirit. The Spirit becomes the crucial epistemological linchpin of his soteriology. The Holy Spirit links the historical Jesus with the ascended Lord and through the communion of the Spirit we can identify the historical absence and actual presence of Christ. Affirming a doctrine of *theosis* Torrance writes: 'Through the Spirit Christ is nearer to us than we are to ourselves, and we who live and dwell on earth are yet made to sit with Christ "in heavenly places", partaking of the divine nature.'[114]

Torrance insists that God's self-revelation and self-communication in the incarnation cannot be understood apart from God's self-giving to us in the Spirit. Hence revelation and reconciliation are correlative. It is in and through the Holy Spirit that 'we are united to Christ the incarnate Son of the Father, and are made through this union with him in the Spirit to participate, humans though we are, in the Communion which the Father, the Son and the Holy Spirit…are in themselves'.[115] He insists that,

> The Holy Spirit interiorizes the knowledge of God within us, but He does this by actualizing within us God's own witness to Himself. The Holy Spirit is the eternal Communion of the Father and the Son and therefore when He is sent into our hearts by the Father in the name of the Son we are made partakers with the Son in His Communion with the Father and thus of God's own self-knowledge.[116]

This description of *theosis* thus summarises the pneumatological work of God in reconciliation in terms of both epistemology and ontology.

While Torrance deals at length with epistemological issues, especially in his articulation of the Spirit of truth, it would be a grave misunderstanding to restrict his theology to epistemic concerns. The Holy Spirit brings knowledge of *Christ*, and through Christ of the triune communion.[117] Through the gift of the Spirit of

---

[113] Thomas F. Torrance, *Space, Time and Resurrection* (1976. Edinburgh: T & T Clark, 1998), pp. 134–5.

[114] Ibid., p. 135.

[115] Torrance, *The Christian Doctrine of God*, p. 148.

[116] Torrance, *God and Rationality*, pp. 173–4.

[117] The Triune nature involves an inherently relational ontology, as developed in Torrance, *The Trinitarian Faith*. See an analysis of this theme by Grenz, *Rediscovering the*

Christ, who is also the Spirit of God, we are drawn into a holy communion in which God by the Spirit, 'is made present to us within the conditions of our creaturely existence in such a healing and creative way as to open our hearts and minds to receive and understand his self-revelation as Father, Son and Holy Spirit'.[118] While Torrance's soteriology does tend to overemphasise issues of epistemology, it does not do so at the expense of ontology as this study on the mutual mediation of Christ and Spirit highlights.

The Spirit, Communion and Adoption

It is Torrance's contention that the Greek patristic theologians' doctrine of the Holy Spirit profoundly altered the notions of person, reason, ontology and epistemology. In Nicene theology a 'profound epistemological inversion'[119] took place, one that was governed by the 'transcendental determination' of humanity to an *objective other*, primarily in God but also in fellow humans. Contrary to the Greek view of humans as the embodiment of an immortal soul, Torrance maintains the patristic theologians' conception of the human person is as an indivisible union of body and soul created by God and for God through his Spirit. Accordingly the real intent of what the Nicene theologians called *theosis* or *theopoiesis* is not, technically speaking, the 'deification' or 'divinisation' of *humanity*, but the immediate presence of the Holy Spirit through whom we participate in the revealing and saving activity of God in the vicarious humanity of Jesus Christ.[120] By rejecting the language of 'deification' and 'divinisation' in favour of *theosis* and *theopoiesis*, Torrance once again makes it clear that no confusion or mixture of natures is in view.

The way the believer is incorporated into Christ by the Spirit is through adoption. While Torrance does speak of adoption/sonship on a number of occasions there is no fully developed doctrine of adoption worked out in his theology. It seems that most of what can be said regarding our adoption as 'sons' has already been said in relation to the vicarious humanity of Christ. While Christ alone is *the* Son, believers incorporated into him by the Spirit become 'sons/children of God' (Rom 8.14, 17). As sons/children of God believers participate in the divine nature by grace – by adoption – while the Son, Jesus Christ is divine by nature.

Adoption is used by Torrance as a cognate for *theosis*; so for instance, we read, 'Athanasius pointed to the very heart of the matter in the incarnation of the Son of God, which by its very nature involved the union of God and man in Christ, and at

---

Triune God, pp. 200–215, and 221–3.

118 Torrance, *The Mediation of Christ*, p. 111.

119 Torrance, 'The Soul and Person in Theological Perspective', p. 112.

120 Ibid., pp. 112–13. For a concise overview which links the radical objectivity of the Spirit to Torrance's doctrine of *theosis* see Deddo, 'The Holy Spirit in T.F. Torrance's Theology', pp. 94–6.

the same time our "deification" or adoption as sons of God in Christ'.[121] Adoption is important for a doctrine of *theosis* as the constant reminder that the union between believers and Christ is not one of nature but grace. Torrance is quick to insist that we are incorporated into Christ's *humanity*: 'Since this takes place in Christ, the incarnate Son, however, it involves a somatic and not just a spiritual union in and with him.'[122] This is what makes the church the body of Christ. Torrance affirms the teaching of Athanasius that as Christ is the true vine and we are the branches, we have bodies that are 'connate (ὁμογενη) with the Lord's Body, receive out of his fullness and have that body as the root of our resurrection and salvation'.[123]

The adoption of believers is specifically into the perfected *humanity* of Christ, and thereby with the Godhead.[124] This does not mean humans are made divine; rather, as Torrance allows Athanasius to remind us, 'our being in the Father is not ours but is the Spirit's who is in us and abides in us…It is the Spirit, then, who is in God, and not we viewed in ourselves'.[125]

The Spirit is Christ's *Alter Advocatus*, even Christ's *Alter Ego*[126] 'who seals our adoption as children of God in Christ and so unites us to Christ that we come to share by grace in Christ's own filial relationship with the Father realized vicariously within Christ's earthly human life on our behalf'.[127] The language of adoption reminds us that the purpose of life is a transforming relationship with God in which the Spirit calls and enables us to become children of God in and alongside the Son and to join in his self-surrender to the Father. With a direct allusion to the language of Torrance, Pinnock writes, 'God has not left us outside the circle of his life. We are invited inside the Trinity as joint heirs together with Christ. By the Spirit we cry "Abba" together with the Son, as we are drawn into the divine filial relationship and begin to participate in God's life'.[128] Pinnock, like Torrance, recalls that this is what the church fathers meant by the doctrine of *theosis*.[129]

Not only is adoption important in the theology of the early church upon which Torrance draws but also, closer to home, it is important to the Reformed tradition within which Torrance operates. Writing prior to Torrance, McLeod Campbell

121 Torrance, *The Trinitarian Faith*, p. 264. Torrance then cites passages from Athanasius including *De decr.* 14, 31; *Con Ar.* 1.9, 37ff, 46ff; 2.47, 53, 59, 63ff; and *De syn.* 51.

122 Ibid. See Athanasius, *Con. Ar.* 3.22f.

123 Ibid., p. 266. Torrance is referring to Athanasius, *De sent. Dion.*,10.

124 Ibid., p. 267.

125 Ibid., p. 268, citing Athanasius, *Con. Ar.* 3.24f.

126 Ibid., p. 249.

127 Colyer, *How To Read T.F. Torrance*, p. 230. Cf. Torrance, *The Mediation of Christ*, pp. 115–17.

128 Pinnock, *Flame of Love*, p. 153. Pinnock's entire chapter on 'Spirit and Union' (pp. 149–83) shows an obvious but unreferenced reliance upon Torrance's theology.

129 Ibid., p. 154.

beautifully describes adoption as 'orphans who have found their lost father'.[130] The logic is that believers participate in Christ, the eternal Son, and so participate in the filial relationship with the Father (Jn 8.19). It is the intimate relationship between the Father and the Son that is communicated to humanity through the Spirit of the Son (Rom 8.29). It is in this sense that Torrance defines salvation as 'sonship'. In similar fashion Walls writes:

> Through the Holy Spirit the innermost mystery of the life of God the Holy Trinity is opened in sheer unmerited gift to us. We become the adopted sons in the Son of God. We become this not by mere imitation but by sharing in this new form of being – being as communion, being constituted by self-giving. So in our created way we reflect and share in the divine nature (2 Pet 1.4). This is eternal life, this is salvation: to be brought within the unbroken circle of God's being in communion. Just as God's being is a consummated distinction in a union of mutual life, so this too is the work of the Holy Spirit in the church as communion of persons.[131]

Such is precisely the vision to which Torrance subscribes.

Adoption depends on the vicarious humanity of Jesus Christ 'who for our sakes became poor that we through his poverty might become rich' (2 Cor 8.9). Torrance explains that '...the Son of God united himself with us in our actual human condition so intimately and profoundly that through his healing and sanctifying of our human nature in himself we may be made with him sons of God'.[132] On this basis Christ acts with us, for us, and on our behalf towards the Father in all our distinctive experiences as children of God:

> such as confession, penitence, sorrow, chastisement, submission to the divine judgement, and faith, obedience, love, prayer, praise, adoration, that we may share with him what he is in his ascension and self-presentation before the Father as the beloved Son in whom he is well pleased.[133]

Collectively, the children of God form the church, the body of Christ, within which *theosis* becomes a reality made possible by the Holy Spirit. For this reason

---

130 Cited in Christian D. Kettler, 'The Vicarious Repentance of Christ in the Theology of John McLeod Campbell and R. C. Moberly', *Scottish Journal of Theology* 38 (1985): p. 540.

131 R. Walls, 'The Church: A Communion of Persons', in *Christ in Our Place: The Humanity of God in Christ for the Reconciliation of the World: Essays Presented to Professor James Torrance*, eds Trevor A. Hart and Daniel P. Thimell (Exeter: Paternoster, 1981), p. 104.

132 Torrance, *Theology in Reconciliation*, p. 136.

133 Ibid.

our attention must turn to the church, the communion of saints, for a more specific application of *theosis* in Torrance's theology.

The Church as a Communion of *Theosis*

The mutual mediation of Christ and Spirit is extended into ecclesiology constituting the church as the *communion* of *theosis* in Torrance's theology. Union with God, most comprehensively subsumed under a doctrine of *theosis*, is realised by the Spirit through the church's sacraments, ministry and worship. Torrance does not consider Pentecost the birth of the church but its re-birth, not its beginning but its transformation. However, he does consider Pentecost as the birth of the *Christian* church and so in this chapter all references to 'church' refer more technically to what Torrance terms the 'Christian Church'.[134]

Kärkkäinen reminds us that, 'Ecclesiologies have traditionally been built on either of the two classical rules, that of Ignatius of Antioch or of Irenaeus'. He explains:

> Ignatius suggested the ecclesiality of the church could be secured by reference to Christ's presence: 'Wherever Jesus Christ is, there is the universal church.' According to Irenaeus what is decisive is the presence of the Spirit of God: 'Wherever the Spirit of God is, there is the church, and all of grace.'[135]

Rather than affirm one model and deny the other, Torrance shows how Ignatius and Irenaeus shared a common conception of the church but approached it from two complementary perspectives.[136] Building on their work, Torrance's ecclesiology is christocentric, pneumatological and trinitarian. Torrance affirms the christological grounding of the church (Ignatius), but essentially follows the Irenaean conception of the church as the communion of saints, and thus christology and pneumatology must be seen as mutual not exclusive.[137] Following the Nicene Creed, Torrance places the church as an aspect of the Spirit's work.[138]

Once more Torrance repeats a familiar Reformed emphasis upon the mutual mediation of Word and Spirit, derived principally from Calvin, who writes,

---

134 See Torrance, *Theology in Reconstruction*, p. 204; and *Royal Priesthood*, pp. 23–42.

135 Veli-Matti Kärkkäinen, 'Toward a Pneumatological Ecclesiology', in *Toward a Pneumatological Theology: Pentecostal and Ecumenical Perspectives on Ecclesiology, Soteriology, and Theology of Mission*, ed. Amos Yong (Lanham: University Press of America, 2002), p. 83.

136 Torrance draws from Ignatius and Irenaeus in *The Trinitarian Faith*, pp. 252–63, but notes the same basic teaching was common in the early centuries, as seen for instance in Clement, Hermas, *Didache*, Hippolytus, Tertullian and Origen.

137 Torrance describes this in *Royal Priesthood*, p. 24.

138 Torrance, *The Trinitarian Faith*, pp. 252–301; *Royal Priesthood*, p. 23, and *Theology in Reconstruction*, pp. 192–208.

'Wherever we see the Word of God purely preached and heard, and the sacraments administered according to Christ's institution, there, it is not to be doubted, a church of God exists'.[139] Thus Torrance combines the 'two-hands' theology of Irenaeus with Calvin's 'marks' of the church in his construction of a pneumato-ecclesiology.

The trinitarian renaissance that has affected every major *locus* of theology has more recently been applied to ecclesiology. In particular, relational or community-centred themes have become the focus of the new work.[140] Torrance's ecclesiology is an anticipation of many of these newer insights. Torrance presents the church as the sphere of God's deifying activity of believers in which the Spirit unites us to Christ and through Christ with the Father so that this community becomes 'the place in space and time where knowledge of the Father, the Son and the Holy Spirit becomes grounded in humanity, and union and communion with the Holy Trinity becomes embodied within the human race'.[141]

Torrance works out a self-consciously corporate vision of salvation where the Spirit unites us to Christ through incorporation into his body, the church.[142] The Holy Spirit actualises union and communion with God through Christ in the structure of our physical, personal, and social being. Torrance views the work of the Spirit as creating and calling forth from humanity a response of faith and obedience, worship and prayer. The central purpose of the church is to glorify God through the progressive 'deification' of his people: that is – the church exists for *theosis*, 'so that through union with [Christ] in Spirit and Body the Church participates in the divine nature and engages in Christ's ministry of reconciliation'.[143]

Torrance remarks, 'In a profound sense atonement is the insertion of the hypostatic union into the very being of our estranged and fallen humanity. That insertion of oneness by atonement results in κοινωνια, in the Church as the communion in which we are made partakers of the divine nature'.[144] Here we have a direct attestation to *theosis*, which is intimately linked to the communion-fellowship making work of the Spirit, seen supremely within the context of the church. As Torrance remarks in *The Trinitarian Faith*,

---

139 Calvin, *Institutes*, 4.1.9. Cf. 4.2.3; 4.2.1; and John Calvin, *A Reformation Debate: Sadoleto's Letter to the Genevans and Calvin's Reply*, ed. John C. Olin (Grand Rapids: Baker, 1966), p. 63. See Torrance, *Royal Priesthood*, p. 24.

140 See for instance on personhood John D. Zizioulas, *Being as Communion: Studies in Personhood and the Church* (Crestwood, NY.: St Vladimir's Seminary Press, 1997); and on community Stanley J. Grenz, *Theology for the Community of God* (Carlisle: Paternoster, 1994), pp. 601–742; Miroslav Volf, *After Our Likeness: The Church as the Image of the Trinity* (Grand Rapids, Cambridge: Eerdmans, 1998); and Craig Van Gelder, *The Essence of the Church: A Community Created by the Spirit* (Grand Rapids: Baker, 2000).

141 Torrance, *The Trinitarian Faith*, pp. 256–7. See *Theology in Reconstruction*, p. 252.

142 This is emphatic in Torrance, *Royal Priesthood*, pp. 34–6, cf. pp. 28–9.

143 Ibid., p. 29. For a remarkably similar argument see Pinnock, *Flame of Love*, p. 117.

144 Torrance, *Conflict and Agreement in the Church*, vol. 2. pp. 90–91.

> Through the incarnation and Pentecost the Holy Spirit comes to us from the inner communion of the Father, Son and Holy Spirit, creates union and communion between us and the Holy Trinity. In other words, the Spirit creates not only personal union but corporate communion between us and Christ and through Christ with the Holy Trinity, so that it is the Holy Spirit who creates and sustains the being and life of the church, uniting the Church to Christ as his one body.[145]

Torrance's ecclesiology at this point shows a marked similarity to distinctively Eastern forms of thought. As is evident in the East, the church is necessary since all the conditions required for believers to attain union with God (*theosis*) are received through the church.[146] Nikos Nissiotis states, 'It is not sufficient to confess God's unique revelation in Christ and our reconciliation with Him. The christocentric approach cannot be valid unless it is thought out in connection with the work of the other two persons of the Trinity, who are revealed through Him and with Him'.[147] According to a plethora of contemporary thinkers, including Nissiotis, what is required is a pneumatological christology that results in a reconstituted pneumato-ecclesiology. Torrance offers such a reformulated ecclesiology when he works out in detail how believers are gathered by the Spirit around Christ to be conformed to the image of the Son and made partakers of the divine nature. 'It is then that the true nature of the Church becomes manifest', writes Torrance, 'as the work of the three divine Persons, as the holy place appointed by God where diseased and sinful men are healed and saved through encountering the ultimate objectivity of God himself in Incarnation and Atonement.'[148]

Salvation, as understood by the term *theosis*, occurs in Christ, by the Spirit, within the church. It is an eschatologically oriented salvation initiated in space-time. Torrance develops these themes in his ecclesiology, and in the process provides resources contributing to the further development of a communio-ecclesiology in both Reformed theology and wider ecumenical discussion. The fact that this aspect of his theology has not been widely recognised attests to the long way Protestant theology still has to travel in understanding how pneumatology is constitutive of christology and ecclesiology.[149] A pneumatologically constituted ecclesiology cannot be construed apart from a christological and a trinitarian orientation: 'The

---

145 Torrance, *The Trinitarian Faith*, p. 9.

146 For a detailed example see Bartos, *Deification in Eastern Orthodoxy*, pp. 252–328.

147 Nikos A. Nissiotis, 'Pneumatological Christology as a Presupposition of Ecclesiology', in *Oecumenica: An Annual Symposium of Ecumenical Research* (Minneapolis: Augsburg, 1967), p. 235.

148 Torrance, *Theology in Reconstruction*, p. 233.

149 It is noteworthy that Pannenberg, *Systematic Theology* (especially vol. 3, pp. 12–27) works towards making pneumatology constitutive of christology and ecclesiology and as such the Holy Spirit plays a crucial role in the doctrine of the Trinity, salvation and ecclesiology.

foundational triad is the relationship between Christ and Spirit, Christ and Church and Spirit and Church.'[150] Adopting a foundational triad in this way will help the West avoid a 'Christomonism' (Nissiotis) that results in a hierarchical church, and in the East a 'Spritomonism' (Kärkkäinen)[151] where Christ as the foundation of the church and head of his body is eclipsed.

Torrance's ecclesiology is constructed on a pneumatological and christological foundation, as one would expect. The result, however, is surprising. Torrance accomplishes in ecclesiology what he does with his christology, trinitarian theology, and scientific theology as a whole: he builds bridges to various traditions while retaining the essentials of his own Reformed tradition. Torrance's pneumato-ecclesiology upholds the affirmation that the Spirit is the divine agent who unites the believer to Christ and through Christ to the Father. As such the Spirit applies the benefits of salvation to the believer in space-time. Torrance, however, does not get caught up in Western individualistic notions of salvation or pietistic notions of church, avoiding both in a realistic appreciation of *koinonia* and community. Torrance also avoids the temptation to identify Christ with the church as an institution and so he does not view Christ's authority as invested directly in church hierarchy. In the first approach the Spirit is reduced to the agent of Christ for individual salvation only, while in the second the Spirit is invoked as a guarantee of a pre-existing order *de jure divino* of the church institution. Torrance's pneumato-ecclesiology thus draws heavily on Protestant soteriology, Reformed ecclesiology, and certain Eastern Orthodox perspectives on both. Within such a framework the theme of the church as the *locus* of *theosis* becomes evident and requires a more direct examination.

Church as Locus *of* Theosis

Because the church 'partakes of the divine nature'[152] Torrance conceives of it as the *locus* of *theosis*. The church is the earthly, historical reflection of the Divine *perichoresis*, 'the heavenly Communion of Love with the Trinity'.[153] In rejecting all accounts of the church as an extension of the incarnation, or of the institutional church acting as the dispenser of grace,[154] Torrance focuses on the role of the Holy Spirit in ecclesiology where he wishes to employ the doctrine of *theosis*. Torrance maintained in his early ministry the utter supremacy of Jesus Christ and

150 Kärkkäinen, 'Toward a Pneumatological Ecclesiology', p. 93. See Volf, *After Our Likeness*.

151 Ibid.

152 Torrance, *Conflict and Agreement in the Church*, vol. 1, p. 109. Cf. p. 224; *Conflict and Agreement in the Church*, vol. 2, pp. 83–4, 89; *Theology in Reconstruction*, p. 204; and *Theological Science* (London: Oxford University Press, 1969), p. 212.

153 Torrance, *Reality and Scientific Theology*, p. 187.

154 See Torrance, *Theology in Reconstruction*, p. 176.

the church as the Body of Christ, drawing somewhat narrowly on the *Filioque*,[155] and arguing that the Spirit reveals Christ; therefore the revealing work of the Spirit is bounded throughout the history of the church by the particularity of the incarnation. Thus the doctrine of the church must be formulated as a correlate of the doctrine of Christ. A result is that the church is the body of Christ, not the body of the Spirit – the approach, according to Torrance, of both Roman Catholicism and Pentecostalism, albeit in different ways. On the contrary, the doctrine of the Spirit holds an indispensable place, for the church is a communion of love, a fellowship of people living the reconciled life. 'The Church is thus the way in which the communion of the Spirit functions within the social relations of creation by creating a supernatural fellowship, in their midst through which, while still within creation, they share in the divine life and love poured out upon them from above in and through Jesus Christ.'[156] As such the church is the sphere within which *theosis* takes place in time-space.[157]

Because of Torrance's stress upon the priority of grace, the Christian experience of *theosis* is not fundamentally an exercise in self-purification, as it tended to be viewed by non-Christian Neoplatonists.[158] Instead, it is an act of the triune God in transforming men and women into the *imago Dei*. This transformation affects more than the mind; it affects the whole person, even the body.

As the body of Christ *and* the communion of saints, the church is the place created by the intersection of the vertical and horizontal dimensions of union with Christ. The vertical dimension relates to communion with God and the horizontal relates to communion with each other. As such 'the Church is the atonement becoming actual among men in the resurrection of a new humanity corresponding to the resurrected Body of Jesus'.[159] This is part of the transformation into Christ-likeness (Christification), the sanctification of the believer, or *theosis*. The process of *theosis* is also the church's means of mission in the world as it lives the resurrected life of Christ. That is to say:

---

155 'Narrow' because Torrance had not yet come into sustained contact with Eastern Orthodoxy or sought to integrate his Reformed theology with distinctive Orthodox emphases as he does in later works such as *Theological Dialogue*, vols 1 and 2; *Trinitarian Perspectives*; and *The Trinitarian Faith*.

156 Torrance, *The School of Faith*, p. cxvii.

157 On church as the context for *theosis* in Eastern Orthodoxy see, Emilianos Timiadis, 'The Trinitarian Structure of the Church and its Authority', in *Theological Dialogue*, vol. 1. pp. 121–56. On Gregory Palamas, who defines church as a 'communion of deification', see Daniel M. Rogich, *Becoming Uncreated: The Journey to Human Authenticity: Updating the Spiritual Christology of Gregory Palamas* (Minneapolis: Light and Life Publishing Company, 1997), p. 87.

158 Consult Stephen Finlan, 'Second Peter's Notion of Divine Participation', in *Theōsis: Deification in Christian Theology*, eds Stephen Finlan and Vladimir Kharlamov (OR.: Pickwick Publications, 2006), pp. 33–40.

159 Torrance, *Conflict and Agreement in the Church*, vol. 1, p. 221.

> [T]he existence of the Church as Church is grounded in the work of the Saviour in abolishing the sin and guilt which have estranged the human race and in overcoming the enmity and disunity between man and God; and the being of the Church consists in the redeemed life of those who being reconciled to God in Christ are therein also reconciled to one another, and are compacted together into one living community in which each member is what he is through the common participation of all in Christ and in mutual sharing in the life of others in love.[160]

By showing how persons commune with God, or the way in which God incorporates creatures into the inner divine life, even if only briefly, Torrance demonstrates a personal engagement with *theosis* as a practice and not simply as a theory. According to Torrance, the sacraments and worship form the indispensable outward form by which 'divinisation' occurs. It is these themes which occupy our attention in the next section.

Theosis *and the Sacraments*

There is, technically, only one sacrament, the Lord Jesus Christ, according to Torrance. The sacraments of Baptism and Eucharist thus point away from themselves toward Christ, the true *mystērion*. Consequently, sacraments may only be called a *mystery* in a secondary sense. For this reason Calvin and others in the Reformed tradition, Torrance included, prefer the terms *mystērion* and *seal* to *res* and *signum* in reference to the sacraments.[161] This is the 'depth dimension' of the sacraments to which Torrance often refers.[162] Baptism is the sign of initiation into Christ, while the Eucharist is the sign of the continual feeding upon Christ until he comes again. Together, they witness powerfully to the reality of union with Christ and the ongoing transformation of believers into christlikeness. As such, both Baptism and Eucharist form the central ecclesial acts in which believers participate and thus *theosis* occurs.

Torrance's doctrine of union with Christ relates that the benefits of Christ are applied to the believer in the church, through faith, and by means of the sacraments

---

160 Torrance, *Theology in Reconciliation*, p. 21.

161 Torrance, *Conflict and Agreement in the Church*, vol. 2, pp. 92, 141–2, 156, 162–3; George Hunsinger, 'The Dimension of Depth: Thomas F. Torrance on the Sacraments of Baptism and the Lord's Supper', *Scottish Journal of Theology* 54 (2001): pp. 169–70, suggests, however, that Torrance's work supports the view that the relations of *signum* and *res* are more nearly instrumental than parallel or symbolic. Lee, *Living in Union With Christ*, p. 278, sees the relation as analogical, as does Spjuth, *Creation, Contingency and Divine Presence*, p. 127. Both positions are correct, for analogy and instrumentality are not mutually exclusive in Torrance's sacramentalism. Torrance himself asserts that the elements of the Eucharist remain what they are and yet are 'converted into instruments of the real presence', Torrance, *Conflict and Agreement in the Church*, vol. 2, p. 188.

162 See Torrance, *Theology in Reconciliation*, pp. 82–3.

of Baptism and the Eucharist. He finds support for this in the *Institutes*, where Calvin writes, 'For all the gifts of God proffered in baptism are found in Christ alone'.[163] As Hunsinger points out, the baptismal gifts Calvin identified were forgiveness of sins, dying and rising with Christ, and communion with Christ himself (*Institutes*, 4.15.1, 5, 6) although, communion with Christ 'was in effect the one inestimable gift that included within itself the other two benefits of forgiveness and rising with Christ from the dead'.[164] He continues: 'Only by participating in Christ through communion could the divine gifts set forth in baptism be truly received'.[165] Hence salvation is conceived as participating baptismally and eucharistically in the incarnate Christ by the Spirit. This is how union with Christ is initiated in the life of the individual believer and how *theosis* is personalised.

Hunsinger highlights the fact that within Calvin's thought, and Reformed theology after him, there is an inherent tension concerning what he terms the 'complex temporality of salvation'.[166] There are two ways of speaking of salvation: 'either salvation must be spoken of as *essentially* in the perfect tense, or else also in the present tense *alongside* the perfect tense'.[167] He continues:

> If salvation is essentially in the perfect sense, then its present and future tenses must be seen as *modes of receiving and participating in* the one salvation already accomplished in Christ. If on the other hand, salvation occurs *essentially* also in the present tense alongside the perfect tense, then its present and future tenses must somehow *supplement and complete a process* that Christ initiated in his earthly existence, but did not entirely fulfil.[168]

Framing the two views in terms of their relation to the perfect tense is helpful.[169]

The entire tenor of Torrance's theology places it firmly within the first model, that salvation must be spoken of essentially in the *perfect tense*, based as it is upon the completed work of Christ, a work into which we enter. How then does Torrance integrate this objective aspect of salvation in the *perfect* tense with what was mentioned earlier, the progressive growth or maturing of the believer? In short: through an emphasis upon participation in the vicarious humanity of Christ

---

163 Calvin, *Institutes*, 4.15.6.

164 Hunsinger, 'The Dimension of Depth: Thomas F. Torrance on the Sacraments of Baptism and the Lord's Supper', p. 155.

165 Ibid.

166 Ibid., p. 156.

167 Ibid., p. 157. George Hunsinger elaborates on the 'tenses of salvation' in 'Baptism and the Soteriology of Forgiveness', *International Journal of Systematic Theology* 2 (2000): pp. 247–69. In *How to Read Karl Barth: The Shape of His Theology* (Oxford: Oxford University Press, 1991), pp. 185–8, 201–18, Hunsinger traces the 'perfect tense' theme back through Barth to the early church in what he calls 'the Chalcedonian pattern'.

168 Ibid.

169 See Lee, *Living in Union With Christ*, p. 312.

and his sanctification. In addressing this issue, Hunsinger considers Torrance's thought is 'surely the most creative Reformed breakthrough on the sacraments in twentieth-century theology, and arguably the most important Reformed statement since Calvin'.[170] Hunsinger finds Torrance's sacramental theology attractive precisely because of its consistent christocentric soteriology.[171]

Throughout our study much has been made of the term communion (*koinonia*) and its cognates. The New Testament principle is that union, fellowship, participation and communion are achieved by Christ in the Holy Spirit. As has been pointed out, 'The principal theological use concerns the communion with God which – through participation in Christ the redeemer and mediator, and in the Holy Spirit the sanctifier – makes believers "partakers of the divine nature" (*theias koinōnoi physeōs*; 2 Peter 1.4)'.[172] In line with Torrance's thought, Wainwright explains that baptism brings a person 'into Christ', and through the Eucharist they 'participate' in the body and blood of Christ. Hence, 'a sacramental sharing creates a fellowship among the participants'.[173] *Theosis* is progressively realised through the corporate relationship with Christ made visible through the sacraments. Thus Torrance incorporates a sacramental view of *theosis* into his ecclesiology and soteriology. This also reflects his clearly defined theology of the mediation and high priestly ministry of Christ.[174]

The sacramental context provides a prime example of how *theosis* occurs, of how the transcendent God can be experienced, participated in, and known by finite human persons. In his sacramental theology Torrance affirms the close unity-in-distinction between human activity and divine presence as he works within a thoroughly Reformed theology which integrates act and passivity, human giving and receiving, justification and sanctification, in one sacramental movement. Torrance argues that 'The holy sacraments, Baptism and Eucharist, are also acts of human response to the proclamation of the Gospel, dramatic answers given to the Word of God incarnate in Jesus Christ'.[175] He reminds us that '…they are above all divinely provided, dominically appointed ways of response and obedience of a radically vicarious kind'.[176] Torrance stresses the vicarious humanity of Christ and human inclusion in God's activity (*theopoiesis*), which allows an active participation by the believer in Christ's vicarious work.

---

170 Hunsinger, 'The Dimension of Depth: Thomas F. Torrance on the Sacraments of Baptism and the Lord's Supper', p. 160.

171 On Torrance's sacramental theology see Spjuth, *Creation, Contingency and Divine Presence*, pp. 125–65.

172 Geoffrey Wainwright, 'The Nature of Communion', *Ecumenical Trends* 28 (1999): p. 81.

173 Ibid.

174 See the concise treatment of this in Torrance, *The Mediation of Christ*, pp. 89–92.

175 Ibid., p. 89.

176 Ibid.

Baptism and the Eucharist are kept in the closest proximity by Torrance's argument that strictly speaking there is only one sacrament (Christ) and Baptism and Eucharist belong to one indivisible whole. 'It is the sacrament of the *Word made flesh*, of the *Christ-event*, which includes the life, teaching, death and resurrection of Jesus Christ.'[177] Both Baptism and Eucharist have to do with incorporation into Christ; Baptism is all-inclusive and final while the Eucharist is the continual renewal of that incorporation in time.[178]

Torrance's ecclesiology is of importance here because the church is not only the place where Christ comes to us but also the place in creation where Christ through the Spirit actualises 'abiding communion' with us.[179] The church thus takes on a sacramental being as the body of Christ in which a real communion between believers and Christ through the Spirit is experienced. This communion is experienced in two ways: firstly, in an outward form of communion through the sacraments; secondly, through an inward and invisible communion in the Holy Spirit.[180] In an article on Orthodoxy Torrance explains that the vertical *koinonia* with Christ 'is our participation in the Holy Spirit, in which we come under the direct impact of God's uncreated energies'.[181] Clearly Torrance is using *energies* here in a personal sense, not the impersonal *energies* of Palamite theology. The mediation of redemption is not just the interrelation between a transcendental constitution 'from above' with a historical movement 'from below'; it is above all the offer and realisation of immediate communion with Christ; a unity the Spirit communicates mainly through Word and sacrament.[182] Hunsinger correctly points out that:

> What Torrance accomplishes is in effect, to bring Calvin and Barth together into a brilliant new synthesis. Like Calvin (but unlike Barth), Torrance sees baptism and the Lord's Supper as forms of God's Word, establishing and renewing the church in its union and communion with Christ. Like Calvin, that is, he sees the sacraments as vehicles of testimony that impart the very Christ whom they proclaim (by the gracious operation of the Holy Spirit), as opposed to Barth, who insists on seeing them 'ethically' as no more than a grateful human response to a prior divine grace not mediated or set forth by the sacraments themselves… However, like Barth (but unlike Calvin), Torrance has an unambiguous grasp on how salvation must be spoken of essentially in the perfect tense.[183]

---

177 Torrance, *Conflict and Agreement in the Church*, vol. 2, p. 156.

178 Ibid., pp. 165–90.

179 Torrance, *Royal Priesthood*, p. 33.

180 Torrance, *Conflict and Agreement in the Church*, vol. 1, p. 26.

181 Thomas F. Torrance, 'The Relevancy of Orthodoxy', in *The Relevancy of Orthodoxy*, ed. J.B. Logan (Stirling: The Drummond Press, 1970), p. 13.

182 This point was made by Spjuth, *Creation, Contingency and Divine Presence*, p. 162.

183 Hunsinger, 'The Dimension of Depth: Thomas F. Torrance on the Sacraments of Baptism and the Lord's Supper', p. 159.

In all of the Spirit's activity, Torrance maintains, there is an immediate presence and activity of God.[184] Torrance criticises any tendency to distinguish God's immediate presence by making differentiations between God's being (*essentia*) and his divine energies (*energeia*), or what he calls the introduction of 'an economic reserve'.[185] Torrance affirms an immediate divine presence of the Holy Spirit through ecclesial acts, especially those of Baptism and Eucharist.

Baptism The magisterial reformers and contemporary Reformed thought emphasise that the sacraments initiate and sustain the faith and spiritual growth of the believer in Christ. By the Spirit the believer is baptised into the community of faith, united to Christ, and set upon the path of glorious transformation. In order to penetrate this theological nexus Torrance develops a doctrine of baptism which revolves around three main movements: first, the objective (extra nos) elements with an emphasis on the vicarious humanity of Christ; second, the subjective (in nobis) elements which centre on the believer's participation in the vicarious humanity of Christ; and third, the eschatological orientation toward which the sacraments point. As with the rest of his theology, Torrance's doctrine of baptism is inherently christocentric and works within a trinitarian framework.

Torrance finds the origin of Christian Baptism in the Old Testament rite of proselyte baptism; it is not that Christian baptism depends on proselyte baptism, but simply that it provides an explanatory key to it. In proselyte baptism three main elements were involved: circumcision, the sprinkling of sin-offering water, and immersion. Behind this rite lay the 'powerful theology' of participation in the Exodus redemption out of Egypt, the crossing of the Red Sea, and of sanctificatory cleansing in the establishment of the Covenant at Mt Sinai.[186]

When Torrance turns specifically to the New Testament rite of Baptism (*baptisma*)[187] he turns to John the Baptist. John's baptism represented a process of initiation into the eschatological community of the Messiah and so Torrance considers it beyond doubt that 'John the Baptist supplied the church with its ritual act, the rite of initiation by water into the messianic Age and Community, into the New Covenant…'.[188] Because Jesus was baptised by John, this is paradigmatic for Christian Baptism, so Baptism involves not just immersion into water from below but also immersion into the Spirit from above.[189] Torrance sees this vividly portrayed at Pentecost when the Spirit was

184 Torrance, *Trinitarian Perspectives*, p. 25.

185 Ibid., p. 40.

186 Torrance, *Conflict and Agreement in the Church*, vol. 2, p. 96.

187 βαπτισμος refers to a repeatable *rite* of ablution or ceremonial cleansing while βαπτισμα is the word exclusively used in the New Testament and refers to the reality signified in baptism – the unique saving event in Christ on which the rite rests. Torrance, *The Trinitarian Faith*, pp. 293–5.

188 Torrance, *Conflict and Agreement in the Church*, vol. 2, p. 108.

189 In not separating water baptism from Spirit baptism Torrance is consciously departing from the theology of Karl Barth. See Barth, *CD*, IV/3, p. 350; IV/4, pp. 30–40;

poured out in baptism upon the church and immediately the apostles summoned men and women to be baptised in water.[190] When the life, death, and resurrection of Christ are taken with full seriousness, he maintains, the rite of Baptism highlights the language of both descent and ascent – descent into Christ's life and death and ascent into Christ's resurrection and ascension.

Torrance develops his doctrine of Baptism around three themes or movements already identified: perfect (past), present and future tenses, or alternatively: objective, subjective and eschatological dimensions. The first in order of chronology and importance is the *perfect tense*. Christ's baptism becomes ours, because of his vicarious life, death, and resurrection. *Objectively*, we are baptised into Christ and his action for us. Considered from the perfect tense, Christ has achieved salvation completely and our baptism or response adds nothing to salvation:

> ...our part is only to receive it, for we cannot add anything to Christ's finished work. Rather does he act upon us through his Spirit in terms of his atoning and sanctifying incorporation of himself into our humanity in such a way that it takes effect in us as our ingrafting into Christ and as our adoption into the family of the heavenly Father.[191]

Subjectively, we are baptised in the Spirit. The present tense manifests and fulfils the perfect tense:[192]

> Thus we have to say that the great baptismatic event includes the once and for all Baptism of Blood on the Cross and the once and for all Baptism of the Spirit upon the Church at Pentecost. There is *One Baptism*, and *One Body*, common to Christ and His Church, but each participates in it differently – Christ actively and vicariously as Redeemer, the Church passively and receptively as the redeemed Community.[193]

Torrance's baptismal theology contains the now thoroughly familiar theme that the incarnation may be identified with Christ's saving activity, and more than this,

---

144–58. Cf. Hunsinger, 'Baptism and the Soteriology of Forgiveness', pp. 256–7; and John Webster, 'Baptism in the Holy Spirit', in *Barth's Ethics of Reconciliation* (Cambridge: Cambridge University Press, 1995), pp. 116–47.

190 Torrance also provides Titus 3.5 as an example. Torrance, *Conflict and Agreement in the Church*, vol. 2, p. 109.

191 Torrance, *Theology in Reconciliation*, p. 88. This raises the vexed question of infant baptism, something Torrance is highly supportive of. For discussion see Hunsinger, 'Baptism and the Soteriology of Forgiveness'; and 'The Dimension of Depth: Thomas F. Torrance on the Sacraments of Baptism and the Lord's Supper'.

192 Hunsinger, 'The Dimension of Depth: Thomas F. Torrance on the Sacraments of Baptism and the Lord's Supper', p. 160.

193 Torrance, *Conflict and Agreement in the Church*, vol. 2, p. 114.

that the Trinity is intimately involved in our salvation, inaugurated experientially through Baptism. Baptism into the name of the Father, Son and Spirit (Mat 28.19) is highly significant. We are not only baptised into Christ's death, argues Torrance, but into his life as well – a life lived in obedience to the Father and empowered by the Spirit. Torrance concludes: 'The significance of this will be apparent if we say that while Baptism is usually spoken of only as the Sacrament of our incorporation into Christ, it is ultimately grounded upon the fact that in Jesus the Son of God incorporated Himself into our humanity.'[194] Torrance's now familiar appeal to a doctrine of *theosis* considers it as ultimately a reality in the incarnate Christ. Through Christ we participate in *his* communion through the Spirit with the Father. Baptism is the initial sacrament of *this* participation. It is baptism into Christ, and specifically, a participation in *Christ*'s vicarious baptism. This explains the title of one of his major essays on the topic, 'The One Baptism Common to Christ and His Church'.[195]

Because of his emphasis on the perfect tense of salvation Torrance is not averse to using the language of 'baptismal regeneration'.[196] However, Torrance is quick to assert that this does not mean the believer is regenerated through *his or her* baptism itself, nor that one is regenerated through the right administration of this sacrament (*ex opere operato*).[197] 'It is not of course the rite of Baptism which regenerates, but in Baptism our regeneration in Christ is declared, and shown forth, and promised: it is *sacramentally* enacted as an image and likeness of the birth and resurrection of Christ.'[198] This is not, however, to be read as implying a mere symbolic representation. In the act of baptism the reality of regeneration is made ours, it is a manifestation of what has already taken place.

Torrance argues in the strongest possible terms that there is no additional act of salvation outside of what Christ has achieved in his incarnation.[199] Baptism is thus integral to soteriology because it mediates the *Christus praesens* to the worshipping community. Thus the *Christus praesens* and the *Christus futuris* are both grounded in the *Christus adventus* in Torrance's theology. His doctrine of the sacraments is merely an elaboration and explanation of that.[200] In baptism the *believer* is brought into a new relationship – the relationship or communion between the Son and the Father, and it is that communion that we are able to share by the Spirit.[201] Baptism thus serves as the liturgical mediation of forgiveness.

---

194 Ibid., p. 117.

195 In ibid., pp. 82–105.

196 Ibid., pp. 111, 127.

197 See Torrance, *Theology in Reconciliation*, pp. 83, 88, 95–9, 124; *God and Rationality*, p. 57; and *The Mediation of Christ*, p. 90.

198 Torrance, *Conflict and Agreement in the Church*, vol. 2, p. 131.

199 Ibid., p. 118.

200 See Hunsinger, 'Baptism and the Soteriology of Forgiveness', pp. 247–9.

201 Torrance, *Conflict and Agreement in the Church*, vol. 2, p. 123.

By using the language of baptismal regeneration Torrance opens himself up for serious misinterpretation. In order to counter any possible misunderstandings he makes certain qualifications clear: the concept of regeneration is applied first of all to Christ, who in his spiritual birth and his resurrection from the dead is the one in whom the regeneration of our humanity has already taken place. In addition, regeneration is applied to Christ's Second Advent when he will return in power to judge the quick and the dead. Therefore Baptism as the sacrament of regeneration is the ordinance of promise given by Christ to his church in its life *between* the two Advents. As Torrance states, salvation comes to us 'more by way of realization or actualization in us of what has already happened to us in [Christ] than as a new effect resulting from [his finished work]'.[202]

On the basis of the perfect salvation secured in the assumption of human nature, Christ's one baptism becomes ours, as we participate in it through the Spirit. As such 'our baptism involves a twofold movement of simultaneity – from Christ to us and from us to him'.[203] Because Christ's work of reconciling humanity to God is complete, believers now participate in that one completed salvation. This is the present or subjective aspect of baptism. 'In baptism, the perfect tense of our salvation in him becomes present to us for what it is – by making us present to itself; its objective reality becomes, as it were, subjectively accessible and actual.'[204] This explains the importance of Torrance's doctrine of Baptism for a doctrine of *theosis*. 'Baptism in the name of the Father, Son and Holy Spirit initiates people into the sphere in which all the divine blessings of forgiveness of sins, resurrection and eternal life are bestowed and become effective… .'[205] This has both subjective and objective implications, but which is to take priority? While Torrance acknowledges both aspects are involved in a doctrine of Baptism, he sides with Athanasius, as one would expect, and considers the fundamental meaning behind baptism in the name of the Holy Trinity to be 'understood as partaking through the Spirit in the one unrepeatable baptism of Christ which he underwent, not just in the Jordan River, but throughout his life and in his death resurrection [*sic*], on our behalf'.[206] Torrance directly relates baptism to the doctrine of *theosis*:

> the central truth of baptism, therefore, is lodged in Jesus Christ himself and all that he has done for us within the humanity he took from us and made his own, sharing to the full what we are that we may share to the full what he is. *Baptism is the sacrament of that reconciling and atoning exchange in the incarnate Saviour.*[207]

---

[202] Torrance, *Theology in Reconciliation*, p. 89.

[203] Hunsinger, 'The Dimension of Depth: Thomas F. Torrance on the Sacraments of Baptism and the Lord's Supper', p. 163.

[204] Ibid.

[205] Torrance, *The Trinitarian Faith*, p. 292.

[206] Ibid., p. 293. Cf. *The Mediation of Christ*, pp. 90–91.

[207] Ibid., p. 294 (italics in original). The language of 'exchange' is also used in relation to the sacraments in *The Mediation of Christ*, p. 90.

Baptism, for Torrance, is our participation in the incarnate Son's *theopoiesis*. It is our subjective participation in the objective work of Christ, both of which were secured by the Holy Spirit, the One Spirit common to Christ and the church. Because baptism is into Christ, the God-man and Saviour, it has an ontological implication. 'It is', writes Torrance, 'to have our frail transient existence taken up into Christ himself in such a way that, without any loss to our creaturely reality but rather with its perfecting through his Spirit, it is united to God and established in union with his eternal reality.'[208] Once again *theosis* is clearly in view, for the creature, without ceasing to be created, participates in the divine nature by grace and adoption through the Son in the Spirit. These are the benefits that the believer enjoys in Christ through baptism. Because baptism inaugurates *theosis* in the believer it is impossible to separate the individual from the community. While believers are baptised individually, they are baptised into the one body of Christ and together share in him and his benefits.

Living communion with the triune God is achieved through the vicarious life of Christ. Our subjective participation in that life by the Spirit does not add to the work of salvation but is, instead, the application of salvation to the believer, hence the stress upon the perfect tense. 'Christ's self-communication involves at least three things simultaneously: our receiving *of him* into our hearts, our participating *in him* personally, and our communion *with him* eternally.'[209] This leads Hunsinger to suggest tentatively that reception is oriented to the past, participation to the present, and communion to the future: 'Reception of Christ means acknowledging who he is and what he has done for our sakes. Participation in Christ means being clothed and renewed by his perfect righteousness. Communion with Christ is eternal life itself.'[210] While this is not the language that Torrance uses it is in line with his thought. Torrance characterises Baptism as the sacrament that reflects our once-and-for-all union and communion with Christ while the Eucharist reflects our continuous union and communion with him. Baptism thus reflects the theme of Christ's complete substitution while the Eucharist reflects the theme of Christ's complete representation.[211]

Baptism also has a future tense or an eschatological orientation. The depth dimension of the sacraments is both retrospective and prospective because they involve participation in Christ's life, death, resurrection and ascension. 'Because the Church is the Body of the risen and ascended Christ who will come again, all that is said about one baptism for the remission of sins is proleptically conditioned by the future.'[212] To be united to the crucified and risen Christ through the baptism of his Spirit, necessarily carries with it sharing with him in the resurrection of the

---

[208] Ibid., p. 297.

[209] Hunsinger, 'The Dimension of Depth: Thomas F. Torrance on the Sacraments of Baptism and the Lord's Supper', p. 164.

[210] Ibid., pp. 164–5.

[211] Torrance, *The Mediation of Christ*, pp. 90–91.

[212] Torrance, *The Trinitarian Faith*, p. 300.

dead and the life of the world to come.[213] Through baptism we enter into union and communion with Christ, the dead-but-now-risen One. Through baptism we have the assurance that in the *eschaton* we too shall be resurrected to experience the future and final form of *theosis*, a form that we know and experience provisionally now, but that will openly embrace all things in the form that is yet to come.

Theosis concerns the whole of salvation, retrospective and prospective elements included, precisely because it is participation in Christ. Baptism functions as a sign and seal of the reality of Christ's once-for-all salvation so Torrance writes:

> Through his incarnation the Son of God took up into himself our physical existence enslaved to sin, thereby making our corruption, death and judgment his own and offering himself as a substitute for us, so that through the atoning sacrifice of his own life, he might destroy the power that corruption and death have over us. Through the resurrection of our physical human nature in himself Christ has set us upon an altogether different basis in relation to God in which there is no longer any place for corruption and death.[214]

Christ has overcome mortality, corruption, sin, and enslavement and through baptism into Christ the believer is incorporated into his Body, his work, himself. Torrance is simply highlighting how, through baptism, what Christ has done for us is actually made a reality in us. By reminding us of the eschatological nature of Baptism the sacrament assures us that in our union with Christ through one Baptism and one Spirit, the one church cannot but look through its participation in the saving death of Christ to its participation in his resurrection from the dead, when 'at the return of its risen Lord and Saviour…its whole existence will be transformed and it will enjoy to the full the sanctity and eternal life of God himself'.[215] Here we see Torrance articulate a concept of *theosis* which enables him to unite the various aspects of salvation into a coherent theology in which the great regeneration (*palingenesia*) points forward to the reality of which baptism into Christ by the Spirit speaks – full creaturely participation in the triune God.

Because the goal of Christian life is *theosis*, Baptism represents the sacrament that by the Spirit binds the believer to the incarnate Christ and to his vicarious baptism. Hence Baptism is administered in the name of the Father, the Son and the Holy Spirit, leading Torrance to maintain the doctrine of *theosis* in his discussion of Baptism because God has 'opened his divine being for human participation'.[216]

Eucharist Like Baptism, the Eucharist is also a sacramental means of theosis, the incorporation of the believer into Christ and of communion through Christ by the Spirit with the Father. As with Baptism, the keynote is on the once-and-for-all,

213 Ibid., p. 299.

214 Torrance, *The Trinitarian Faith*, p. 299.

215 Ibid., p. 300.

216 Torrance, *Theology in Reconciliation*, p. 101.

objective work of Christ into which the church enters. Further, like Baptism, the Eucharist points to the true mystērion, Jesus Christ.[217] Through the sacraments the church participates in the person and work of Christ in such a way that his work becomes ours; the wonderful exchange elaborated in Torrance's doctrine of reconciliation takes on a sacramental cast. Torrance explains this by highlighting the asymmetrical participation of Christ and the church in the Eucharist: 'In the upper room Jesus and his disciples all shared the loaf, and all drank of the cup, but in different ways: Christ actively and vicariously as Redeemer, the disciples receptively and obediently as the foundation of the redeemed community.'[218] Torrance's sacramental theology is an attempt to explicate the actio of Christ and the re-actio of the church in such a way that the actio of Christ retains priority and is the objective grounding of the secondary, but no less important, subjective participation or re-actio of the believer (church) in his vicarious humanity. As such,

> …the mystery of the Eucharist is to be understood in terms of our participation through the Spirit in what the whole Jesus Christ, the incarnate, crucified, risen and ascended Son, is in himself, in respect both of his activity from the Father towards mankind and of his activity from mankind towards the Father.[219]

The twofold movement of God-to-humanity and humanity-to-God realised in the incarnate Christ is applied to the sacraments, and the result closely reflects what Torrance has already worked out in his doctrines of incarnation and reconciliation.

Hunsinger considers Torrance's sacramental theology to be strongest at the point at which it maintains the 'Protestant principle' of salvation in and by Christ alone, while still upholding a form of 'Catholic substance' in which Baptism and Eucharist are specific sacramental forms of the one saving act of God in Christ through the Spirit.[220] He is right. Torrance's construction of salvation in the perfect tense does not diminish the ongoing importance of the Eucharist but explains more clearly how salvation is mediated to believers. The Eucharist is a mediating form of saving action, not a constitutive form. Like preaching, the Eucharist is secondary and derivative in relation to the finished work of Christ and as such, the sacraments manifest, attest, mediate and participate in the one central form of salvation, for Christ's finished work allows of no supplementation.[221] Thus Torrance makes sense of the real presence of Christ in the Eucharist for it reflects the twofold

---

217 This is made clear in the essay 'The Paschal Mystery of Christ in the Eucharist', in ibid., pp. 106–38.

218 Ibid., p. 106.

219 Ibid., p. 117.

220 Hunsinger, 'The Dimension of Depth: Thomas F. Torrance on the Sacraments of Baptism and the Lord's Supper', p. 167.

221 Torrance, *The Mediation of Christ*, pp. 91–2.

movement evident in the incarnation itself and in the high priestly work of Christ. Torrance works out this twofold movement by emphasising that in the Eucharist the command to do this 'in *anamnesis* of me' is done in holy analogue to and in union with what Christ has done for us in his self-offering and self-consecration to the Father, through the Spirit.[222]

With Calvin, Torrance affirms the view of the *sursum corda*,[223] that we are elevated by the Spirit to participate in the incarnate Son's self-offering to the Father, but he goes beyond Calvin in affirming that at the same time Christ in and with the bread and wine is present to the church by the same Spirit, in the vicarious humanity of his body and blood.[224] This twofold movement by the Spirit through Christ to the Father and from the Father through Christ in the Spirit is what Torrance refers to as the 'dimension of depth' in the Eucharist.[225]

The Eucharist is the great unveiling of the new age in our midst through the Spirit. This means that 'we have to distinguish in a doctrine of "the real presence" between the Eucharistic Parousia of Christ and His final Parousia in judgment and new creation'.[226] It is here that 'memorialist' and 'mystical' views go astray according to Torrance. The first involves an 'un-christological' separation between the sign and the thing signified and treats the sign as a symbol of what happened historically in the past, while the other involves an 'un-christological' confusion between the sign and the thing signified through a doctrine of transubstantiation. This is one reason Torrance rejects certain notions of deification, especially deification through the liturgy, as it posits a union with the *divine* nature of Jesus Christ rather than with his *human* nature; something he calls the problem of 'Apollinarianism in the liturgy'.[227] Instead, 'The Eucharist involves at its very heart the *sursum corda*, of our union with Christ in history and yet out of history is a reality that utterly transcends all our categories of space and time'.[228]

---

222 Torrance, *Theology in Reconciliation*, pp. 117–18.

223 See Christopher B. Kaiser, 'Climbing Jacob's Ladder: John Calvin and the Early Church on our Eucharistic Ascent to Heaven', *Scottish Journal of Theology* 56 (2003): pp. 247–67.

224 Torrance, *Theology in Reconciliation*, pp. 118, 128; and *Royal Priesthood*, pp. 86, 96.

225 Torrance, *Theology in Reconciliation*, pp. 108, 119. Related to this discussion is the doctrine of the *extra Calvinisticum* which Torrance endorses. See Torrance, *Space, Time and Resurrection*, p. 124; *Space, Time and Incarnation* (1969, Edinburgh: T & T Clark, 1997); and Habets, 'Putting the "Extra" Back into Calvinism'.

226 Torrance, *Conflict and Agreement in the Church*, vol. 2, p. 139. See Torrance, *Royal Priesthood*, p. 23.

227 See Thomas F. Torrance, 'The Mind of Christ in Worship: Apollinarianism in the Liturgy', in *Theology in Reconciliation*, pp. 139–214. A recent commentator concurs, see Graham Redding, *Prayer and the Priesthood of Christ in the Reformed Tradition* (Edinburgh: T & T Clark, 2003), p. 72.

228 Torrance, *Conflict and Agreement in the Church*, vol. 2, p. 189.

Following Calvin, Torrance applies a christological analogy to the Supper: 'In participating in [Christ] we become conformed to Him so that we participate also in our own way in the union of the divine and human natures in Christ. Thus the mode of sacramental relation reflects the mode of hypostatic union in Christ.'[229] To be one with Christ is to be caught up into the Triune *perichoresis* to share in the life of God.[230]

> This is an elevation or exaltation into fellowship with the divine life through the amazing condescension of the Son who has been pleased to unite Himself with us in our poverty and unrighteousness, that through redemption, justification, sanctification, eternal life and all the other benefits that reside in Christ we may be endowed with divine riches, even with the life and love that overflow in Christ from God Himself.[231]

Sacramental union is thus another of Torrance's conceptual equivalents for *theosis*: partaking of the divine nature through the Son in the Spirit.

> There can be no doubt that as yet we walk by faith and not by sight, nevertheless the significance of eucharistic communion lies in the fact that by the act of the eternal Spirit the believing Church is given to step over the eschatological boundary, and to partake of the divine nature.[232]

How close is the union that believers have with God in *theosis* by means of the Eucharist? Torrance answers, 'No union, save that of the Persons of the Holy Trinity, could be closer, without passing into absolute identity, than that between Christ and His Church as enacted in the Holy Eucharist'.[233] The union is, accordingly, 'ontological', and even, using the language of Calvin, 'substantial'.[234] Once again we find at the heart of Torrance's theology a commitment to *theosis*, worked out around the twofold mediation of Christ by the Spirit, this time unfolded through a sacramental theology in which we step over the eschatological boundary to partake of the divine nature.

According to Torrance, 'the key to the understanding of the Eucharist is to be sought in the *vicarious humanity of Jesus, the priesthood of the incarnate Son*'.[235]

---

229 Ibid., p. 139.

230 This is the meaning of the Eucharist as Torrance explains in *The Mediation of Christ*, p. 92.

231 Torrance, *Conflict and Agreement in the Church*, vol. 2, p. 145.

232 Ibid., pp. 187–8. One of the weaknesses of Lee's study *Living in Union With Christ*, p. 282, is that in limiting his focus to union and communion he fails to grasp the full implications of *theosis* and the genuinely trinitarian structure of Torrance's theology.

233 Ibid., p. 189.

234 Ibid., p. 188.

235 Torrance, *Theology in Reconciliation*, p. 110 (italics in original).

This priestly intercession is also twofold: first, Christ interceded for us in the incarnation by his sacrificial life and death on our behalf, and second, he continues to intercede for us in his resurrection and ascension by offering himself, and believers with himself, to the Father. Thus by establishing complete kinship with us, Jesus Christ acts as our High Priest both in vicarious receiving and in vicarious offering.[236] In the incarnation God comes to us in Christ and participates in the depth of the human condition, redeeming humanity in his perfect life and death. By his incarnation he has bound himself to believers and believers to himself, removing all sin and corruption and endowing believers with divine holiness.[237] The second aspect of his work is the God-ward response of humanity offered vicariously 'as our own act towards God'. Hunsinger's analysis of Torrance's Eucharistic theology is expressed in aphoristic form:

> [W]ith the Incarnation, heaven participates in earth that earth might participate in heaven. God participates in human flesh that human flesh might participate in God. Holiness participates in corruption that corruption might be uncorrupted by participating in holiness. Christ binds us to himself in his incarnational self-giving unto death in order that he might bring us into living union and communion with himself in his eternal self-offering to God.[238]

Torrance's sacramentology is a further articulation of *theosis* when understood in light of his entire theology. As Baptism is the initiation of Christian life Eucharist is the continual renewal of our communion with Christ in the church. It is interesting to note that the fathers spoke of the Eucharist as a *pharmakon* or medicine.[239] The Eucharist is the service of healing where the Lord bids believers to partake of his being, to become one with him. The reference to *pharmakon* in the fathers is accompanied by the classical theme that 'the unassumed is the unhealed', a theme Torrance often adopts.[240] Through the incarnation God in Christ healed the human

---

236 In his explanation of this Torrance draws once again upon Athanasius when, in *Contra Arianos,* IV.6, he writes, 'he became Mediator between God and men in order that he might minister the things of God to us and the things of ours to God', see ibid., p. 110.

237 Ibid., p. 117.

238 Hunsinger, 'The Dimension of Depth: Thomas F. Torrance on the Sacraments of Baptism and the Lord's Supper', p. 171.

239 See Stanley S. Harakas, *Health and Medicine in the Eastern Orthodox Tradition* (New York: Crossroads, 1990), p. 91; and Kenneth L. Bakken, 'Holy Spirit and Theosis. Toward a Lutheran Theology of Healing', *St Vladimir's Theological Quarterly* 38 (1994): pp. 419–21.

240 See Gregory Nazianzen, *Epistolae*, 101, and *Orations* 1.13; 13.21. See Torrance, *Theology in Reconciliation*, pp. 139–214; and *Karl Barth: Biblical and Evangelical Theologian*, pp. 103–5, 160, 202–5, 231–4.

condition. The Eucharist is an expression of that healing, as believers are united to Christ and to his perpetual intercession on our behalf before the Father.[241]

This perpetual offering of our worship to the Father by the Son in the Spirit does not diminish the perfect tense of salvation but shifts the focus to the perpetual validity of that eternal and perfect salvation. In Torrance's estimation Christ presents us continuously to the Father in a way that calls for 'our continuous living communion with him as the Son'.[242] Without the flesh and blood of Christ there would be no offering acceptable to the Father and so this offering, which the Spirit unites to Christ in our eucharistic worship, parallels and complements the uniting work of the Spirit of Christ with the believer.

'This is the Church of the triune God', Torrance writes,

> embodying under the power of the Spirit, the Lord and Giver of life, the divine *koinonia* within the conditions of human and temporal existence. For the church to be *in the Spirit* in an objective and ontological sense, is to be *in God.* It belongs to the nature and life of the Church in space and time to partake of the very life and light and love which God is.[243]

In the mystery of the Holy Spirit 'we are brought into such a communion with the Father through the Son and in the Spirit, that we are made to participate in the real presence of God to himself'.[244] Participation in the sacraments is thus the path to participation in the divine nature, a mystery of the faith that unites the believer to Christ by the Spirit, and by the same Spirit and through the same Christ, enables the believer to commune with God. In short, the vision of sacramental participation in God Torrance articulates is consistent with a concept of *theosis* inherent in the rest of his theology.[245]

Given such a sacramental vision of union with God, *theosis* acts as a controlling motif in Torrance's theology. The Holy Spirit is seen as the mediator of *theosis* in all its forms: union, communion and participation. In this context, as in all others for Torrance, *theosis* is mediated by the Holy Spirit, is grounded in Christ as its definitive object, and our sacramental participation in salvation is affirmed in fully christocentric, trinitarian and eschatological terms. Through the divinely appointed means (Word and sacrament), the Holy Spirit joins us to Christ (and with one another as Christ's body), and it is this union that initiates and sustains the process

---

241 Torrance, *Theology in Reconciliation*, p. 111.

242 Ibid., p. 111.

243 Torrance, *The Trinitarian Faith*, p. 251.

244 Thomas F. Torrance, 'The Ministry of Women', in *The Call to Serve: Biblical and Theological Perspectives on Ministry in Honour of Bishop Penny Jamieson*, ed. Douglas A. Campbell (Sheffield: Academic Press, 1996), p. 282.

245 This is made explicit in Torrance, *Theology in Reconciliation*, p. 121.

of *theosis* in the believer. While believers currently await the consummation of *theosis*, they already begin to share eternal life with the Holy Trinity.[246]

Kärkkäinen speaks of a 'pneumatological anemia' in relation to the Eucharist;[247] specifically, a lack of reflection on how the Spirit mediates the presence of Christ in the Lord's Supper. This pneumatological anaemia is not shared by Torrance, for his sacramental theology is permeated by the identity and mission of the Spirit who mediates the presence of God in Christ to believers. This does not mean that Torrance explicitly describes *how* the real presence of Christ is present in the Eucharist any more than Calvin does. For Torrance, the Eucharist is, like the mystery of the Trinity or the mystery of the Incarnation, more the place for adoration than explanation.[248] Missing in Torrance's theology of the sacraments are not the foundational principles upon which a doctrine of *theosis* may be built – they are clearly present – but the substance of what *theosis* may mean in practice for the church. Nevertheless, Torrance's sacramentology is consistent with what has been developed elsewhere in his theology.

Approaching God in Worship

Because Christ is the true Man, the last Adam, the Word and Light, his life forms the paradigm for ours. To advance this Torrance consistently emphasises Christ's High Priesthood. Christ is our *leitourgos* (Heb 7.28; 8.1–3), who, as the term suggests, completes the work (*ergon*) of the people (*laos*).[249] Salvation consists in being incorporated into Christ by the Spirit in order to participate in the Son's worship of the Father. Consequently Christ is not only the initiator of salvation but also the model and the perfector of it. His bodily resurrection and ascension to the right hand of the Father means that he continues to serve as Priest on our behalf. This is his 'Royal Priesthood' into which believers progressively participate. This provides the context in which Torrance speaks of the church's response in faith, sacraments, evangelism, ministry, prayer, and worship; a response that is essentially eucharistic. A brief examination of Torrance's articulation of the Royal Priesthood of Christ and the derivative priesthood of the church highlights a final area in which an understanding of *theosis* informs his theology, subsumed under the category of worship.

---

246 This paragraph was a deliberate adaptation of thesis 51 in Hunsinger, 'Baptism and the Soteriology of Forgiveness', p. 266. I am indebted to this article for its insights into Barth's sacramental theology and *koinonia* relations which Hunsinger brings out.

247 Veli-Matti, Kärkkäinen, 'The Spirit and the Lord's Supper', in *Toward a Pneumatological Theology: Pentecostal and Ecumenical Perspectives on Ecclesiology, Soteriology, and Theology of Mission*, ed. Amos Yong (Lanham: University Press of America, 2002), p. 136.

248 Torrance, *Theology in Reconciliation*, pp. 120, 126–7.

249 Torrance, *Royal Priesthood*, p. 15.

Torrance deals very little with the actual response of *a* believer to God, an omission that has the effect of weakening the import of the participatory nature of salvation he constructs. While the theology of the identity of the Holy Spirit is rigorously maintained, Torrance does not go on to suggest in detail ways in which the mission of the Spirit is equally crucial. There is no extended treatise on ministry, mission, or spiritual disciplines such as we may find in the practical theology of the Orthodox, Catholic or Evangelical traditions. It is not that Torrance is unconcerned about such things – clearly he is[250] – but rather the theological foundation has been provided and he considers that he can add little in theological terms.[251] Because of his emphasis on the vicarious humanity of Christ and our incorporation into his human life, Torrance's work is largely concerned with establishing the God-human relationship in Christ, from which the believer's relationship is derived.

Christ is all in all and Torrance wishes the church to understand that reality in all its profundity. This accounts for Torrance's emphasis on the vicarious humanity of Christ and the concept of reconciling exchange that works its way through his theology. This also accounts for his acceptance of *theosis*, for this concept escapes the captivity into which many other theories of the atonement fall and retains the mystery of salvation central to Christian soteriology.

In terms of ministry Torrance believes the church participates in the ministry of Jesus Christ. This does not mean the church has an identical ministry to Christ, for then the church would replace Christ and thus undermine the Gospel. On the other hand the ministry of the church is not *other than* the ministry of Christ or separable from it; something Torrance considers endemic in 'sectarian' views of the church. This apparent conflict between the ministry of the church and the ministry of Christ is resolved by referring to the relation of the church to Christ as one of Head to body, Lord to servant, King to herald, Householder to steward; from beginning to end it is a relation of subordination and obedience as the church participates in Christ's ministry as Prophet, Priest and King. As Torrance presents it, 'The ministry of the church is related to the ministry of Christ in such a way that in and through the ministry of the Church it is always Christ Himself who is at work, nourishing, sustaining, ordering, and governing His Church on earth'.[252] This is made possible through the presence of the Holy Spirit who enables, conforms, empowers, appoints, commands, and governs the life of believers so that 'throughout the whole prophetic, priestly, and kingly ministry of the Church, it is Christ himself who presides as Prophet, Priest, and King, but He summons the Church to engage in *His* ministry

---

[250] As a pastor, preacher, son of a missionary and self-proclaimed disciple of Jesus Christ, Torrance's commitment to ministry, mission and spiritual disciplines is unquestioned. It is the infrequency of these themes in his work which is observed here.

[251] For a rare example see Thomas F. Torrance, 'Crisis in the Kirk', in *St Andrews Rock: The State of the Church in Scotland*, ed. Stewart Lamont (London: Bellew Publishing, 1992), pp. 13–23.

[252] Torrance, *Royal Priesthood*, pp. 37–8.

by witness (ματυρια) by stewardship (ὀικονομια) and by service (διακονια)'.[253] The derivative priesthood of the church becomes a significant form in which Torrance indicates what a practical vision of *theosis* may look like.

Having laid such a foundation Torrance does little to build upon it. Had Torrance undertaken to develop at least the rudiments of a practical theology many of his critics might have been appeased and more of his theology would perhaps have been accessible to a wider readership. This being said, it is obvious that Torrance's thinking lends itself to practical and applied theology, as is evident in the ever-growing secondary literature.[254] Torrance obviously did not consider any of this important enough for him to address, however, he was fully supportive of those who felt it was their vocation to undertake such an endeavour.

Alongside an understanding of the High Priesthood of Christ, Torrance affirms a Reformed view on the orders of the ministry, or the royal priesthood of the church. Within the Church of Scotland these orders are expressed through the institution of presbyter and elders.[255] Torrance affirms a somewhat High Church position in this matter, emphasising that the presbytery brings God before the congregation in Word and sacrament and the deacons help people give their faithful response back to God.[256] He explains the relationship between the High Priest, Jesus Christ, and the royal priesthood of the church thus:

> That sacrificial act of Christ once and for all performed and enduring in His endless life in the presence of God, is realised in the life of His people, not by repetition of His substitutionary sacrifice, but by their dying and rising with Christ in faith and life, and by the worship of self-presentation to God…This sacrifice of the Church in worship, ministry, and life is entirely non-propitiatory, non-piacular. It is essentially eucharistic.[257]

---

[253] Ibid., p. 38.

[254] For example consult the following: *Union in Christ: A Commentary with Questions for Study and Reflection,* eds Andrew Purves and Mark Achtemeier (Louisville: Witherspoon, 1999); Ray S. Anderson, 'Reading T.F. Torrance as a Practical Theologian', in *The Promise of Trinitarian Theology: Theologians in Dialogue with T.F. Torrance*, ed. Elmer M. Colyer (Lanham, Md.: Rowman & Littlefield, 2001), pp. 161–83; Christian D. Kettler, *The God Who Believes: Faith, Doubt, and the Vicarious Humanity of Christ* (Eugene, Or.: Wipf & Stock, 2005); Leonard J. Vander Zee, *Christ, Baptism and the Lord's Supper: Recovering the Sacraments for Evangelical Worship* (Grand Rapids: IVP, 2004); and Gerrit S. Dawson, *Jesus Ascended: The Meaning of Christ's Continuing Incarnation* (Phillipsburg: P & R Publishing, 2004).

[255] Torrance prefers to have 'deacons' rather than 'elders'. See Torrance, *Conflict and Agreement in the Church*, vol. 1, pp. 126–34, 141–5; and *Royal Priesthood*, p. 102.

[256] Torrance, *Royal Priesthood*, pp. 80–81.

[257] Ibid., p. 17.

As a royal priesthood the church is created to offer 'spiritual sacrifices' (*pneumatikai thusai*) to God (1 Pet 2.5), which Torrance links with the Pauline concept of 'rational worship' (*logikē latreia*) found in Rom 12.1. What unites both concepts is the twofold work of Christ and the Spirit. The sacrifice of Christ has cleansed our conscience from fear and anxiety for legal justification, and the Spirit has liberated us from the dead works and carnal ordinances of ritual so that worship comes to stand for the life of the people, the living sacrifice that is spiritual worship. This leads Torrance to the conclusion that '*Latreia* is worship of God in Spirit and in Truth (John 4.22f)'.[258]

Spiritual worship, conducted by the church as the royal priesthood, is significant because its life of worship on earth conforms to a heavenly pattern (Heb 12.22–4, 28, 29). While this was true also of Old Testament worship (Heb 8.5; 9.23), the radical nature of New Testament worship is found in the relationship established between the ascended Christ, our *Leitourgos*, and the yet-to-be-perfected-and-resurrected church. Avoiding the language of the Septuagint or Platonic philosophy, Hebrews 9.23 pointedly uses *hupodeigma* as opposed to *paradeigma* or *eidos* to show that worship on earth is 'not a transcription of the heavenly reality, but a pointer in observable form to a higher reality'.[259] Our *hupodeigma* is an imperfect reality that will one day pass away, whose efficacy lies in liturgical obedience to what God has done in Christ on the cross.

By highlighting both the High Priesthood of Christ and the royal priesthood of the church, Torrance makes the familiar point that what the church does on earth, summarised as worship, is done in the power of the Spirit who unites our imperfect sacrifice with that of Christ, the perfect sacrifice, our *Leitourgos*. On this basis:

> …the Church is given to participate in His ministry, in word, deed, and life; in word, by proclaiming the Gospel to the nations, by prayer and worship and praise and thanksgiving; in life and deed, by self-sacrifice, by ministering humbly to the needs of others, and by presenting our bodies in worship to God.[260]

The now familiar theme of our response being incorporated into Christ's means that the believer's real participation in spiritual ascension is acknowledged, but this is interpreted as empowered by the Spirit and made acceptable only through the incarnate Son.

Good works thus play an important part in *theosis*, not as the means to *theosis*, but as a result of it. As Dawson, highly influenced by Torrance, remarks:

> The most daring and engaged ministries of compassion and evangelism will mark churches living in vivid awareness of the continuing incarnation of Jesus. Our Lord is in heaven, but he is also here among the least of the least. Remaining

---

258 Ibid., p. 19.

259 Ibid, pp. 20–21.

260 Ibid., p. 22.

> incarnate, he directs us to cherish all those with whom he is a brother after the flesh. Thus, no one is to be left out of the sphere of the Church living in the power of the Spirit of the ascended Jesus.[261]

According to Torrance this is evident in the church's prayer and worship.

Unfortunately Torrance offers no extended discussion of Christian ministry and its relation to salvation, justification or good works. Conspicuous by its absence is also any specific discussion of what *theosis* 'looks like' in everyday life. We might speculate that if asked to account for this absence Torrance would respond that other concerns, namely epistemic clarity, occupied his time to the exclusion of applying the principles of his theology to practical questions. Perhaps this is so. However, to not attempt to work out in practice one's soteriology, especially when it is as consciously and rigorously constructed as his, is surely a serious omission. In lieu of a developed 'practical theology' what we do find is a discussion of the life of the Christian formed by prayer and worship. The treatment of these themes is sparse but it does at least give some guidelines to anyone seeking to apply Torrance's theology to Christian spirituality, something a doctrine of *theosis* would normally commit one to.

Both prayer and worship are intimately related to the sacraments in Torrance's thought:

> In so far as the Eucharist is the act of the Church in his name and is also a human rite, it must be understood as act of prayer, thanksgiving and worship, i.e. as essentially *eucharistic* in nature, but as act in which through the Spirit we are given to share in the vicarious life, faith, prayer, worship, thanksgiving and self-offering of Jesus Christ to the Father, for in the final resort it is Jesus Christ himself who is our true worship.[262]

The theme of Jesus Christ as our true worship and the Spirit as the one who enables communion between the church and Christ is a hallmark of Torrance's use of *theosis*.[263]

Torrance appeals to John McLeod Campbell's definition of worship as the presentation of 'the mind of Christ' to the Father, for what God accepts as our true worship is Christ himself.[264] 'Worship of the Father in spirit and in truth is the life of the Son in us that ascends to the Father in such worship.'[265] Outside

---

261 Dawson, *Jesus Ascended*, p. 178.

262 Torrance, *Theology in Reconciliation*, p. 109.

263 It is also a hallmark of Eastern Orthodox theology as seen in the essay by Bradley Nassif, 'Are Eastern Orthodoxy and Evangelicalism Compatible? Yes', in *Three Views on Eastern Orthodoxy and Evangelism*, eds Stanley N. Gundry and James Stamoolis (Grand Rapids: Zondervan, 2004), pp. 40–48.

264 Torrance, *Theology in Reconciliation*, p. 139.

265 Ibid.

of Christ *nothing* is acceptable to the Father, so prayer and worship can only be offered in and through Christ. 'All our prayer and praise and worship are sinful and unworthy but through the Holy Spirit breathed upon us they are cleansed in the sacrifice of Christ and absorbed into intercession and praise and worship within the veil.'[266] The Spirit thus creates the bond between the believer and Christ and takes what is ours to Christ and what is Christ's to us so that *his* prayer and *his* worship of the Father becomes *ours*. In the light of this perhaps the most specific statement regarding worship that we find in Torrance is the following: 'Jesus Christ is our worship, the essence of it and the whole of it, and we may worship God in Spirit and in Truth as we are made partakers of his worship.'[267] This parallels the definition of worship referred to earlier, provided by James Torrance: 'Christian worship is, therefore, our participation through the Spirit in the Son's communion with the Father, in his vicarious life of worship and intercession.'[268] Both James and Thomas Torrance see worship as central to the life of the church. As James Torrance explains:

> When we see that the worship and mission of the church are the gift of participating through the Holy Spirit in the incarnate Son's communion with the Father and the Son's mission from the Father to the world, that the unique center of the Bible is Jesus Christ, 'the apostle and high priest whom we confess' (Heb 3.1), then the doctrines of the Trinity, the incarnation, the atonement, the ministry of the Spirit, Church and sacraments, our understanding of the kingdom, our anthropology and eschatology, all unfold from that center.[269]

This perspective is no less true for Thomas Torrance.

The Spirit breathed upon the disciples by Christ is the Spirit of our response to Christ and, through him, to the Father. This is the trinitarian frame of worship, this is life, and this is *theosis*. The vision of the Christian life lived on earth for Torrance is empowered by the breath of the Holy Spirit, the Spirit of God and the Spirit of Christ:

> On our lips the prayer, *Come, Creator Spirit*, is a prayer of commitment to what God has already done in Jesus Christ, and a prayer of participation in the divine nature, in the faith that it is only the power of God which can redeem fallen man, and that nothing short of the very life and breath of God can renew the life of his people.[270]

---

266 Ibid., p. 249.

267 Ibid.

268 James B. Torrance, *Worship, Community and the Triune God of Grace*, p. 15.

269 Ibid., p. 9.

270 Torrance, *Theology in Reconstruction*, p. 242.

For the church to worship God means that the Spirit draws it within the circle of the life of God in Christ Jesus in order to 'live out that divine life on earth…a life of praise and witness to his glory'.[271]

Had Torrance taken greater care to explain the relationship between the Spirit and Christ during Christ's earthly ministry, specifically the way the Spirit was able to lead, inspire, and keep Christ faithful to God as he grew in wisdom and grace (Lk 2.40) and learnt obedience through his sufferings (Heb 5.8), he would have been able to apply this more directly to the Spirit-filled and Spirit-led life of the believer in these in-between times as we await the glorious return of the risen Christ. Unfortunately, such a discussion is absent and students of Torrance are left to work out such a practical theology for themselves.[272] However, that said, Torrance does provide the theological resources such an enterprise can draw upon, and this in itself is a major achievement.

Prayer and worship complete our examination of how Torrance incorporates *theosis* into his theology for with them we come full circle back to our participation in the completed work of Christ, through union with the incarnate Son, by the Holy Spirit. We pray and worship in the Spirit of Christ who takes our prayer and worship and unites it with Christ's own self-consecration and so offers us to the Father as Offerer and Offering, Gift and Giver. In the final analysis what God accepts as our true worship is Christ himself.[273] True worship is to have the mind of Christ in worship (Phil 2.5).[274] 'Through the indwelling Spirit, who himself completes the adorable and blessed Trinity, the worshipping church is, so to speak, the doxological correlate of the Triunity of God.'[275]

Conclusion

Torrance reminds us of the heart of the Gospel as he sees it – the significance of the vicarious humanity of Jesus Christ:

> In conclusion, let me direct you to those striking words of St Paul in his Epistle to the Galatians, 2.20, which give succinct expression to the evangelical truth which we have been trying to clarify. 'I am crucified with Christ: nevertheless I live, yet not I but Christ lives in me; and the life which I now live in the flesh I live by faith, the *faithfulness* of the Son of God who loved me and gave himself for me.' This is surely the insight that we must allow to inform all our human

---

271 Ibid.

272 Compare this with the work of his brother James B. Torrance, *Worship, Community and the Triune God of Grace*, who applies much the same theology to the way believers pray, worship, and minister.

273 Torrance, *Theology in Reconciliation*, p. 113.

274 Ibid.

275 Torrance, *The Trinitarian Faith*, p. 269.

> responses to God, whether they be in faith, conversion and personal decision, worship and prayer, the holy sacraments, or the proclamation of the Gospel: *'I yet not I but Christ'*...this applies to the whole of my life in Christ and to all my human responses to God, for in Jesus Christ they are laid hold of, sanctified and informed by his vicarious life of obedience and response to the Father. They are in fact so indissolubly united to the life of Jesus Christ which he lived out among us and which he has offered to the Father, as arising out of our human being and nature, that they are *our responses* toward the love of the Father poured out upon us through the mediation of the Son and in the unity of his Holy Spirit.[276]

While Torrance has more to say about community and communion, the principles outlined above are sufficient to indicate what *theosis* entails for believers and the church. *Theosis* is worship from beginning to end, for it is an active participation in Jesus Christ made possible by the Spirit. In reconciliation with God believers are caught up into the life of the Son's response to the Father and in that communion they participate in the Divine nature. Christ's vicarious life thus sanctifies believers so that what Christ has done and continues to do is communicated to them, and his worshipful response to the Father becomes theirs. The communion of the Holy Trinity is imaged on earth in the communion of saints – the church, of which its members are called and transformed into Christlikeness, in order that they may participate in the Divine communion.

---

[276] Torrance, *The Mediation of Christ*, p. 98.

Conclusion
The 'Danger of Vertigo'?

The 'Danger of Vertigo'?

The central argument of this study is that although the formal language of *theosis* may appear rather infrequently in Torrance's work, its material content is pervasive. Torrance considers *theosis* to be biblical, orthodox, Reformed, and appropriate for contemporary theology, as long as it is defined within specific parameters.

Torrance explores what *theosis* affirms while defining the limits to this soteriological analogy. Neoplatonic ideas of divinisation are consistently dismissed as foreign accretions to the Christian gospel as Torrance believes such forms of divinisation posit the immediate participation of the creature with Divinity so that the creature literally becomes divine in its essence. In its place Torrance argues that the Christian gospel supports the fact that God himself became man in the incarnation and in that unique theandric person, deification took place. Therefore, through participation in Christ by the Holy Spirit believers may also be 'deified'. The eternal Son is 'deified' by nature; the believer in Christ is 'deified' by grace. As such, salvation consists in being incorporated into the humanity of the incarnate Christ and through his humanity one may experience, participate in, and know the triune God.

Jesus Christ alone is the *imago Dei* in its fullness. As the *Alpha* and the *Omega* the incarnate Son is the true image of God. This has several implications for Torrance's articulation of theological anthropology. First, the incarnate Son is the *imago Dei* in whose image Adam and Eve were created. Second, the incarnate Son is the image into which all believers will one day be conformed. Third, salvation is the full participation of creatures in the *humanity* of Jesus Christ.

> The hypostatic union of the divine and human natures in Jesus preserves the human and creaturely being he took from us, and it is in and through our sharing in that human and creaturely being, sanctified and blessed with him, that we share in the life of God while remaining what we are made to be, humans and not Gods.[1]

This is an emphatic rejection of any reading of *theosis* that would suggest humanity ceases to be human even at the *telos* of salvation.

As a consequence of Torrance's theological anthropology believers may participate in the divine nature because humanity is, in part, compatible with divinity, as the incarnation proves. This compatibility is located in the person of the

---

[1] Thomas F. Torrance, *Space, Time and Resurrection* (1976, Edinburgh: T & T Clark, 1998), p. 136.

incarnate Son through whom we have a genuine human relation with God. In the person of the incarnate Son, through his life, death, and resurrection, reconciliation occurred between God and humanity. The Son became human, even, if Torrance is to be believed, taking on the form of *fallen* human nature, and redeemed humanity through his obedient life, death, resurrection, and ascension. The life of this man, the last Adam, was, from first to last, vicarious. In him humanity and divinity were perfectly reconciled resulting in true personhood and full salvation.

Recent thinkers have presented ideas similar to Torrance's, however, none have done so as consistently or as comprehensively. Despite this, problems remain regarding many of Torrance's ideas. Given Torrance's equivocation on the issue of the Primacy of Christ many would rather relegate his positive discussion of the Scotistic hypothesis and dismiss any claims that Torrance followed Scotus at all. Studying Torrance's isolated comments on this alone will not resolve the debate. Rather, examining his work within the context of his entire theology proves more fruitful. However, differences remain amongst his commentators.[2]

In addition, Torrance forcefully contends that the patristic phrase, 'the unassumed is the unhealed' unambiguously means that the Son assumed a *fallen* human nature, and thus salvation is about healing *that* human nature in his own person. While coherent within Torrance's own theology, this reading of patristic theology is highly debatable. Although such notions as these are not required in order to accept Torrance's theology, he emphasises these themes in his own work. He was, however, not able to provide a satisfactory defence of these ideas and so they require further consideration.

Central to Torrance's soteriology is the emphasis upon the *vicarious* humanity of Christ. Jesus Christ has accomplished communion with God perfectly by uniting humanity with divinity, without dissolving either nature. Jesus Christ is *homoousios* with God and humanity and he alone establishes twofold mediation between the two. By means of *hypostatic union* the incarnate Son has entered into the depths of the human condition, healed it, united it with divinity, and established a communion between the two in which neither nature – divine nor human – ceases to be what it is. This, argues Torrance, is what doctrines of *theosis* are meant to suggest, and nothing less.

A closer reading of Torrance's theology does raise certain questions. Eschewing certain notions of a physical theory of redemption aspects of it remain. Torrance does not make union and communion with God merely a mechanical process, however, his stress upon the incarnation over the atonement lends support to such a reading. Reformed theologians especially, the tradition within which Torrance works, will want to see a more rigorous interaction with the doctrines of sin and guilt, the cross and imputation, and of sin and grace. These themes are present in Torrance's theology but do not occupy a prominent position. This consistently leads his critics to question how much Torrance actually endorses a Reformed

[2] Myk Habets, 'On Getting First Things First: Assessing Claims for the Primacy of Christ', *New Blackfriars* 90 no. 1027 (2009), pp. 343–64.

soteriology. Unfortunately, a thorough articulation of how compatible *theosis* is with Reformed theology is not provided by Torrance, although his work goes a long way in establishing such a relation.

While cogent and even compelling, Torrance's soteriology, working as it does within a Western, Reformed context, offers only an initial explanation of how a model of *theosis* is compatible with a doctrine of justification by faith, for instance. For many, deification and justification are doctrines that inhabit two mutually exclusive theological paradigms and thus it is incoherent bringing the two together. Torrance's work does provide resources to address such allegations, as has been shown, despite the fact that he does not directly interact with these issues in detail. A conception of how the two themes may ultimately be compatible requires development beyond which Torrance provides.

What Torrance does present is a christology and soteriology that reflects what *he* considers to be the core of Reformed theology, namely, the priority of union with Christ from which all the benefits of salvation flow, including *theosis*. *Theosis* expresses a rich biblical truth that helps express the lengths to which God has gone in reconciling humanity to himself. Because Jesus Christ has reconciled God and humanity, the reconciliation he achieved is both objective and subjective. Profoundly utilising a theme of 'exchange', Torrance finds a concept of *theosis* central to a theology of the incarnation. Christ takes to himself what is ours, namely, our fallenness, disobedience and sin, in order to give us what is his, namely, obedient sonship, immortality, knowledge of and participation in the Holy Trinity. Through this 'wonderful exchange' our humanity is healed, redeemed, and perfected in the Son. Furthermore, as we participate in Christ by the Spirit, we too may come to experience the reconciling love of God and partake of the divine nature of love and life.

For reconciliation to become a reality in the life of a believer the Holy Spirit joins believers to Christ and therefore to his perfected humanity. Building upon insights of Athanasius and Calvin regarding believers' union with Christ, Torrance considers *theosis* to be a central feature. When the Spirit joins believers by grace through faith to the Son, they are caught up into *his* obedient life, *his* worship, *his* ministry, and *his* perfect response to the Father. Believers become perfected persons in the Son. Through fellowship with the saints, corporate worship, the ministry of the Word, and partaking of the sacraments, the believer is continually bound to Christ by the Spirit and progressively transformed or 'deified' from glory to glory into Christlikeness. At the *parousia*, believers will be glorified, raised to new life with Christ, and equipped to serve and glorify God joyfully and obediently like the Son.

Torrance's use of *theosis* is not without its problems. The role of the Holy Spirit permeates his theology and is integral to its trinitarian dimensions but it is not given the attention it demands specifically when ideas of *theosis* are articulated. The epistemological role of the Holy Spirit is meticulously developed, as are the trinitarian dimensions of pneumatology, yet Torrance's discussion on the place of the Holy Spirit in the mission of Christ, while indicative, lacks a comprehensive development. In terms of a doctrine of reconciliation, especially one that so rigorously works with a concept of *theosis*, the lack of developed pneumatological thought is a considerable oversight. This is especially true since Torrance is self-consciously drawing upon Eastern theological emphases that have made so much of this aspect, and in view of Barth's pneumatological *lacuna* in this area. It is clear that Torrance lays a solid pneumatological foundation for various aspects of his theological enterprise; however, he does not go far enough in articulating the actual dynamics of how the Holy Spirit 'deifies' believers in practice. The reason for this absence may be that a detailed account of our experience of *theosis* has proved problematic for many in the tradition as these accounts can too easily tend towards the confusion of the Holy Spirit with the human 'spirit' and because such accounts also tend to confuse Christ and Christian experience. It is not human experience that Torrance thinks is important, rather the Christ whom humans experience is the centre of evangelical theology. One wonders if there is a way to speak of human experience without falling into these traps, and if an articulation of *theosis* provides a way to do this? Surely the solution is to speak more of Christ's human experience than Torrance has done.[3]

Torrance's description of a pneumato-ecclesiology is suggestive yet ultimately fails to develop many of the fundamental insights discussed elsewhere in his work. Whereas Eastern Orthodox expressions of *theosis* typically include a direct and well-developed application of the theme, Torrance's theology leaves much of the application open-ended. After defining what *theosis* is and showing its reality in the incarnate Son, Torrance is content to make only general statements about how this may be so in the life of a believer. Torrance's christocentricity apparently threatens to engulf a clear application of his theology to human creatures. While not completely absent,[4] practical theology is clearly not one of Torrance's main considerations. Readers are left to establish the implications of Torrance's theology for themselves. The resulting emphasis Torrance wishes to place upon *theosis* is implicitly undermined.

What is not in question is Torrance's commitment to incorporating the theme of *theosis* throughout his *corpus*. Amongst many Western theologians the concept of *theosis* creates unease or hostility, for it appears to confuse humanity with God. Reformed and evangelical Christians in particular have been wary of the concept. Torrance is sensitive to this unease and while his doctrine of *theosis* never affirms

---

[3] One way to do this is through a Spirit Christology. See Myk Habets, 'Spirit Christology: Seeing in Stereo', *Journal of Pentecostal Theology* 11 (2003): pp. 199–235.

[4] See for instance Torrance's extensive dialogues with the Eastern Orthodox on the Trinity which constitutes a practical effort at church unity in *Trinitarian Perspectives: Toward Doctrinal Agreement* (Edinburgh: T & T Clark, 1994); his theology of the Eucharist where he argues for inter-communion because it is the *Lord*'s Supper and not the *church*'s supper in *Conflict and Agreement in the Church*, vol. 2. *The Ministry and the Sacraments of the Gospel* (London: Lutterworth, 1960), and his discussion on faith and godliness in *The Trinitarian Faith: The Evangelical Theology of the Ancient Catholic Church* (Edinburgh: T & T Clark, 1995), pp. 13–46.

the literal divinisation of humans, he does identify the 'danger of vertigo'[5] that can overwhelm some people when they contemplate being exalted in Christ to partake of the divine nature. The 'vertigo' of which Torrance speaks is the danger of Neoplatonic mysticism or pantheism that identifies human being with the divine being. Torrance argues this is the antithesis of the Christian gospel. And yet, Torrance asserts, this perceived 'danger' is not sufficient for us to reject the idea of *theosis*. This phrase – 'the danger of vertigo' – is critical to this study for it shows Torrance's preparedness to unequivocally espouse the theme of *theosis* despite the misunderstanding it can cause in the West.

Clearly Torrance does not offer the final word on *theosis* any more than he does on epistemology, theology and science, or natural theology. A rigorous examination of his theology has indicated the need to build upon this foundation in order to tease out and apply the implications it suggests. What may emerge is unclear but this is the task Torrance has set the church. Torrance has initiated the building of a bridge between Eastern and Western theologies and he has done so via the central dogmas both share in common: the Trinity, incarnation, reconciliation and *theosis*. By incorporating *theosis* into his theology, Torrance's work has ecumenical and contemporary significance. This makes Torrance's use of *theosis* both important and exciting, but not definitive. Torrance has set an agenda for those who may wish to follow. Gerald Bray echoes this when he writes:

> Indeed, it may not be too much to say that the Reformed approach to the Trinity can provide a bridge between the classical Augustinianism of the Western churches and the newly discovered mystical theology of the Eastern church. It can hardly be an accident that Reformed theologians of the stature of Thomas Torrance, Jürgen Moltmann and the late Colin Gunton have shown themselves so open to receiving the insights of the Eastern Orthodox tradition, while at the same time remaining firmly anchored in the Augustinian West and fully appreciative of Karl Barth's contribution to its continuing theological vigour. Serious engagement with the East may be a recent development, but there are indications even in the theology of John Calvin that point towards an openness in that direction, and it may well be that there is something inherent in the Reformed tradition since the sixteenth century that makes it peculiarly able to reach out to the East in ways that might be able to bridge the gap between what appear to be two irreconcilable theological positions.[6]

Questions regarding some of Torrance's ideas remain, but what he has provided is powerful and persuasive. Torrance's use of *theosis* reminds us that the gift of the Son is a relationship with the triune God. Without ceasing to be human, men and

---

[5] Torrance, *Space, Time and Resurrection*, pp. 136–9.

[6] Gerald Bray, 'The Trinity: Where Do We Go From Here?' in *Always Reforming: Explorations in Systematic Theology*, ed. Andrew T.B. McGowan (Downers Grove: IVP, 2006), p. 29.

women are called and empowered to participate in the divine nature. As Torrance reminds us:

> *Theosis* is an attempt to express the staggering significance of Pentecost as the coming from on high, from outside of us and beyond us, of divine power, or rather as the coming of Almighty God, the Maker of heaven and earth, to dwell with sinful mortal man, and therefore as the emancipation of man from imprisonment in himself and the lifting of him up to partake of the living presence and saving acts of God the Creator and Redeemer.[7]

A study of *theosis* in Torrance's scientific dogmatics offers new insights into his theology and for Reformed thought more generally. While the language may indeed sound strange to Western ears and some may perceive an apparent 'danger of vertigo', Torrance is right to urge us not to quarrel about the word *theosis*, but to honour its intention.

DSE

---

[7] Thomas F. Torrance, *Theology in Reconstruction* (Grand Rapids: Eerdmans, 1965), p. 244.

Bibliography

Select Works of T.F. Torrance

——. *Theological and Natural Science*. Eugene, OR.: Wipf & Stock, 2002.

——. *The Doctrine of Jesus Christ: Auburn Lectures 1938–39*. Eugene, Or.: Wipf & Stock, 2002.

——. 'Thomas Torrance Responds.' In *The Promise of Trinitarian Theology: Theologians in Dialogue with T.F. Torrance*. Ed. E.M. Colyer. Lanham, Md.: Rowman & Littlefield, 2001, 303–40.

——. 'Michael Polanyi and the Christian Faith – A Personal Report.' *Tradition and Discovery: The Polanyi Society Periodical* 27 no. 2 (2000–2001): 26–32.

——. 'The Reconciliation of Mind: A Theological Meditation upon the Teaching of St. Paul.' In *Theology in the Service of the Church: Essays in Honor of Thomas W. Gillespie*. Ed. W.M. Alston. Grand Rapids: Eerdmans, 2000, 196–204.

——. 'The Christ Who Loves Me.' In *A Passion for Christ: Vision that Ignites Ministry*. Ed. G. Dawson and J. Stein. Edinburgh: The Handsel Press, 1999, 9–20.

——. 'Preaching Jesus Christ.' In *A Passion for Christ: Vision that Ignites Ministry*. Ed. G. Dawson and J. Stein. Edinburgh: The Handsel Press, 1999, 23–32.

——. *Scottish Theology from John Knox to John McLeod Campbell*. Edinburgh: T & T Clark, 1996.

——. *The Christian Doctrine of God: One Being Three Persons*. Edinburgh: T & T Clark, 1996.

——. 'From John Knox to John McLeod Campbell: A Reading of Scottish Theology.' In *Disruption to Diversity: Edinburgh Divinity 1846–1996*. Ed. D.F. Wright and G.D. Badcock. Edinburgh: T & T Clark, 1996, 1–28.

——. 'Ultimate and Penultimate Beliefs in Science.' In *Facets of Faith and Science* vol. 1: *Historiography and Modes of Interaction*. Ed. J. van der Meer. Lanham, MD.: University Press of America, 1996, 151–76.

——. *The Trinitarian Faith: The Evangelical Theology of the Ancient Catholic Church*. 1988. Edinburgh: T & T Clark, 1995.

——. *Divine Meaning: Studies in Patristic Hermeneutics*. Edinburgh: T & T Clark, 1995.

——. *Trinitarian Perspectives: Toward Doctrinal Agreement*. Edinburgh: T & T Clark, 1994.

——. *Preaching Christ Today*. Grand Rapids: Eerdmans, 1994.

——. (Ed.). *Theological Dialogue Between Orthodox and Reformed Churches*, vol. 2. Edinburgh: Scottish Academic Press, 1993.

——. 'Introduction.' In *Theological Dialogue Between Orthodox and Reformed Churches*, vol. 2. Ed. T.F. Torrance, Edinburgh: Scottish Academic Press, 1993, ix–xxiv.

——. 'The Triunity of God in the Nicene Theology of the Fourth Century.' In *Theological Dialogue Between Orthodox and Reformed Churches*, vol. 2. Ed. T.F. Torrance, Edinburgh: Scottish Academic Press, 1993, 3–37.

——. and Others, 'Working Paper on the Holy Trinity.' In *Theological Dialogue Between Orthodox and Reformed Churches*, vol. 2. Ed. T.F. Torrance, Edinburgh: Scottish Academic Press, 1993, 109–21.

——. 'The Christian Apprehension of God the Father.' In *Speaking the Christian God: The Holy Trinity and the Challenge of Feminism.* Ed. A.F. Kimel, Grand Rapids: Eerdmans, 1992, 120–43.

——. *The Mediation of Christ.* 1989. New enlarged edition. Edinburgh: T & T Clark, 1992.

——. 'The Atonement the Singularity of Christ and the Finality of the Cross: The Atonement and the Moral Order.' In *Universalism and the Doctrine of Hell.* Ed. N.M de S. Cameron. Carlisle: Paternoster; Grand Rapids: Baker, 1992, 225–56.

——. 'Incarnation and Atonement: Theosis and Henosis in the Light of Modern Scientific Rejection of Dualism.' *Society of Ordained Scientists*, Bulletin No. 7, Edgeware, Middlesex (Spring 1992): 8–20.

——. *Karl Barth: Biblical and Evangelical Theologian.* Edinburgh: T & T Clark, 1990.

——. 'The Distinctive Character of the Reformed Tradition.' In *Incarnational Ministry: Essays in Honor of Ray S. Anderson.* Ed. C.D. Kettler and T.H. Speidell. Colorado Springs: Helmers and Howard, 1990, 2–15.

——. *The Christian Frame of Mind: Order and Openness in Theology and Natural Science.* Edinburgh: Handsel Press, 1985.

——. 'The Soul and Person in Theological Perspective.' In *Religion, Reason, and the Self: Essays in Honour of Hywel D. Lewis.* Ed. S.R. Sutherland and T.A. Roberts, Cardiff: University of Wales Press, 1989, 103–18.

——. 'The Goodness and Dignity of Man in the Christian Tradition.' *Modern Theology* 4 no. 4 (1988): 309–22.

——. 'Hugh Ross Mackintosh: Theologian of the Cross.' *Scottish Bulletin of Evangelical Theology* 5 (1987): 160–73.

——. 'The Doctrine of the Holy Trinity According to St. Athanasius.' *Anglican Theological Review* 71 (1989): 395–405.

——. 'Karl Barth and Patristic Theology.' In *Theology Beyond Christendom: Essays on the Centenary of the Birth of Karl Barth May 10, 1986.* Ed. J. Thompson. Allison Park, PA.: Pickwick, 1986, 215–39.

——. 'My Interaction with Karl Barth.' In *How Karl Barth Changed My Mind.* Ed. D.K. McKim, Grand Rapids: Eerdmans, 1986, 52–64.

——. 'Karl Barth and the Latin Heresy.' *Scottish Journal of Theology*, 39 no. 4 (1986): 461–82.

——. (Ed.). *Theological Dialogue Between Orthodox and Reformed Churches*, vol. 1. Edinburgh: Scottish Academic Press, 1985.
——. *Reality and Scientific Theology*. Edinburgh: Scottish Academic Press, 1985.
——. *Transformation and Convergence in the Frame of Knowledge: Explorations in the Interrelations of Scientific and Theological Enterprise*. Grand Rapids: Eerdmans, 1984.
——. 'The Concept of Order in Theology and Science.' *The Princeton Seminary Bulletin* 5 no. 2 (1984): 130–39.
——. 'The Deposit of Faith.' *Scottish Journal of Theology* 36 no. 1 (1983): 1–28.
——. '"The Substance of the Faith": A Clarification of the Concept in the Church of Scotland.' *Scottish Journal of Theology* 36 no. 3 (1983): 327–38.
——. 'John Philoponos of Alexandria, Sixth Century Christian Physicist.' *Texts and Studies*, vol. 2. London: Thyateira House, 1983, 261–5.
——. *Reality and Evangelical Theology*. Philadelphia: Westminster Press, 1982. Reprint, Downers Grove: IVP, 1999.
——. 'Theological Realism.' In *The Philosophical Frontiers of Christian Theology: Essays Presented to D.M. MacKinnon*. Ed. B. Hebblethwaite and S. Sutherland. Cambridge: Cambridge University Press, 1982, 169–96.
——. (Ed.). *The Incarnation: Ecumenical Studies in the Nicene-Constantinopolitan Creed A.D. 381*. Edinburgh: Handsel Press, 1981.
——. *Christian Theology and Scientific Culture*. New York: Oxford University Press, 1981.
——. *Divine and Contingent Order*. New York: Oxford University Press, 1981. Reprint, Edinburgh: T & T Clark, 1998.
——. 'Divine and Contingent Order.' In *The Sciences and Theology in the Twentieth Century*. Ed. A.R. Peacocke. London: Oriel Press, 1981, 81–97.
——. 'The Framework of Belief.' In *Belief in Science and in Christian Life: The Relevance of Michael Polanyi's Thought for Christian Faith and Life*. Ed. T.F. Torrance; Edinburgh: Handsel, 1980, 1–27.
——. 'The Place of Michael Polanyi in the Modern Philosophy of Science.' *Ethics in Science and Medicine* 7 (1980): 57–95.
——. 'Ultimate Beliefs and the Scientific Revolution.' *Cross Currents* 30 (1980): 129–49.
——. *The Ground and Grammar of Theology*. Charlottesville: University of Virginia Press, 1980. Edinburgh: T & T Clark, 2001.
——. *Space, Time and Resurrection*. 1976. Edinburgh: T & T Clark, 1998.
——. *Theology in Reconciliation: Essays Towards Evangelical and Catholic Unity in East and West*. London: Geoffrey Chapman, 1975. Reprint, Eugene, Or.: Wipf & Stock, 1997.
——. 'The Relation of the Incarnation to Space in Nicene Theology.' In *The Ecumenical World of Orthodox Civilisation. III. Russia and Orthodoxy: Essays in Honor of Georges Florovsky*. Ed. A. Blane. The Hague: Mouton, 1973, 43–70.

——. 'Truth and Authority: Theses on Truth.' *Irish Theological Quarterly* 39 (1972): 215–42.

——. 'Newton, Einstein and Scientific Theology.' *Religious Studies* 8 (1971): 233–50.

——. *God and Rationality.* London: Oxford University Press, 1971. Reprint, Eugene, Or.: Wipf & Stock, 1997.

——. 'The Problem of Natural Theology in the Thought of Karl Barth.' *Religious Studies* 6 (1970): 121–35.

——. 'The Relevance of Orthodoxy.' In *The Relevancy of Orthodoxy.* Ed. J.B. Logan. Stirling: The Drummond Press, 1970, 9–19.

——. *Theological Science.* London: Oxford University Press, 1969. Reprint, Edinburgh: T & T Clark, 1996.

——. *Space, Time and Incarnation.* 1969. Edinburgh: T & T Clark, 1997.

——. 'Dialogue – Grace and Sacraments: The Roman Doctrine of Grace from the Point of View of Reformed Theology.' In P.F. Fransen, *Intelligent Theology.* London: Darton, Longman & Todd, 1969, vol. 3, 46–77.

——. 'Spiritus Creator.' In *Le Traité sur le Saint-Espirit de Saint Basile.* Ed. L. Visher. Taizé: Presses de Taizé, 1969. Reprint: *Verbum Caro* 23 (1969): 63–85.

——. *Theology in Reconstruction.* Grand Rapids: Eerdmans, 1965.

——. *Karl Barth: An Introduction to His Early Theology 1910–1931.* 1962. Reprint, Edinburgh: T & T Clark, 2000.

——. *Conflict and Agreement in the Church: Volume Two: The Ministry and the Sacraments of the Gospel.* London: Lutterworth, 1960.

——. 'The Atoning Obedience of Christ.' *Moravian Theological Seminary Bulletin* (1959): 65–81.

——. 'The Doctrine of Order.' *Church Quarterly Review* 160 (1959): 21–36.

——. *Conflict and Agreement in the Church: Volume One: Order and Disorder.* London: Lutterworth, 1959.

——. *The School of Faith: The Catechisms of the Reformed Church.* Trans. and ed. with Introduction by T.F. Torrance. London: James Clarke and Co, 1959, xi–cxxvi.

——. *The Biblical Doctrine of Baptism.* Edinburgh: The Saint Andrew Press, 1958.

——. 'The Place of the Humanity of Christ in the Sacramental Life of the Church.' *Church Service Society Annual* 26 (1956): 3–10.

——. *Royal Priesthood.* Scottish Journal of Theology: Occasional Papers No. 3. Edinburgh: Oliver and Boyd, 1955.

——. 'The Atonement and the Oneness of the Church.' *Scottish Journal of Theology* 7 no. 3 (1954): 245–69.

——. 'Universalism or Election?' *Scottish Journal of theology* 2 (1949): 310–18.

——. *Calvin's Doctrine of Man.* London: Lutterworth, 1949.

——. *The Doctrine of Grace in the Apostolic Fathers.* Thesis for Basel University. Edinburgh: Oliver and Boyd, 1948.

——. 'The Word of God and the Nature of Man.' In *Reformation Old and New: Festschrift for Karl Barth.* Ed. F.W. Camfield. London: Lutterworth Press, 1947, 121–41.

——. 'Predestination in Christ.' *Evangelical Quarterly* 13 (1941): 108–41.

Select Secondary Works on the Theology of T.F. Torrance

Achtemeier, P.M. 'Natural Science and Christian Faith in the Thought of T.F. Torrance.' In *The Promise of Trinitarian Theology: Theologians in Dialogue with T.F. Torrance.* Ed. E.M. Colyer. Lanham, Md.: Rowman & Littlefield, 2001, 269–302.

——. 'The Truth of Tradition: Critical Realism in the Thought of Alasdair MacIntyre and T.F. Torrance.' *Scottish Journal of Theology* 47 no. 3 (1996): 355–74.

Achtner, W. *Physik, Mystik und Christentum: eine Darstellung und Diskussion der natèurlichen Theologie bei T.F. Torrance.* Frankfurt am Main: P. Lang, 1991.

Anderson, R.S. 'Reading T.F. Torrance as a Practical Theologian.' In *The Promise of Trinitarian Theology: Theologians in Dialogue with T.F. Torrance*. Ed. E.M. Colyer. Lanham, Md.: Rowman & Littlefield, 2001, 161–83.

——. 'Real Presence Hermeneutics: Reflections on Wainwright, Thielicke, and Torrance.' *Theological Students Fellowship Bulletin* 6 no. 2 (1982): 5–7.

——. *Historical Transcendence and the Reality of God: A Christological Critique.* Grand Rapids: Eerdmans, 1975.

Apczynski, J.V. 'Torrance on Polanyi and Polanyi on God: Comments on Weightman's Criticisms – A Review Essay.' *Tradition & Discovery: The Polanyi Society Periodical* 24 no. 1 (1997–98): 32–4.

Bauman, M. *Roundtable: Conversations with European Theologians.* Grand Rapids: Baker, 1990.

Burgess, A. *The Ascension in Karl Barth.* London: Ashgate, 2004, 109–34.

Colyer, E.M. 'The Incarnate Saviour: T.F. Torrance on the Atonement.' In *An Introduction to Torrance Theology: Discovering the Incarnate Saviour.* Ed. G.S. Dawson. London: T & T Clark, 2007, 33–54.

Colyer, E.M. 'Thomas F. Torrance on the Holy Spirit.' *Word and World* 23 no. 2 (2003): 160–67.

——. (Ed.). *The Promise of Trinitarian Theology: Theologians in Dialogue with T.F. Torrance.* Lanham, Md.: Rowman & Littlefield, 2001.

——. 'A Scientific Theological Method.' In *The Promise of Trinitarian Theology: Theologians in Dialogue with T.F. Torrance*. Ed. E.M. Colyer. Lanham, Md.: Rowman & Littlefield, 2001, 205–37.

——. *How To Read T.F. Torrance: Understanding his Trinitarian and Scientific Theology.* Downers Grove: IVP, 2001.

——. *The Nature of Doctrine in T.F. Torrance's Theology.* Eugene, Or.: Wipf & Stock, 2001.

——. 'Thomas F. Torrance.' In *A New Handbook of Christian Theologians*. Ed. by D.W. Musser and J.L. Price, Nashville: Abingdon, 1996, 460–67.

Dawson, G.S. (Ed.). *An Introduction to Torrance Theology: Discovering the Incarnate Saviour.* London: T & T Clark, 2007.

——. 'Far as the Curse is Found: The Significance of Christ's Assuming a *Fallen* Human Nature in the Torrance Theology.' In *An Introduction to Torrance Theology: Discovering the Incarnate Saviour.* Ed. G.S. Dawson. London: T & T Clark, 2007, 55–74.

—— and Stein, J. (Ed.). *A Passion for Christ: Vision that Ignites Ministry*. Edinburgh: The Handsel Press, 1999.

Deddo, G.W. 'The Holy Spirit in T.F. Torrance's Theology.' In *The Promise of Trinitarian Theology: Theologians in Dialogue with T.F. Torrance*. Ed. E.M. Colyer. Lanham, Md.: Rowman & Littlefield, 2001, 81–114.

Del Colle, R. '"Person" and "Being" in John Zizioulas' Trinitarian Theology: Conversations with Thomas F. Torrance and Thomas Aquinas.' *Scottish Journal of Theology* 54 no. 1 (2001): 70–86.

Dragas, G.D. 'Professor T.F. Torrance on his 80th Birthday.' *Church and Theology* 12 (1993): 566–76.

Flett, E.G. 'Priests of Creation, Mediators of Order: The Human Person as a Cultural Being in Thomas F. Torrance's Theological Anthropology.' *Scottish Journal of Theology* 58 no. 2 (2005): 161–83.

Fransen, P.F. 'Dialogue – Grace and Sacraments: Reflections on the Conditions and Possibility of an Ecumenical Dialogue.' In *Intelligent Theology*. London: Darton, Longman & Todd, 1969, vol. 3, 78–100.

Grenz, S.J. *Rediscovering the Triune God: The Trinity in Contemporary Theology.* Minneapolis: Fortress, 2004, 200–215.

Gunton, C. 'Being and Person: T.F. Torrance's Doctrine of God.' In *The Promise of Trinitarian Theology: Theologians in Dialogue with T.F. Torrance*. Ed. E.M. Colyer. Lanham, Md.: Rowman & Littlefield, 2001, 115–37.

Guthridge, J. *The Christology of T.F. Torrance: Revelation and Reconciliation in Christ*. Excerpta ex dissertation ad Lauream. Melbourne: Pontificia Universitas Gregoriana, 1967.

Habets, M. 'Reformed *Theosis*? A Response to Gannon Murphy', *Theology Today* 65 no. 4 (January, 2009), pp. 489–98.

——. 'The Doctrine of Election in Evangelical Calvinism: T.F. Torrance as a Case Study.' *Irish Theological Quarterly* 73 no 3–4 (2008): 334–54.

——. 'How "Creation is Proleptically Conditioned by Redemption".' *Colloquium* (forthcoming).

——. 'Thomas Forsyth Torrance: Mystical Theologian *Sui Generis*', *Princeton Theological Review* 14 no. 2, issue 39 (Fall, 2008), pp. 91–104.

——. 'Naked but Not Disembodied: A Case for Anthropological Duality', *Pacific Journal of Baptist Research* 4 no. 1 (2008), pp. 33–50.

——. 'On Getting First Things First: Assessing Claims for the Primacy of Christ', *New Blackfriars* 90 no. 1027 (2009), pp. 343–64.

——. 'Reforming Theosis.' In *Theosis: Deification in Christian Theology*. Ed. S. Finlan and V. Kharlamov. OR.: Pickwick Publications, 2006, 146–67.

Hardy, D.W. 'Theology and Natural Science.' In *The Modern Theologians*, 2nd edn, ed. D.W. Hardy. Oxford: Blackwell, 1997, 647–68.

——. 'Thomas F. Torrance.' In *The Modern Theologians: An Introduction*. Vol. 1. Ed. D.F. Ford. Oxford: Blackwell, 1989, 71–91.

Harvey, N.P. 'Frames of Reference for the Resurrection [Pannenberg and Torrance].' *Scottish Journal of Theology* 42 no. 3 (1989): 335–9.

Heltzel, P. 'Thomas Torrance.' In *Dictionary of Modern Western Theology*, http://people.bu.edu/wwildman/WeirdWildWeb/courses/mwt/dictionary/mwt_themes785. Accessed 28.8.02.

Heron, A.I.C. 'T.F. Torrance In Relation to Reformed Theology.' In *The Promise of Trinitarian Theology: Theologians in Dialogue with T.F. Torrance*. Ed. E.M. Colyer. Lanham, Md.: Rowman & Littlefield, 2001, 31–49.

——. *A Century of Protestant Theology*. Philadelphia: The Westminster Press, 1980, 209–214.

Hesselink, I.J. 'A Pilgrimage in the School of Christ – An Interview with T.F. Torrance.' *Reformed Review* 38 no. 1 (1984): 49–64.

Hunsinger, G. 'The Dimension of Depth: Thomas F. Torrance on the Sacraments of Baptism and the Lord's Supper.' *Scottish Journal of Theology* 54 no. 2 (2001): 155–76.

——. 'The Dimension of Depth: Thomas F. Torrance on the Sacraments.' In *The Promise of Trinitarian Theology: Theologians in Dialogue with T.F. Torrance*. Ed. E.M. Colyer. Lanham, Md.: Rowman & Littlefield, 2001, 139–60.

——. *Disruptive Grace: Studies in the Theology of Karl Barth*. Grand Rapids: Eerdmans, 2000, 30–34.

Kaiser, C.B. 'Humanity in an Intelligible Cosmos.' In *The Promise of Trinitarian Theology: Theologians in Dialogue with T.F. Torrance*. Ed. E. Colyer. Lanham, Md.: Rowman & Littlefield, 2001, 239–67.

Kang, Phee Seng. 'The Epistemological Significance of ὁμοονσον [*sic*] in the Theology of Thomas F. Torrance.' *Scottish Journal of Theology* 45 no. 3 (1992): 341–66.

Kelly, D.F. 'The Realist Epistemology of Thomas F. Torrance.' In *An Introduction to Torrance Theology: Discovering the Incarnate Saviour.* Ed. G.S. Dawson. London: T & T Clark, 2007, 75–102.

Kettler, C.D. *The Vicarious Humanity of Christ and the Reality of Salvation.* Lanham. MD.: University Press of America, 1991, 121–55.

Klinefelter, D.S. 'God and Rationality: A Critique of the Theology of Thomas F. Torrance.' *Journal of Religion* 53 (1973): 117–35.

Kruger, C.B. 'The Doctrine of the Knowledge of God in the Theology of T.F. Torrance: Sharing in the Son's Communion with the Father in the Spirit.' *Scottish Journal of Theology* 43 no. 3 (1990): 366–89.

Langford, T.A. 'T.F. Torrance's *Theological Science*: A Reaction.' *Scottish Journal of Theology* 25 no. 2 (1972): 155–70.

Lee, K.W. *Living in Union With Christ: The Practical Theology of Thomas F. Torrance*. Issues in Systematic Theology, Volume 11. New York: Peter Lang, 2003.

Louth, A. 'Science and Mystery.' In *Discerning the Mystery: An Essay on the Nature of Theology*. Oxford: Clarendon Press, 1983, 45–72.

Luoma, T. *Incarnation and Physics: Natural Science in the Theology of Thomas F. Torrance*. An American Academy of Religion Book. USA: Oxford University Press, 2002.

McCall, T. 'Ronald Thiemann, Thomas Torrance and Epistemological Doctrines of Revelation.' *International Journal of Systematic Theology* 6 no. 2 (2004): 148–68.

McGrath, A.E. *T.F. Torrance: An Intellectual Biography*. Edinburgh: T & T Clark, 1999.

McKinney, R.W.A. (Ed.). *Creation, Christ and Culture: Studies in Honour of T.F. Torrance*. Edinburgh: T and T Clark, 1976.

Macleod, D. 'Dr T.F. Torrance and Scottish Theology: A Review Article [*Scottish Theology from John Knox to John McLeod Campbell*, 1996].' *Evangelical Quarterly* 72 no. 1 (Jan 2000): 57–72.

——. *Jesus is Lord: Christology Yesterday and Today*. Fearn: Mentor, 2000, 125–34.

——. *The Person of Christ*. Contours of Christian Theology. Leicester: IVP, 1998.

McPake, J.L. 'The Reception of the Theology of Karl Barth in Scotland [diss. abst., Edinburgh, 1994].' *Tyndale Bulletin* 47 no. 1 (1996): 181–4.

Marley, A.G. *T.F. Torrance: The Rejection of Dualism*. Nutshell Series vol. 4. Edinburgh: Handsel Press, 1992.

Martin, R.K. *The Incarnate Ground of Christian Faith: Toward a Christian Theological Epistemology for the Educational Ministry of the Church*. Lanham, MD.: University Press of America, 1998.

Mascall, E.L. *Theology and the Gospel of Christ: An Essay in Reorientation*. London: SPCK, 1977, 46–62.

Molnar, P.D. 'Natural Theology Revisited: A Comparison of T.F. Torrance and Karl Barth.' *Zeitschrift für dialektische Theologie* 20 no. 1 (2005): 53–83.

——. 'The Eucharist and the Mind of Christ: Some Trinitarian Implications of T.F. Torrance's Sacramental Theology.' In *Trinitarian Soundings in Systematic Theology*. Ed. P.L. Metzger. London: Continuum, 2005, 175–88.

——. 'Incarnation, Resurrection and the Doctrine of the Trinity: A Comparison of Thomas F. Torrance and Roger Haight.' *International Journal of Systematic Theology* 5 no. 2 (2003): 147–67.

——. *Divine Freedom and the Doctrine of the Immanent Trinity: In Dialogue with Karl Barth and Contemporary Theology*. London: T & T Clark, 2002, 167–96; 317–30.

——. 'God's Self-communication in Christ: A Comparison of Thomas F. Torrance and Karl Rahner.' *Scottish Journal of Theology* 50 no. 3 (1997): 288–320.

Morrison, J.D. 'Heidegger, Correspondence Truth and the Realist Theology of Thomas Forsyth Torrance.' *Evangelical Quarterly* 69 no. 2 (1997): 139–55.

——. *Knowledge of the Self-Revealing God in the Thought of Thomas Forsyth Torrance.* Issues in Systematic Theology Volume 2. New York: Peter Lang, 1997.

——. 'Thomas Forsyth Torrance's Critique of Evangelical (Protestant) Orthodoxy.' *Evangelical Quarterly* 67 no. 1 (1995): 53–69.

Muller, R.A. 'The Barth Legacy: New Athanasius or Origen Redivivus? A Response to T.F. Torrance.' *Thomist* 54 (1990): 673–704.

Myers, B. 'The Stratification of Knowledge in the Thought of T.F. Torrance.' *Scottish Journal of Theology* 61 no. 1 (2008): 1–15.

Neidhardt, W.J. 'Thomas F. Torrance's Integration of Judeo-Christian Theology and Natural Science: Some Key Themes.' *Perspectives on Science and Christian Faith* 41 no. 2 (1989): 87–98.

Newell, R. 'Torrance, Thomas Forsyth.' In *Dictionary of Historical Theology*. Ed. T. Hart. Grand Rapids: Eerdmans, 2000, 549–51.

Norris, F.W. 'Mathematics, Physics and Religion: A Need for Candor and Rigor.' *Scottish Journal of Theology* 37 no. 1 (1984): 457–70 [465–7].

O'Donoghue, N.D. 'Creation and Participation.' In *Creation, Christ and Culture: Studies in Honour of T. F. Torrance.* Ed. R.W.A. McKinney, Edinburgh: T and T Clark, 1976, 135–48.

Palma, R.J. 'Thomas F. Torrance's Reformed Theology.' *Reformed Review* 38 no. 1 (1984): 2–46.

Peters, T. 'Theology Through Philosophy.' In *The Modern Theologians*, 2nd edn. Ed. D.W. Hardy, Oxford: Blackwell, 1997, 252–85.

Pratz, G. 'The Relationship Between Incarnation and Atonement in the Theology of Thomas F. Torrance.' *Journal for Christian Theological Research*, 3 no. 2 (1998). http://apu.edu/~CTRF/articles/1998_articles/pratz.html (accessed 5.3.02)

Purves, A. 'The Christology of Thomas F. Torrance.' In *The Promise of Trinitarian Theology: Theologians in Dialogue with T.F. Torrance.* Ed. E.M. Colyer. Lanham, Md.: Rowman & Littlefield, 2001, 51–80.

Redding, G. *Prayer and the Priesthood of Christ in the Reformed Tradition.* Edinburgh: T & T Clark, 2003.

Rehnman, S. 'Barthian Epigoni: Thomas F. Torrance's Barth-Reception.' *Westminster Theological Journal* 60 no. 2 (1998): 271–96.

Richardson, K.A. 'Revelation, Scripture, and Mystical Apprehension of Divine Knowledge.' In *The Promise of Trinitarian Theology: Theologians in Dialogue with T.F. Torrance.* Ed. E.M. Colyer. Lanham, Md.: Rowman & Littlefield, 2001, 185–203.

——. 'The Contemporary Renewal of Trinitarian Theology: Possibilities of Convergence in the Doctrine of God.' In *The Nature of Confession.* Ed. T.R. Phillips and D.L. Ockholm. Grand Rapids. IVP, 1996, 183–92, 289–91.

Schubert, F.D. 'Thomas F. Torrance: The Case for a Theological Science.' *Encounter* 45 no. 2 (1984): 123–37.

Shuster, M. 'What is Truth: An Exploration of Thomas F. Torrance's Epistemology.' *Studia Biblica et Theologica* 3 (1973): 50–56.

Siemens, D.F. 'Two Problems with Torrance [reply to W.J. Neidhardt, 41 (1989): 87–98].' *Perspectives on Science and Christian Faith* 43 no. 2 (1991): 112–13.

Spjuth, R. *Creation, Contingency and Divine Presence: In the Theologies of Thomas F. Torrance and Eberhard Jüngel.* Lund: Lund University Press, 1995.

Thiemann, R. *Revelation and Theology: The Gospel as Narrated Promise.* Notre Dame: University of Notre Dame Press, 1985, Chapter 2.

Torrance, D.W. 'Thomas Forsyth Torrance: Minister of the Gospel, Pastor, and Evangelical Theologian.' In *The Promise of Trinitarian Theology: Theologians in Dialogue with T.F. Torrance.* Ed. E.M. Colyer. Lanham, Md.: Rowman & Littlefield, 2001, 1–30.

Torrance, I.R. 'A Bibliography of the Writings of Thomas F Torrance 1941–1989.' *Scottish Journal of Theology* 43 no. 2 (1990): 225–62.

Weightman, C. 'Polanyi and Mathematics, Torrance and Philosophy of Science: A Response to Apczynski's Review.' *Tradition & Discovery: The Polanyi Society Periodical* 24 no. 1 (1997–98): 35–8.

——. *Theology in a Polanyian Universe: The Theology of Thomas Torrance.* New York: Peter Lang, 1994.

Wigley, S.D. 'Karl Barth on St. Anselm: The Influence of Anselm's "Theological Scheme" on T.F. Torrance and Eberhard Jüngel.' *Scottish Journal of Theology* 46 no. 1 (1993): 79–97.

Yeung, J.H-K. *Being and Knowing: An Examination of T.F. Torrance's Christological Science.* Jian Dao Dissertation Series 3. Theology and Culture 1. Hong Kong: China Alliance Press, 1996.

Index